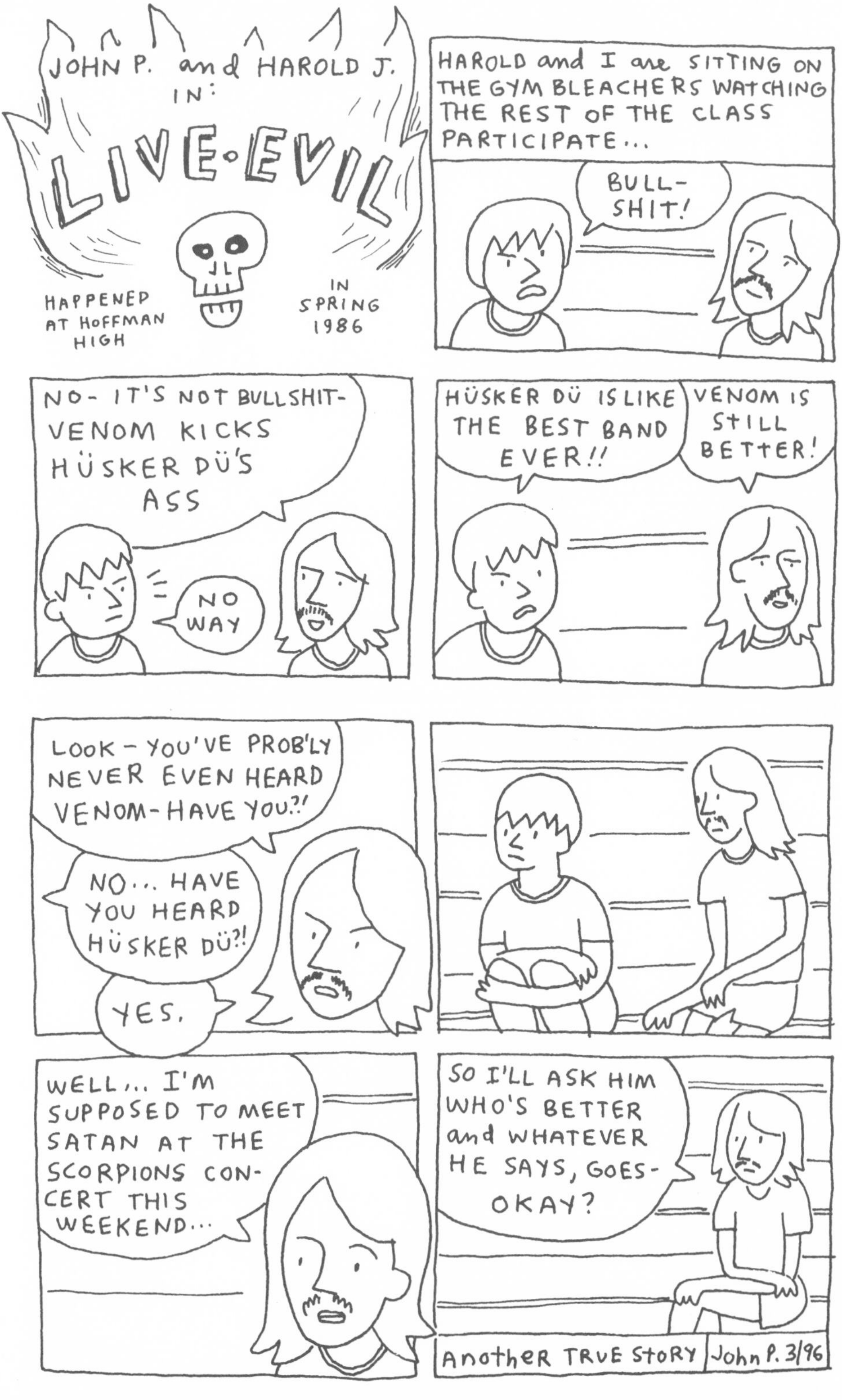
JOHN P. and HAROLD J. IN:
LIVE•EVIL
HAPPENED AT HOFFMAN HIGH
IN SPRING 1986
HAROLD and I are SITTING ON THE GYM BLEACHERS WATCHING THE REST OF THE CLASS PARTICIPATE...
BULL-SHIT!
NO- IT'S NOT BULLSHIT- VENOM KICKS HÜSKER DÜ'S ASS
NO WAY
HÜSKER DÜ IS LIKE THE BEST BAND EVER!!
VENOM IS STILL BETTER!
LOOK - YOU'VE PROB'LY NEVER EVEN HEARD VENOM-HAVE YOU?!
NO... HAVE YOU HEARD HÜSKER DÜ?!
YES.
WELL... I'M SUPPOSED TO MEET SATAN AT THE SCORPIONS CON-CERT THIS WEEKEND...
SO I'LL ASK HIM WHO'S BETTER and WHATEVER HE SAYS, GOES-OKAY?
Another TRUE STORY
John P. 3/96

PERFECT EXAMPLE

By
John Porcellino

Drawn and Quarterly
Montréal

Publication design: Tom Devlin and John Porcellino.
Publisher: Chris Oliveros.
Publicity: Peggy Burns.

Drawn & Quarterly
Post Office Box 48056
Montreal, Quebec
Canada H2V 4S8
www.drawnandquarterly.com

Visit John's website at www.king-cat.net

First Drawn & Quarterly edition: October 2005.
ISBN 1-896597-75-0
Printed in Canada.
Originally published by Highwater Books, March 2000 (ISBN 0-9665363-5-5).

10 9 8 7 6 5 4 3 2 1

Library and Archives Canada Cataloguing in Publication
Porcellino, John
Perfect example / John Porcellino.
ISBN 1-896597-75-0
    I. Title.
PN6727.P67P47 2005   741.5'973   C2005-904423-3

Distributed in the USA by:
Farrar, Straus and Giroux
19 Union Square West
New York, NY 10003
Orders: 888.330.8477

Distributed in Canada by:
Raincoast Books
9050 Shaughnessy Street
Vancouver, BC V6P 6E5
Orders: 800.663.5714

A PERFECT EXAMPLE is
   all the things it's done to me ...
I think I might lose my mind
   But not my memoRy.

(It means a lot to me).

HüskeR Dü "PeRfect Example"   FoRge.

FOR YOU
♡

PERFECT EXAMPLE

LIVE·EVIL

Belmont Harbor

HAIRCUTTING TIME

IN-BETWEEN DAYS

THE FOURTH OF JULY

CELEBRATED SUMMER

Escape to Wisconsin

Belmont Harbor

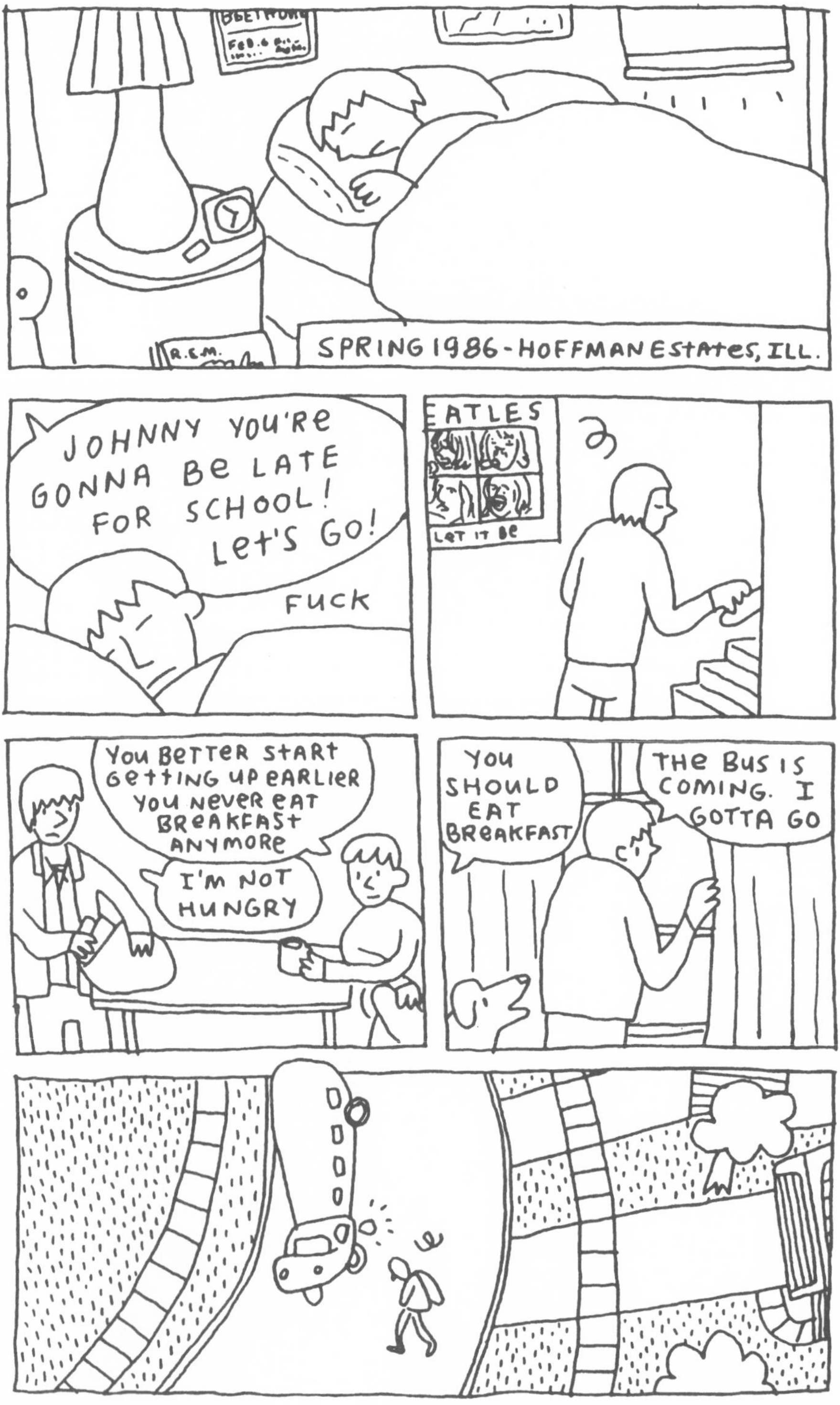

SPRING 1986 - HOFFMAN ESTATES, ILL.
R.E.M.
JOHNNY YOU'RE GONNA BE LATE FOR SCHOOL! LET'S GO!
FUCK
EATLES
LET IT BE
YOU BETTER START GETTING UP EARLIER YOU NEVER EAT BREAKFAST ANYMORE
I'M NOT HUNGRY
YOU SHOULD EAT BREAKFAST
THE BUS IS COMING. I GOTTA GO

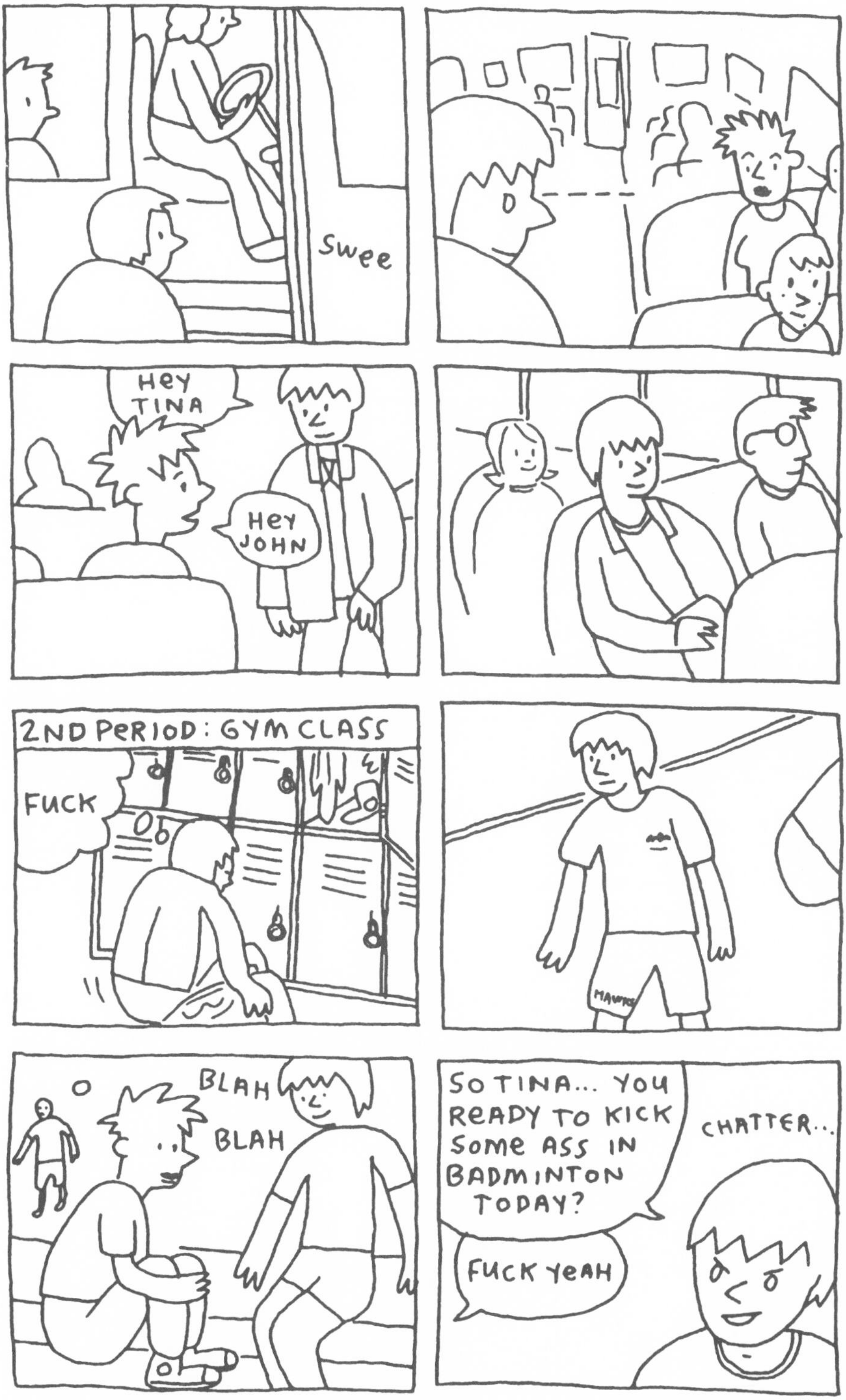

SWEE
HEY TINA
HEY JOHN
2ND PERIOD: GYM CLASS
FUCK
MAWKS
BLAH
BLAH
SO TINA... YOU READY TO KICK SOME ASS IN BADMINTON TODAY?
CHATTER...
FUCK YEAH

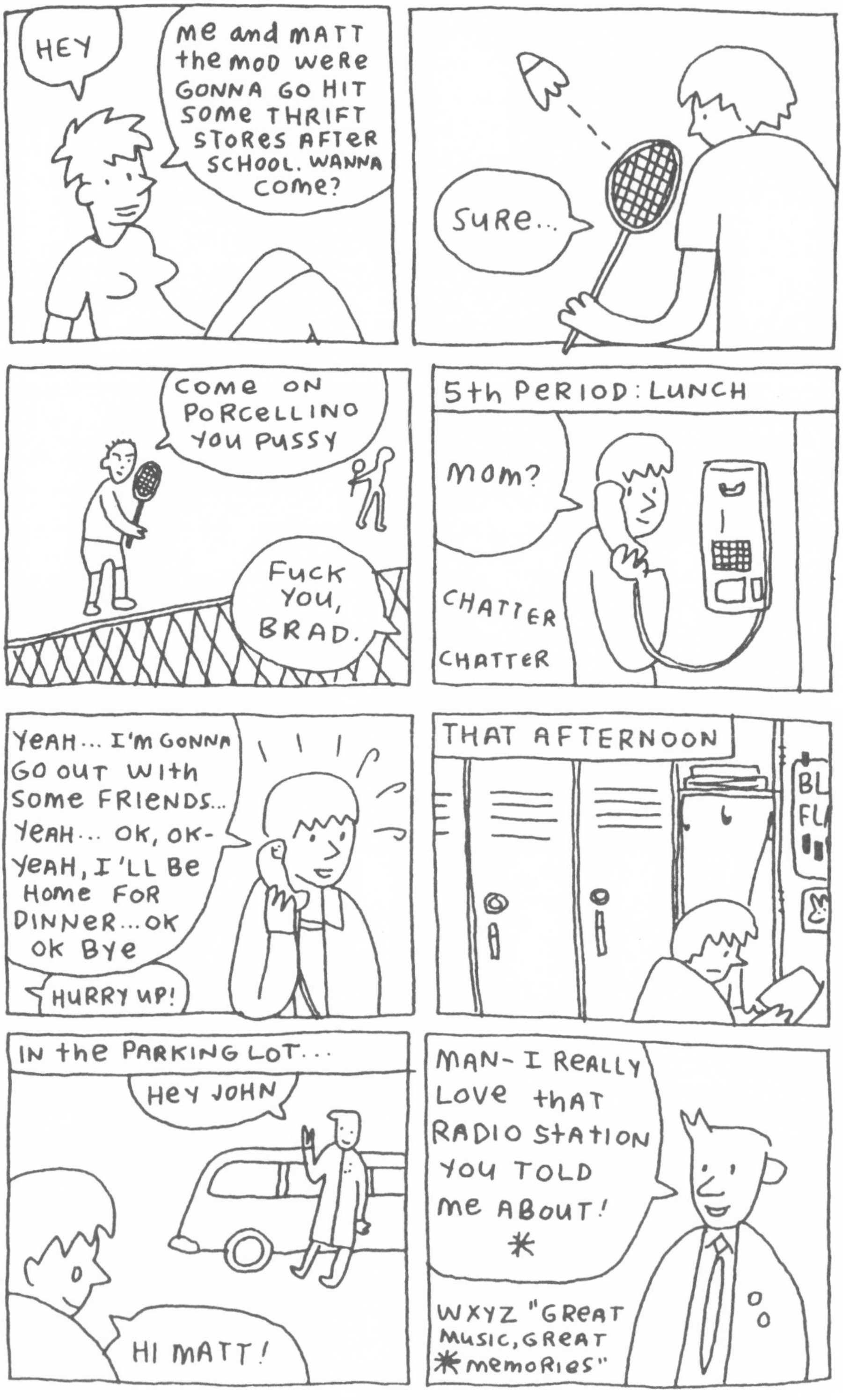
HEY
me and MATT the MOD were GONNA GO HIT some THRIFT STORES AFTER SCHOOL. WANNA come?
SURE...
COME ON PORCELLINO YOU PUSSY
FUCK YOU, BRAD.
5th PERIOD: LUNCH
mom?
CHATTER
CHATTER
YEAH... I'M GONNA GO OUT WITH SOME FRIENDS... YEAH... OK, OK- YEAH, I'LL BE HOME FOR DINNER... OK OK BYE
HURRY UP!
THAT AFTERNOON
IN THE PARKING LOT...
HEY JOHN
HI MATT!
MAN- I REALLY LOVE THAT RADIO STATION YOU TOLD ME ABOUT! *
WXYZ "GREAT MUSIC, GREAT * MEMORIES"

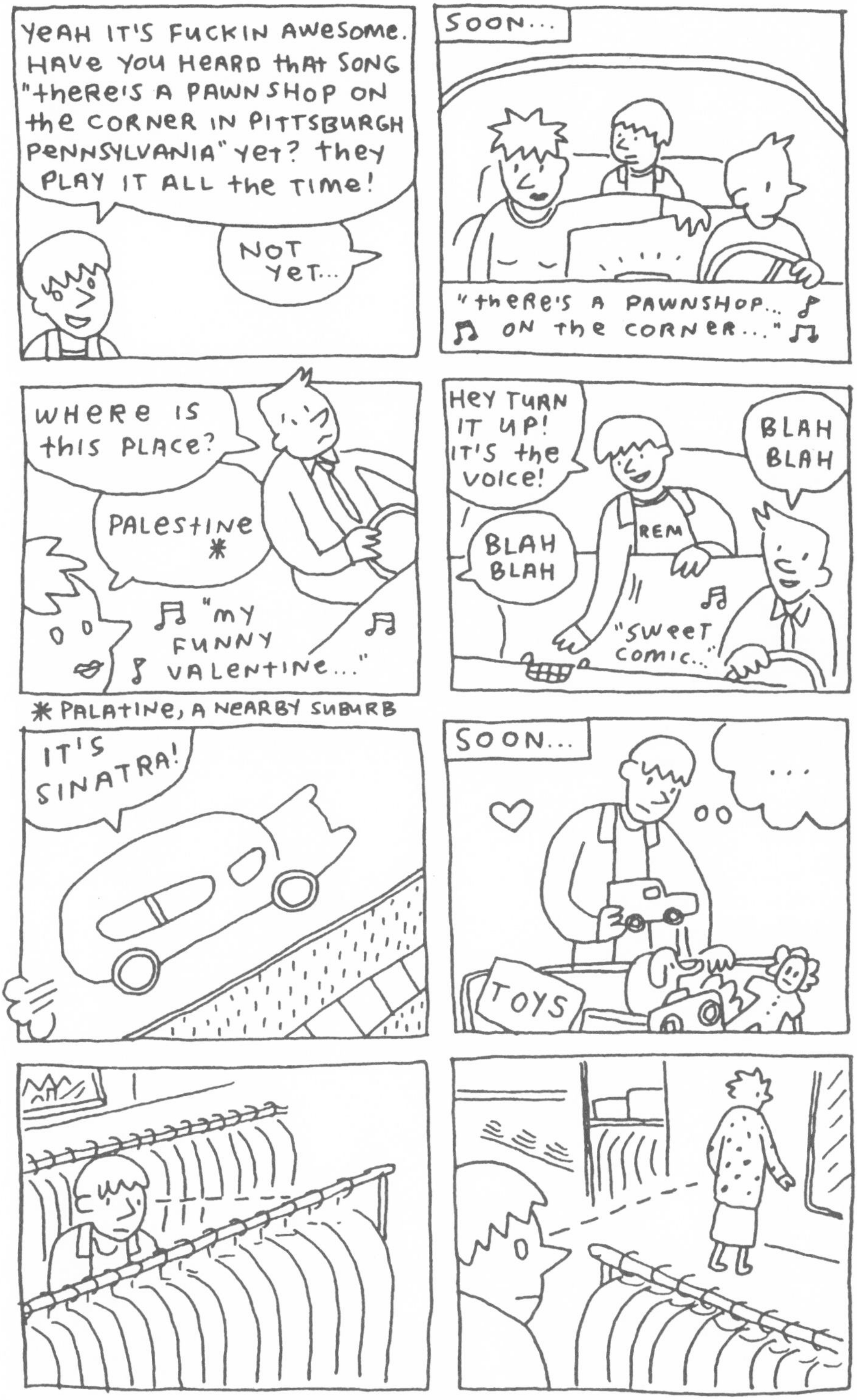
YEAH IT'S FUCKIN AWESOME. HAVE YOU HEARD THAT SONG "THERE'S A PAWNSHOP ON THE CORNER IN PITTSBURGH PENNSYLVANIA" YET? THEY PLAY IT ALL THE TIME!
NOT YET...
SOON...
"THERE'S A PAWNSHOP... ON THE CORNER..."
WHERE IS THIS PLACE?
PALESTINE *
"MY FUNNY VALENTINE..."
HEY TURN IT UP! IT'S THE VOICE!
BLAH BLAH
BLAH BLAH
REM
"SWEET COMIC..."
* PALATINE, A NEARBY SUBURB
IT'S SINATRA!
SOON...
...
TOYS

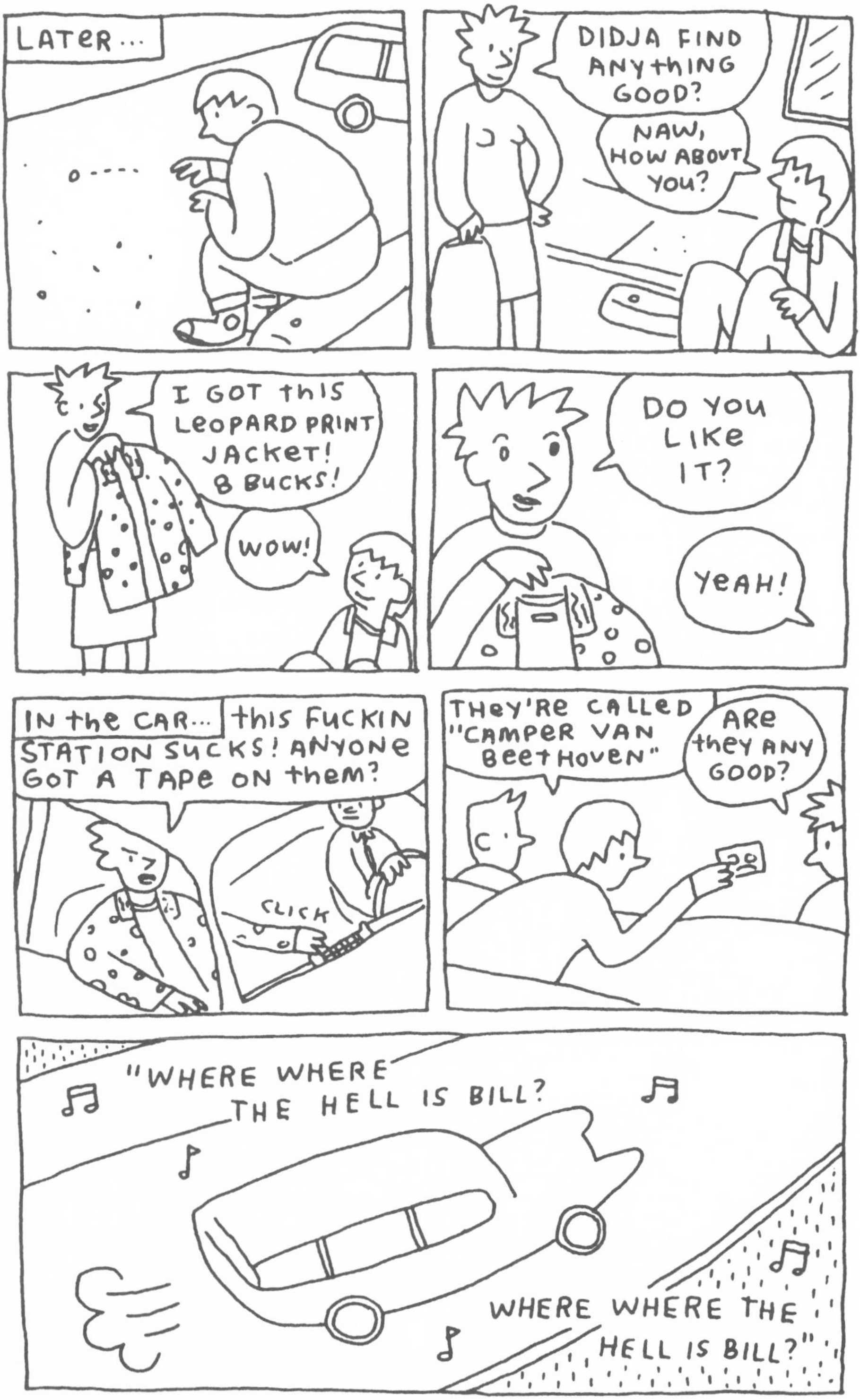
LATER...
DIDJA FIND ANYTHING GOOD?
NAW, HOW ABOUT YOU?
I GOT THIS LEOPARD PRINT JACKET! 8 BUCKS!
WOW!
DO YOU LIKE IT?
YEAH!
IN THE CAR...
THIS FUCKIN STATION SUCKS! ANYONE GOT A TAPE ON THEM?
CLICK
THEY'RE CALLED "CAMPER VAN BEETHOVEN"
ARE THEY ANY GOOD?
"WHERE WHERE THE HELL IS BILL?
WHERE WHERE THE HELL IS BILL?"

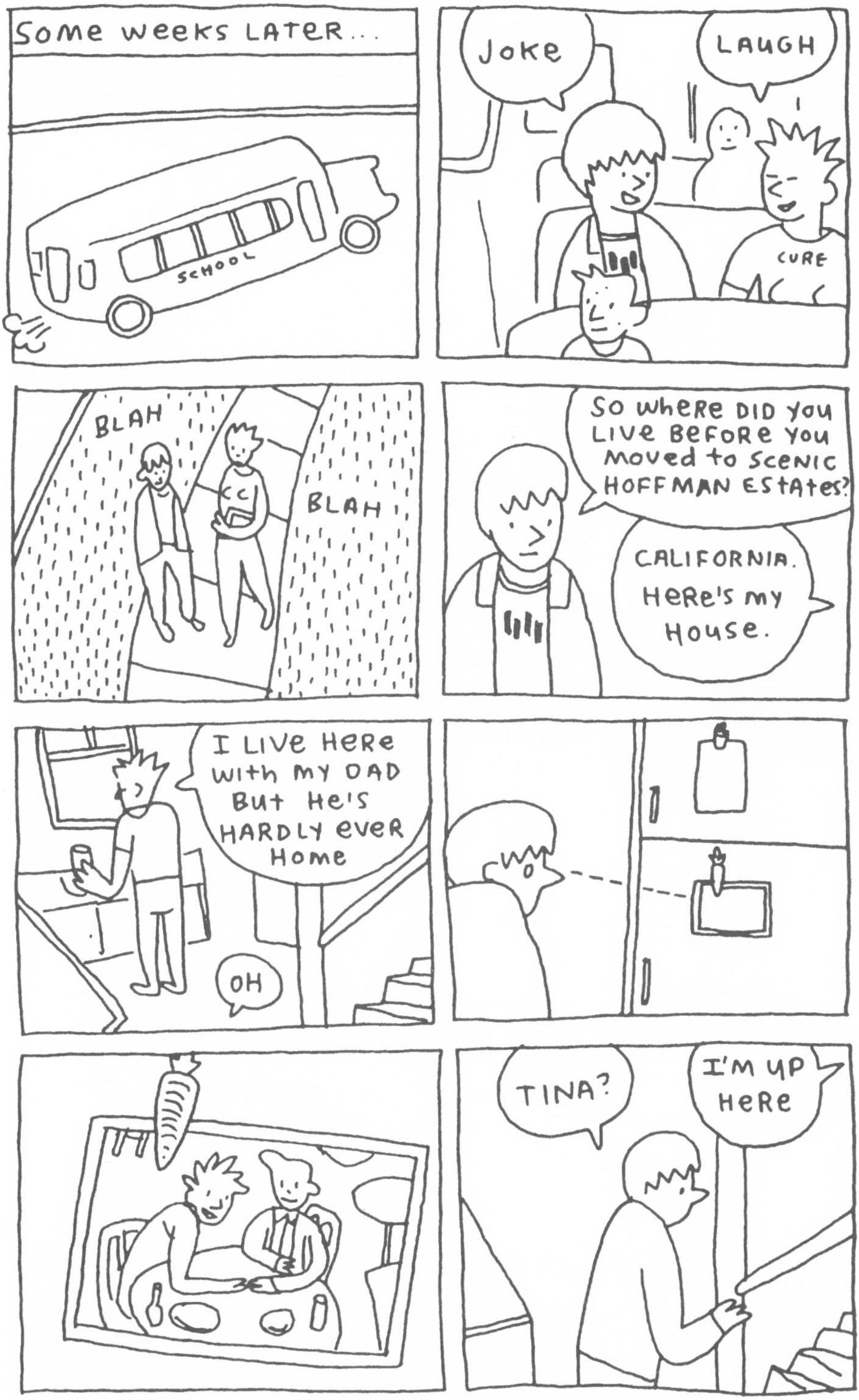
SOME WEEKS LATER...
SCHOOL
JOKE
LAUGH
CURE
BLAH
BLAH
SO WHERE DID YOU LIVE BEFORE YOU MOVED TO SCENIC HOFFMAN ESTATES?
CALIFORNIA. HERE'S MY HOUSE.
I LIVE HERE WITH MY DAD BUT HE'S HARDLY EVER HOME
OH
TINA?
I'M UP HERE

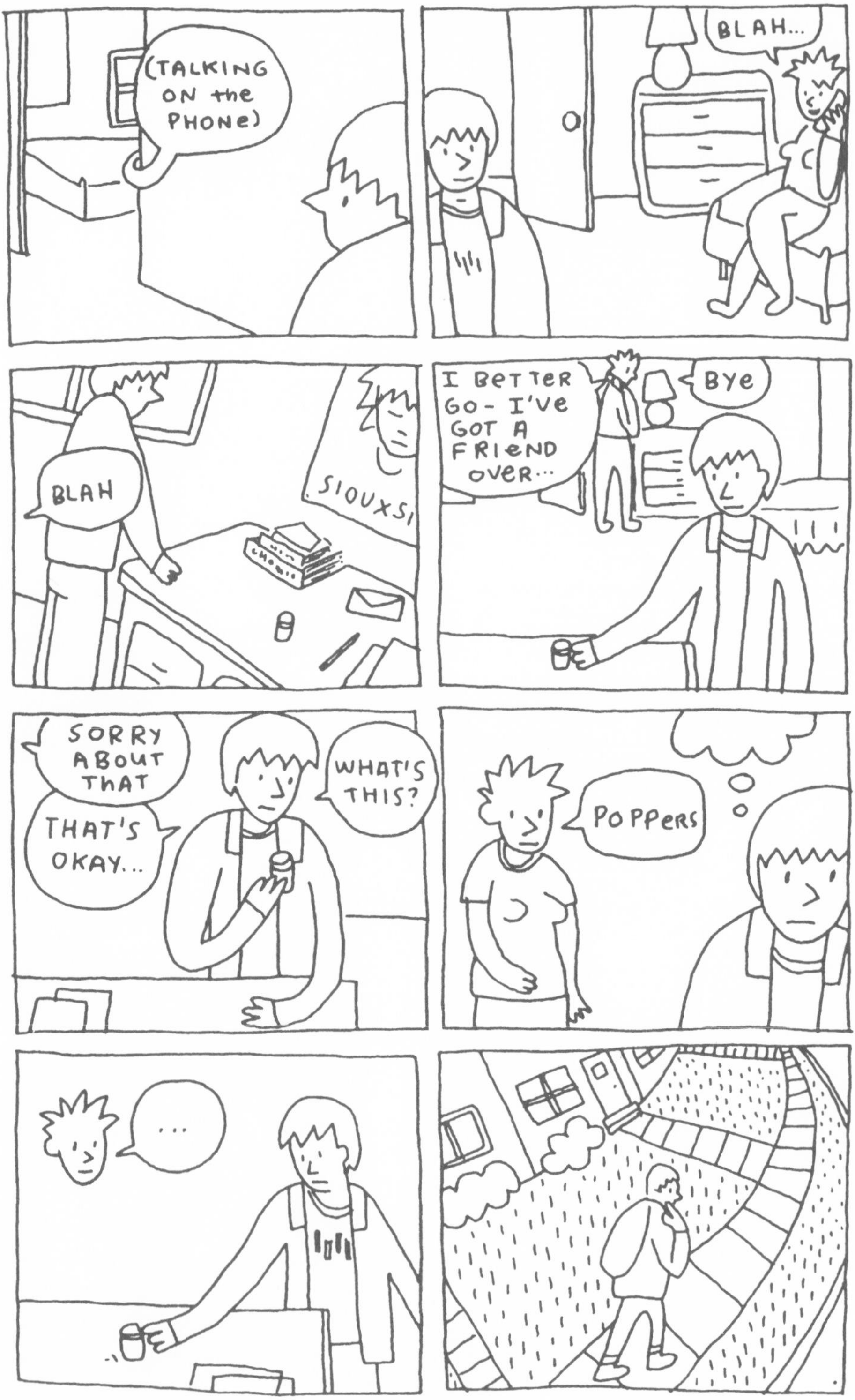

(TALKING ON the PHONE)
BLAH...
BLAH
SIOUXSI
I BETTER GO - I'VE GOT A FRIEND OVER...
BYE
SORRY ABOUT THAT
THAT'S OKAY...
WHAT'S THIS?
POPPERS
...

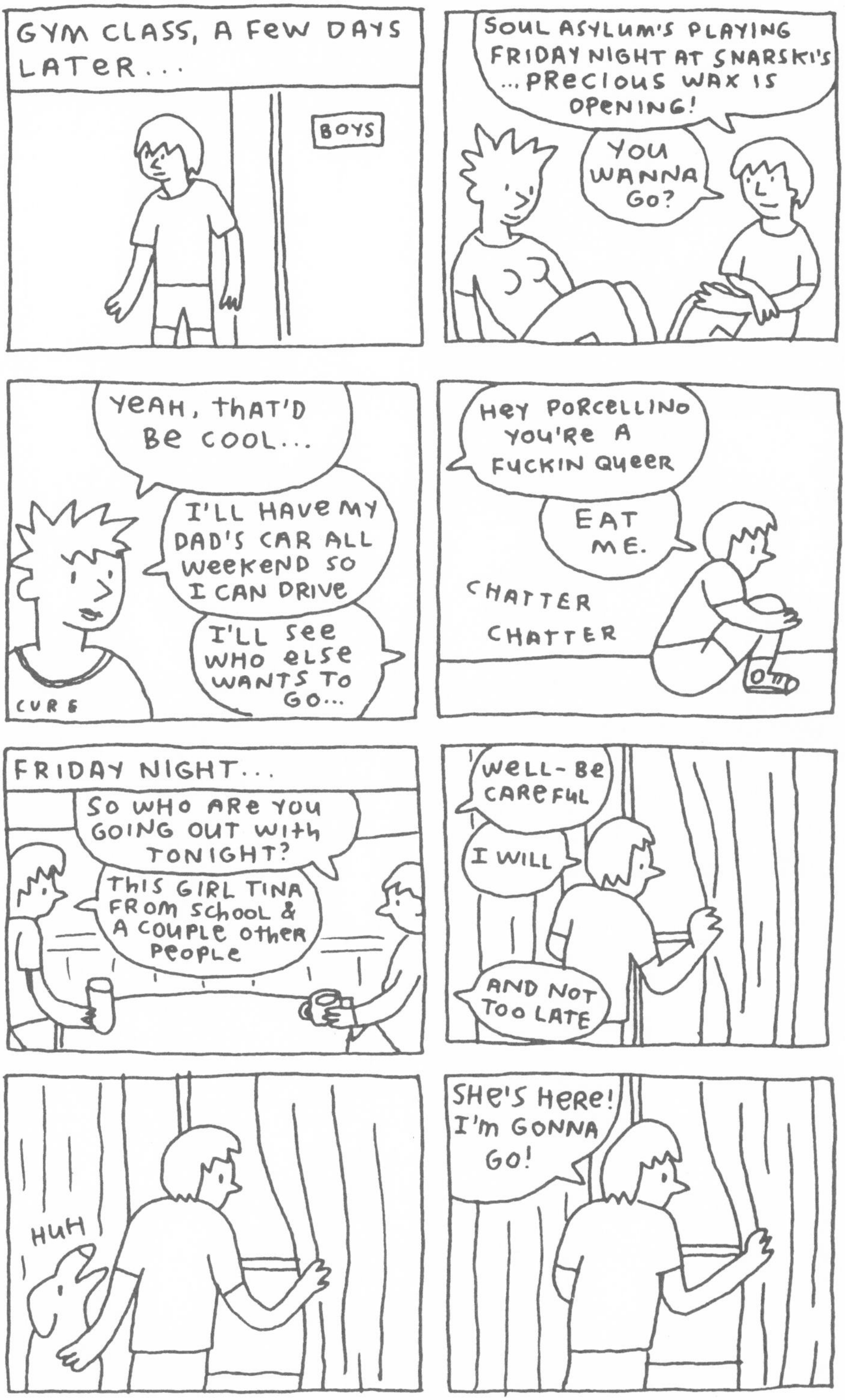
GYM CLASS, A FEW DAYS LATER...
BOYS
SOUL ASYLUM'S PLAYING FRIDAY NIGHT AT SNARSKI'S ...PRECIOUS WAX IS OPENING!
YOU WANNA GO?
YEAH, THAT'D BE COOL...
I'LL HAVE MY DAD'S CAR ALL WEEKEND SO I CAN DRIVE
I'LL SEE WHO ELSE WANTS TO GO...
CURE
HEY PORCELLINO YOU'RE A FUCKIN QUEER
EAT ME.
CHATTER
CHATTER
FRIDAY NIGHT...
SO WHO ARE YOU GOING OUT WITH TONIGHT?
THIS GIRL TINA FROM SCHOOL & A COUPLE OTHER PEOPLE
WELL-BE CAREFUL
I WILL
AND NOT TOO LATE
HUH
SHE'S HERE! I'M GONNA GO!

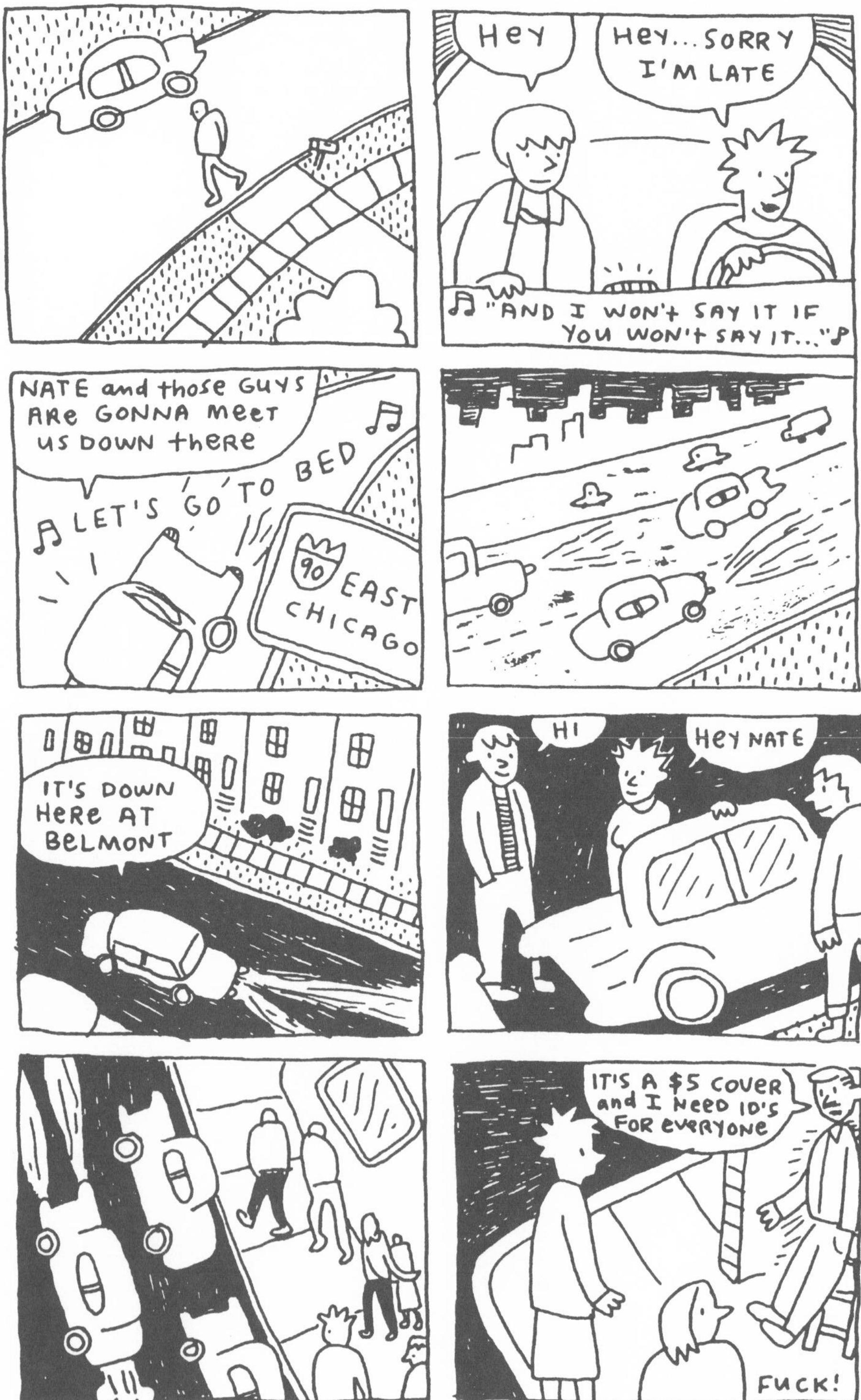
Hey
Hey... SORRY I'M LATE
"AND I WON't SAY IT IF YOU WON't SAY IT..."
NATE and those GUYS ARe GONNA Meet us DOWN there
LET'S GO TO BED
90 EAST CHICAGO
IT'S DOWN HeRe AT BeLMONT
HI
Hey NATE
IT'S A $5 COVeR and I NeeD ID'S FOR eveRYONE
FUCK!

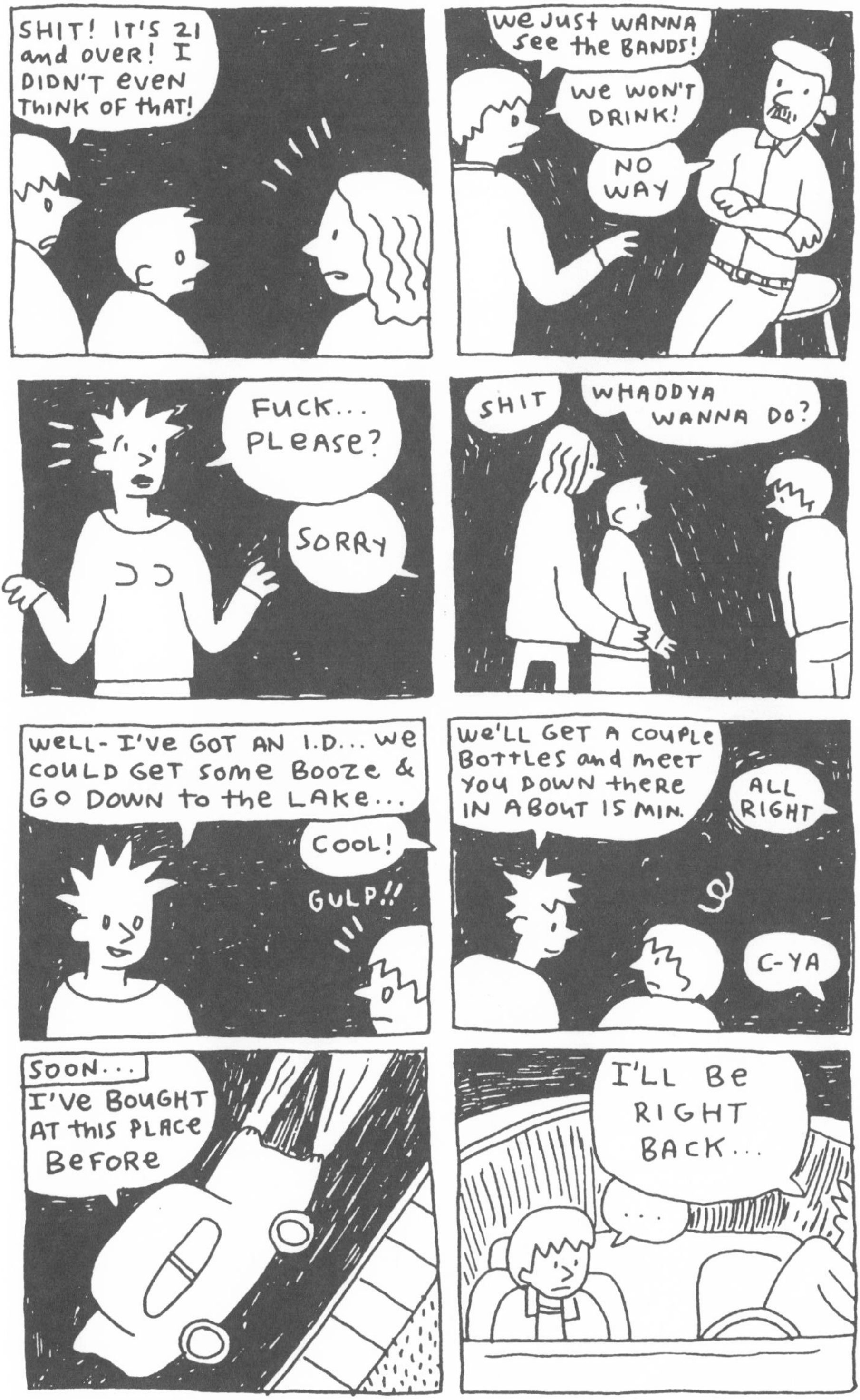
SHIT! IT'S 21 and OVER! I DIDN'T even THINK OF thAT!
we JUST WANNA see the BANDS!
we WON'T DRINK!
NO WAY
FUCK... PLeASe?
SORRY
SHIT
WHADDYA WANNA DO?
weLL- I've GOT AN I.D... we COULD GeT Some Booze & GO DOWN to the LAKe...
COOL!
GULP!!
we'LL GeT A COUPLe BOTTLeS and meeT YOU DOWN there IN ABOUT 15 MIN.
ALL RIGHT
C-YA
SOON...
I've BOUGHT AT this PLACe BeFORe
I'LL Be RIGHT BACK...
...

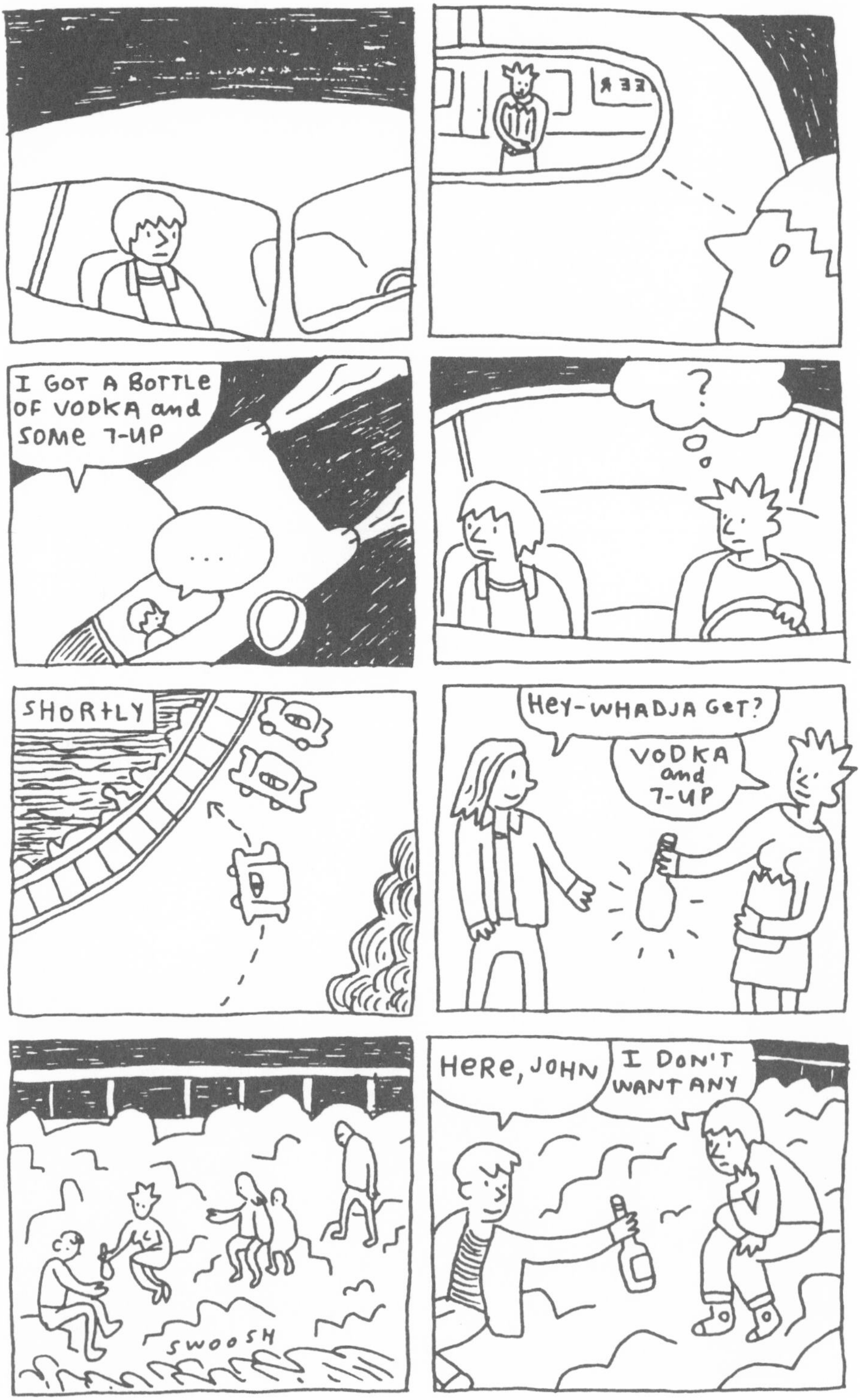
I GOT A BOTTLE OF VODKA and SOME 7-UP
...
?
SHORTLY
Hey-WHADJA GeT?
VODKA and 7-UP
SWOOSH
Here, JOHN
I DON'T WANT ANY

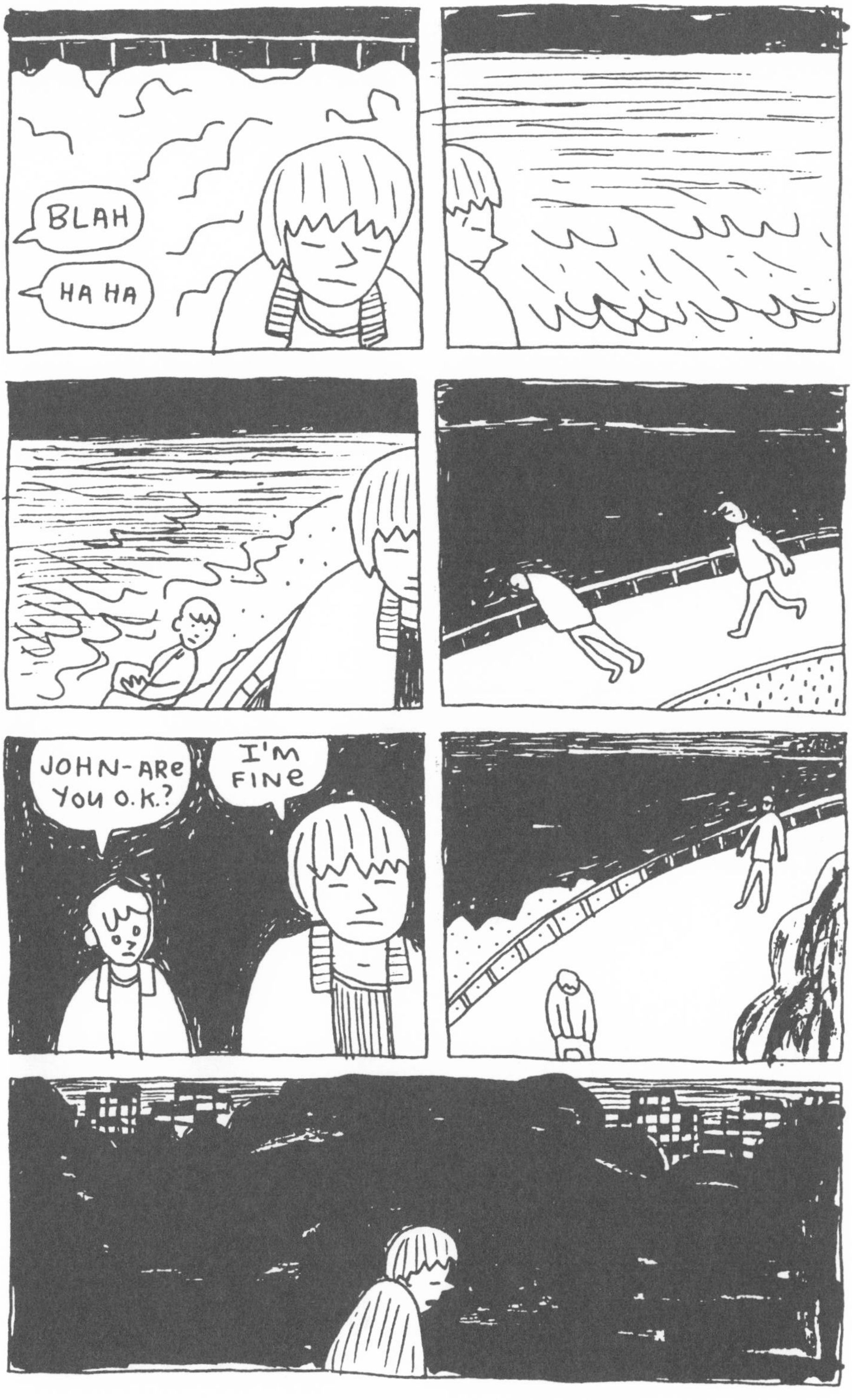
BLAH
HA HA
JOHN-ARE YOU O.K.?
I'M FINE

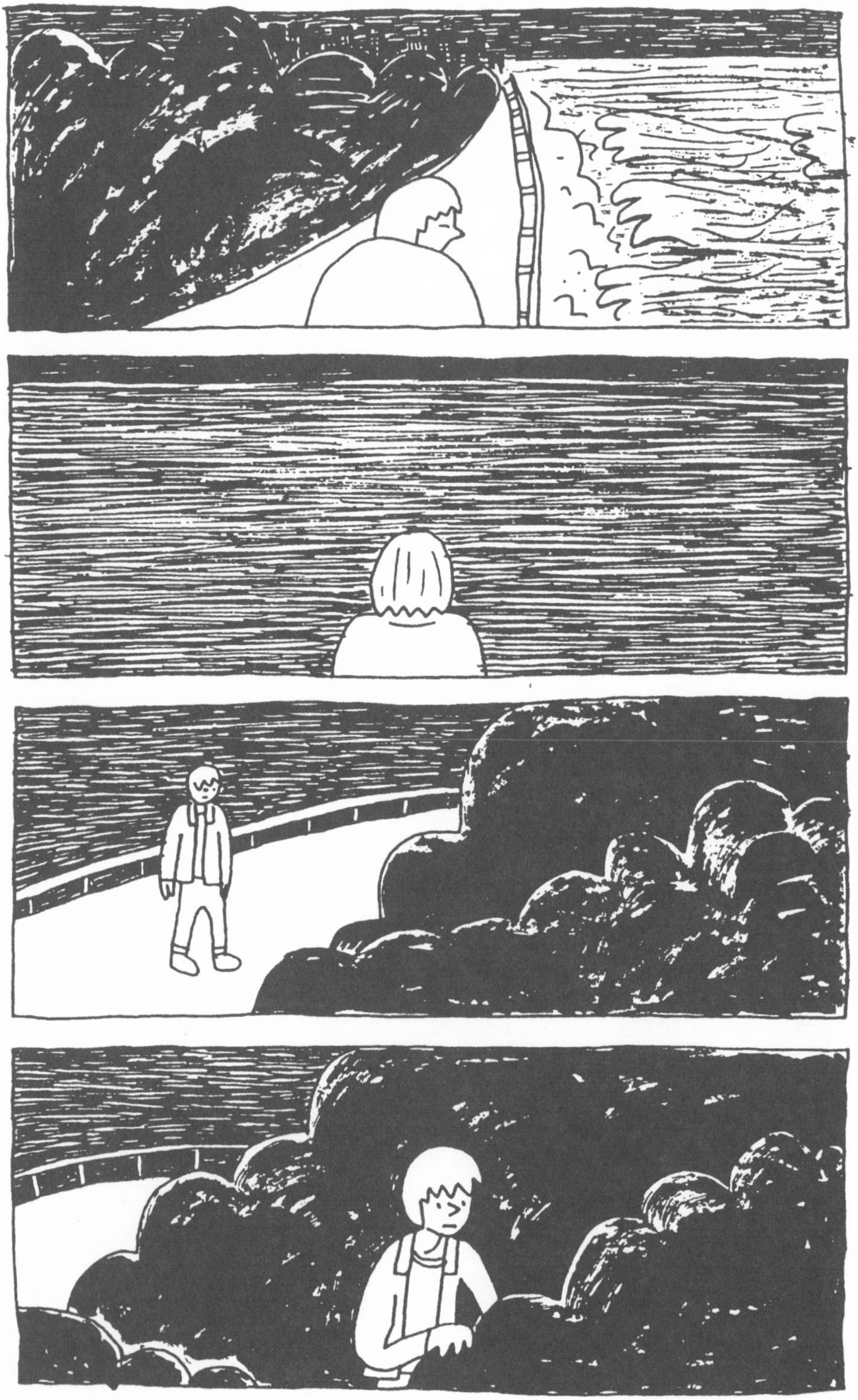

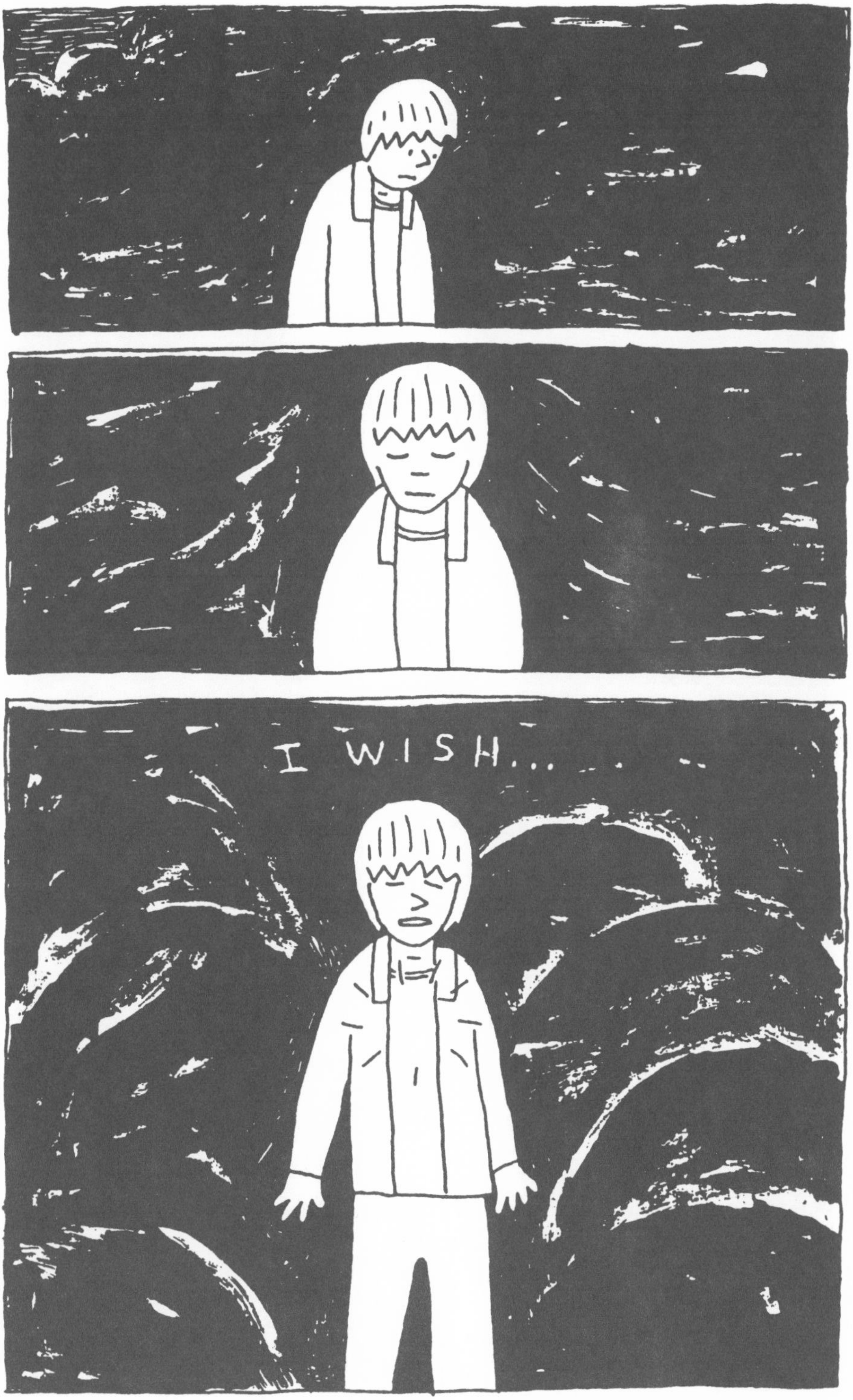
I WISH...

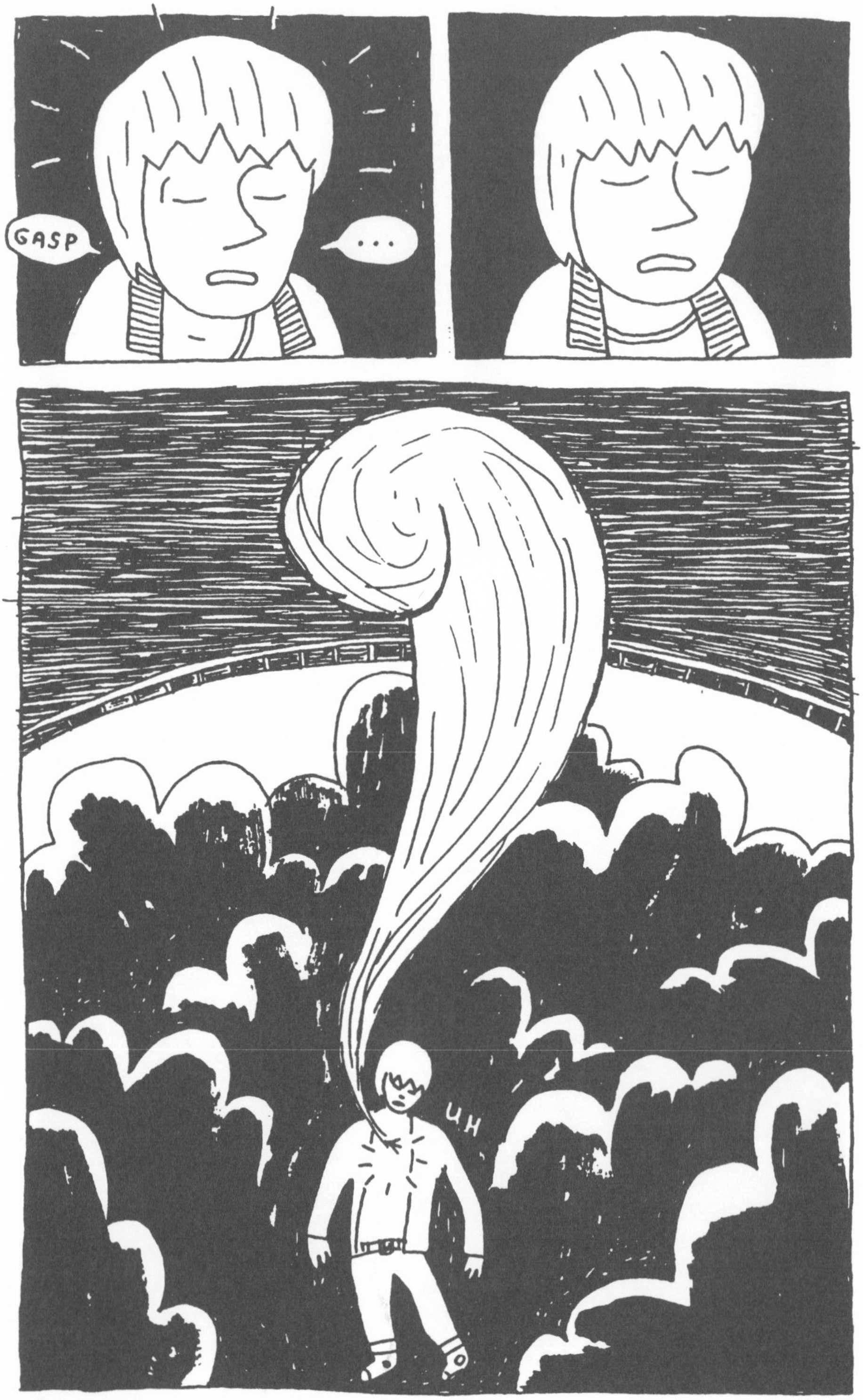
GASP
...
UH

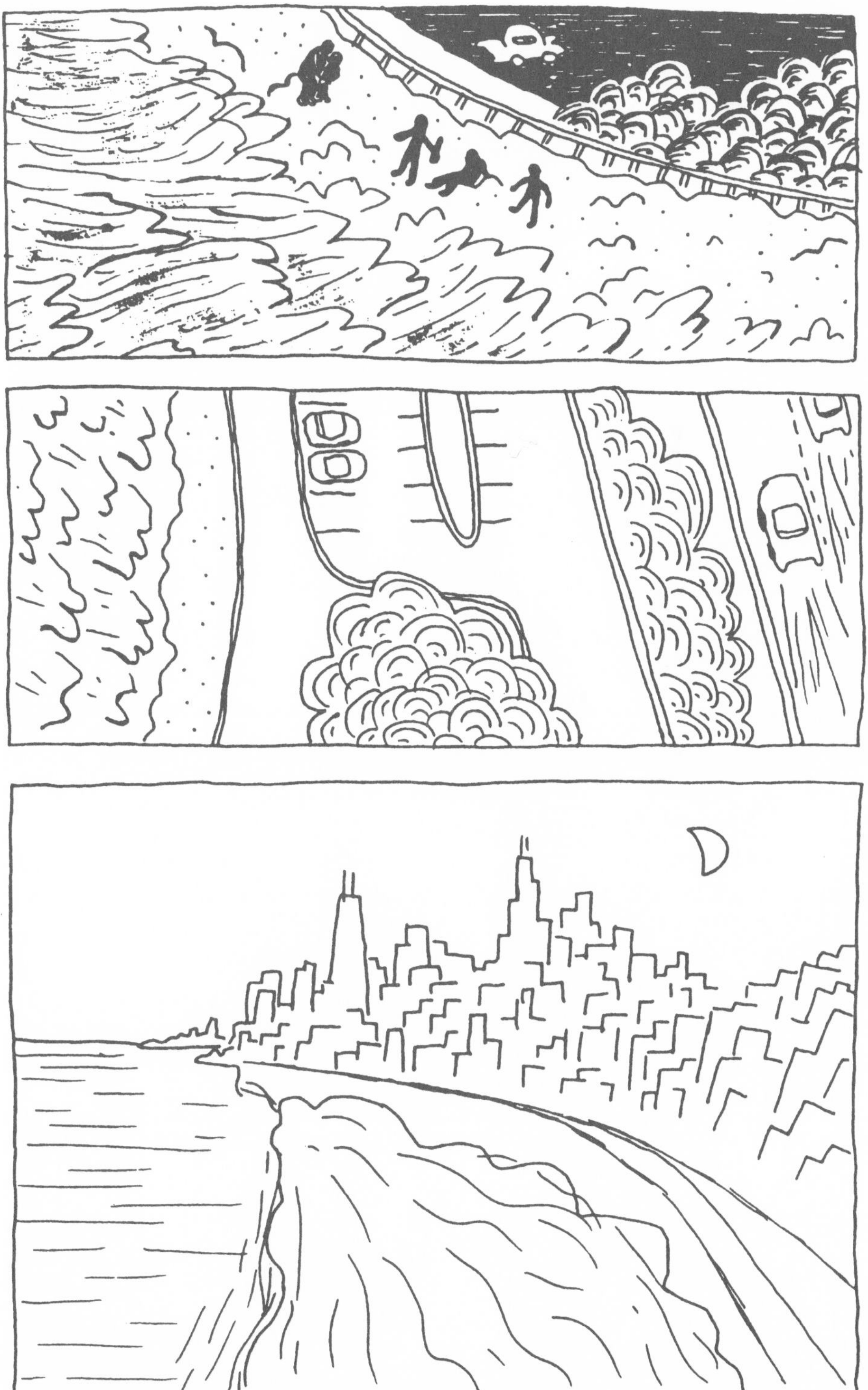

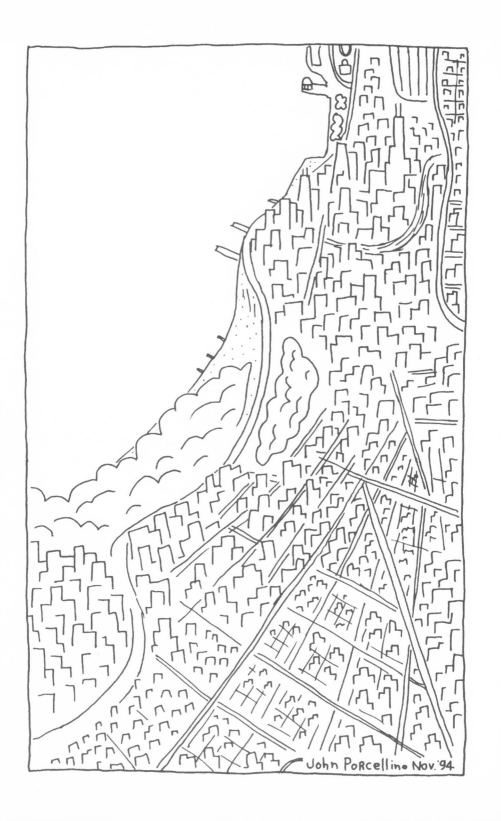

John Porcellino Nov. '94

Part One
HAIRCUTTING TIME

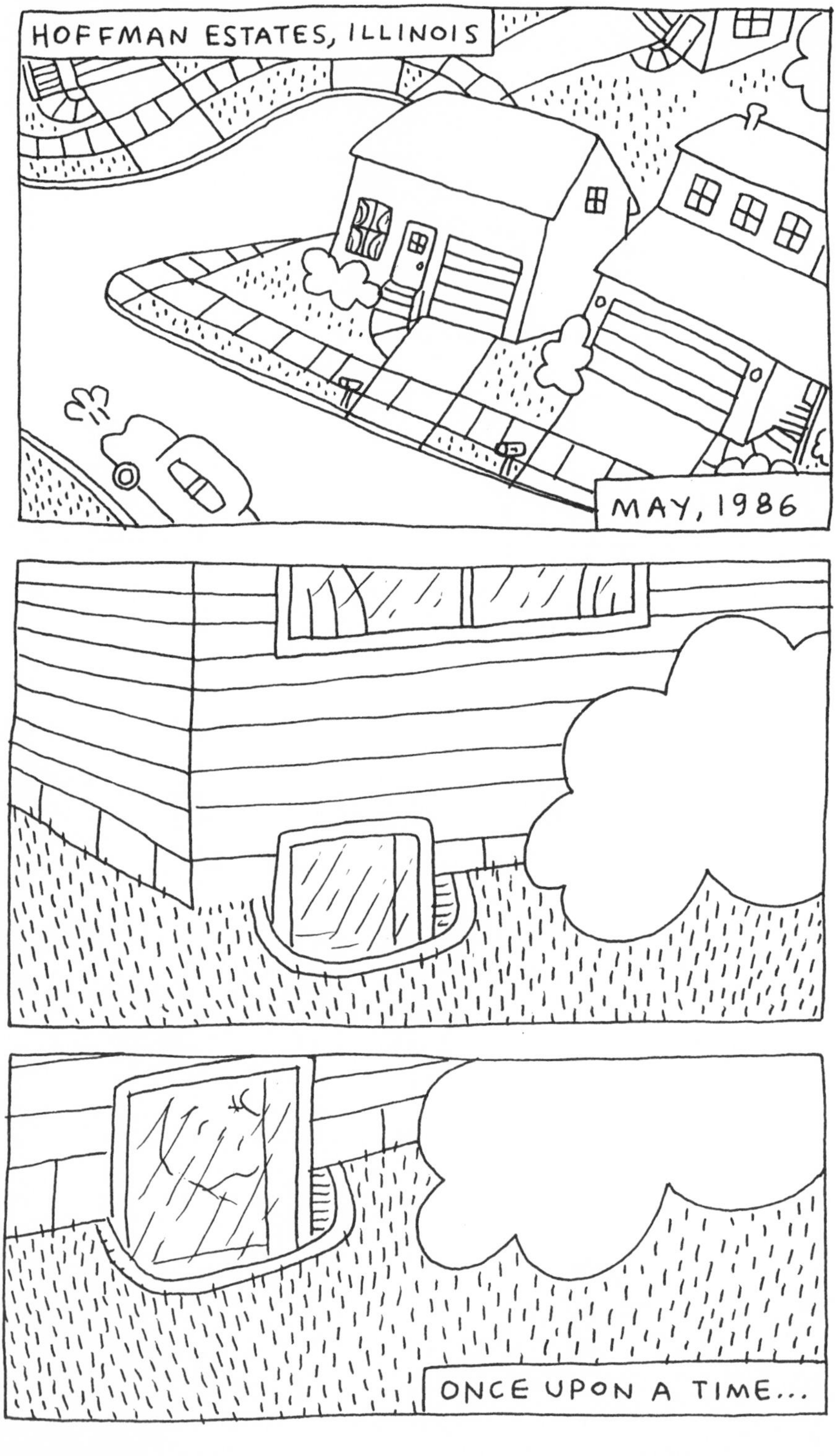
HOFFMAN ESTATES, ILLINOIS
MAY, 1986
ONCE UPON A TIME...

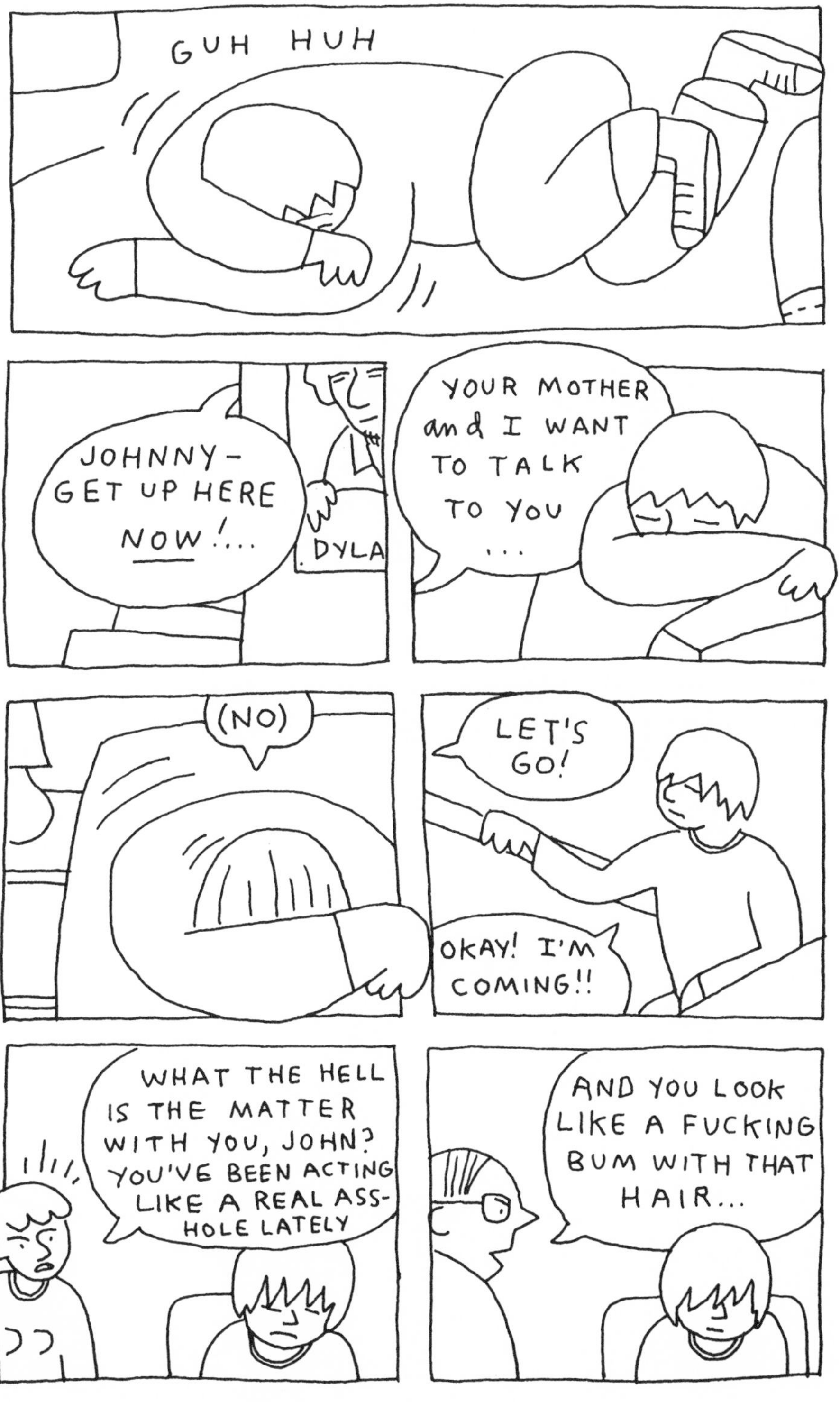
GUH HUH
JOHNNY-
GET UP HERE
NOW!...
DYLA
YOUR MOTHER
and I WANT
TO TALK
TO YOU
...
(NO)
LET'S
GO!
OKAY! I'M
COMING!!
WHAT THE HELL
IS THE MATTER
WITH YOU, JOHN?
YOU'VE BEEN ACTING
LIKE A REAL ASS-
HOLE LATELY
AND YOU LOOK
LIKE A FUCKING
BUM WITH THAT
HAIR...

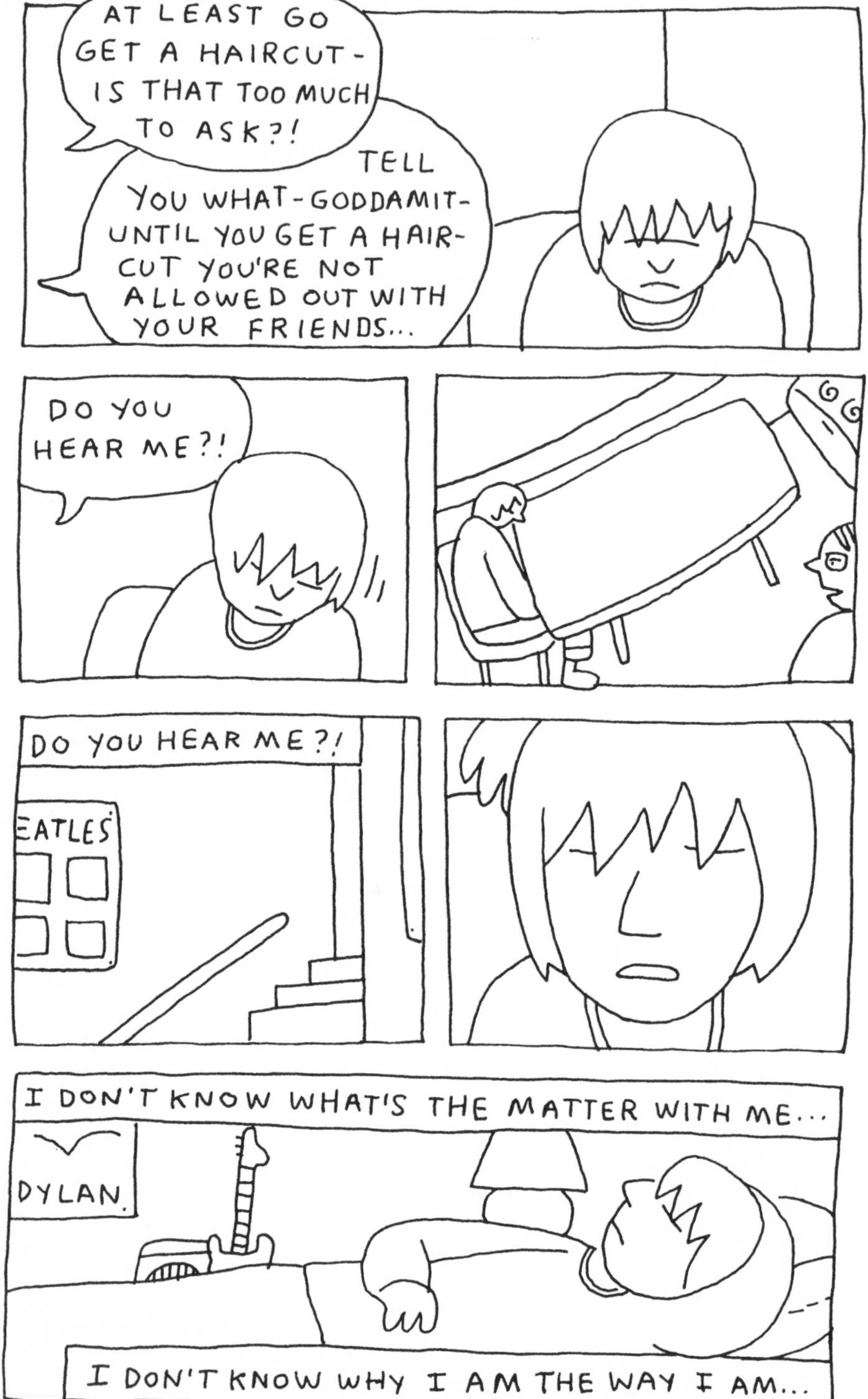
AT LEAST GO GET A HAIRCUT - IS THAT TOO MUCH TO ASK?!
TELL YOU WHAT - GODDAMIT - UNTIL YOU GET A HAIRCUT YOU'RE NOT ALLOWED OUT WITH YOUR FRIENDS...
DO YOU HEAR ME?!
DO YOU HEAR ME?!
EATLES
I DON'T KNOW WHAT'S THE MATTER WITH ME...
DYLAN
I DON'T KNOW WHY I AM THE WAY I AM...

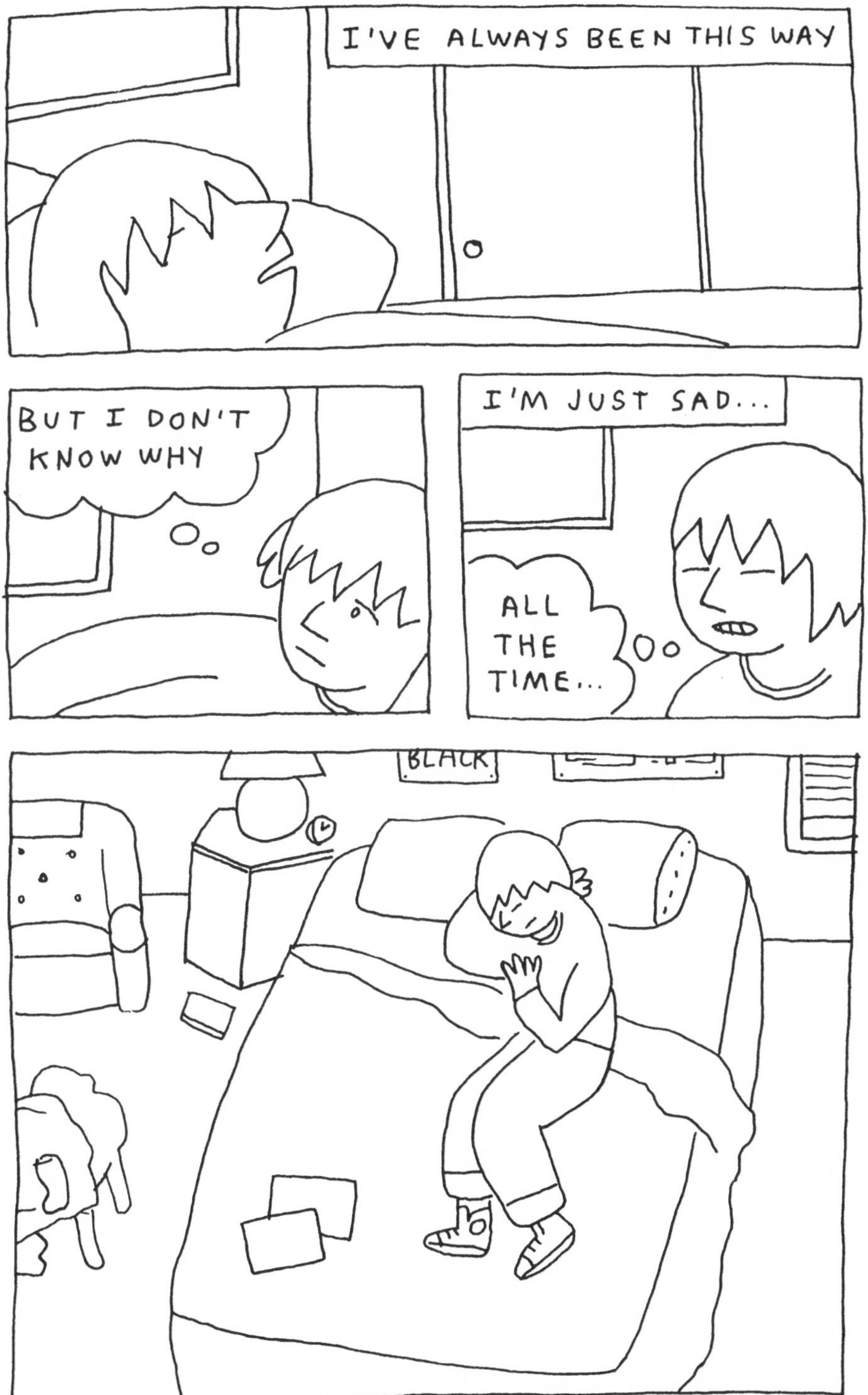
I'VE ALWAYS BEEN THIS WAY
BUT I DON'T KNOW WHY
I'M JUST SAD...
ALL THE TIME...
BLACK
AND I DON'T KNOW WHAT TO DO.

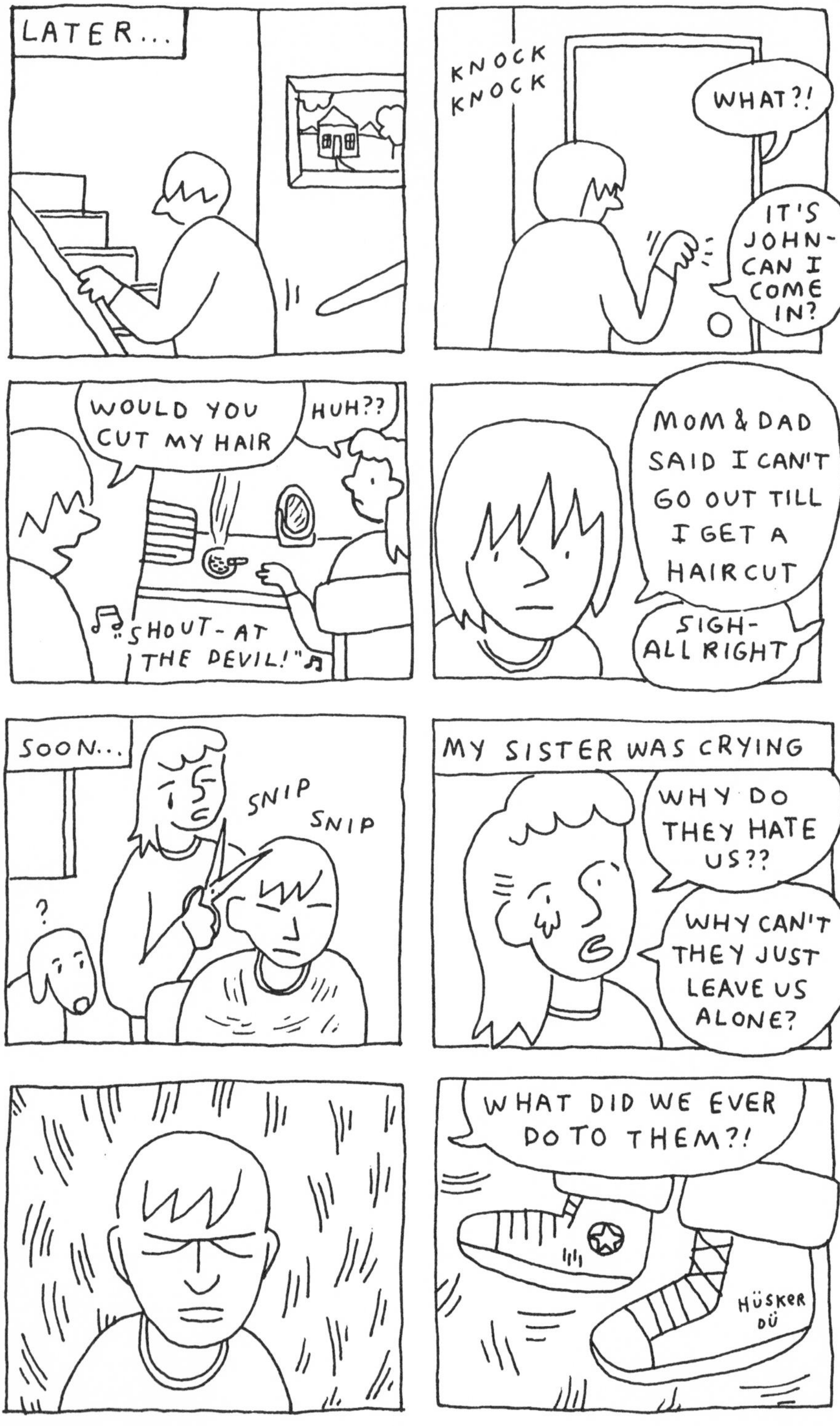
LATER...
KNOCK KNOCK
WHAT?!
IT'S JOHN- CAN I COME IN?
WOULD YOU CUT MY HAIR
HUH??
"SHOUT-AT THE DEVIL!"
MOM & DAD SAID I CAN'T GO OUT TILL I GET A HAIRCUT
SIGH- ALL RIGHT
SOON...
SNIP SNIP
?
MY SISTER WAS CRYING
WHY DO THEY HATE US??
WHY CAN'T THEY JUST LEAVE US ALONE?
WHAT DID WE EVER DO TO THEM?!
HÜSKER DÜ

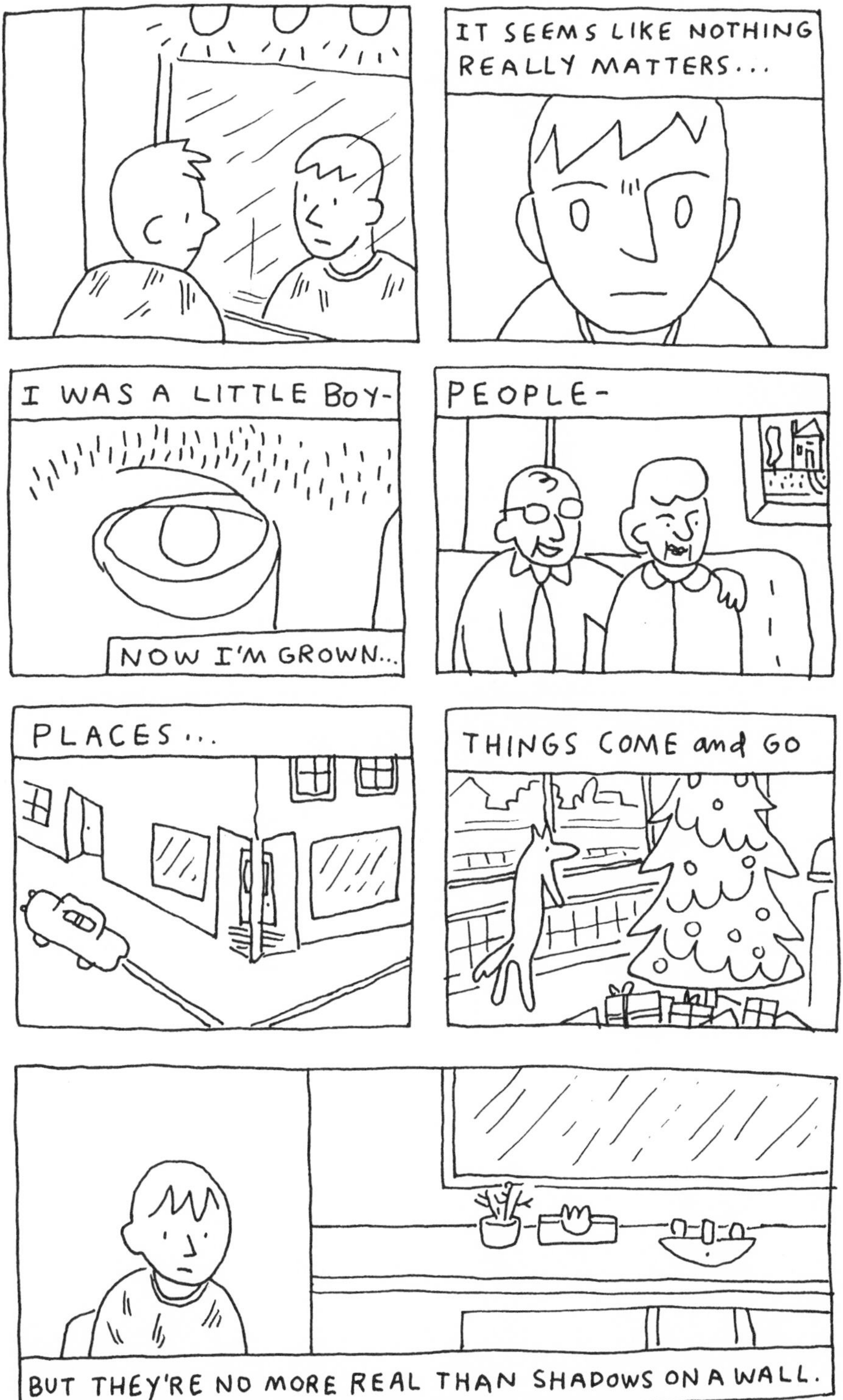
IT SEEMS LIKE NOTHING REALLY MATTERS...
I WAS A LITTLE BOY-
NOW I'M GROWN...
PEOPLE-
PLACES...
THINGS COME and GO
BUT THEY'RE NO MORE REAL THAN SHADOWS ON A WALL.

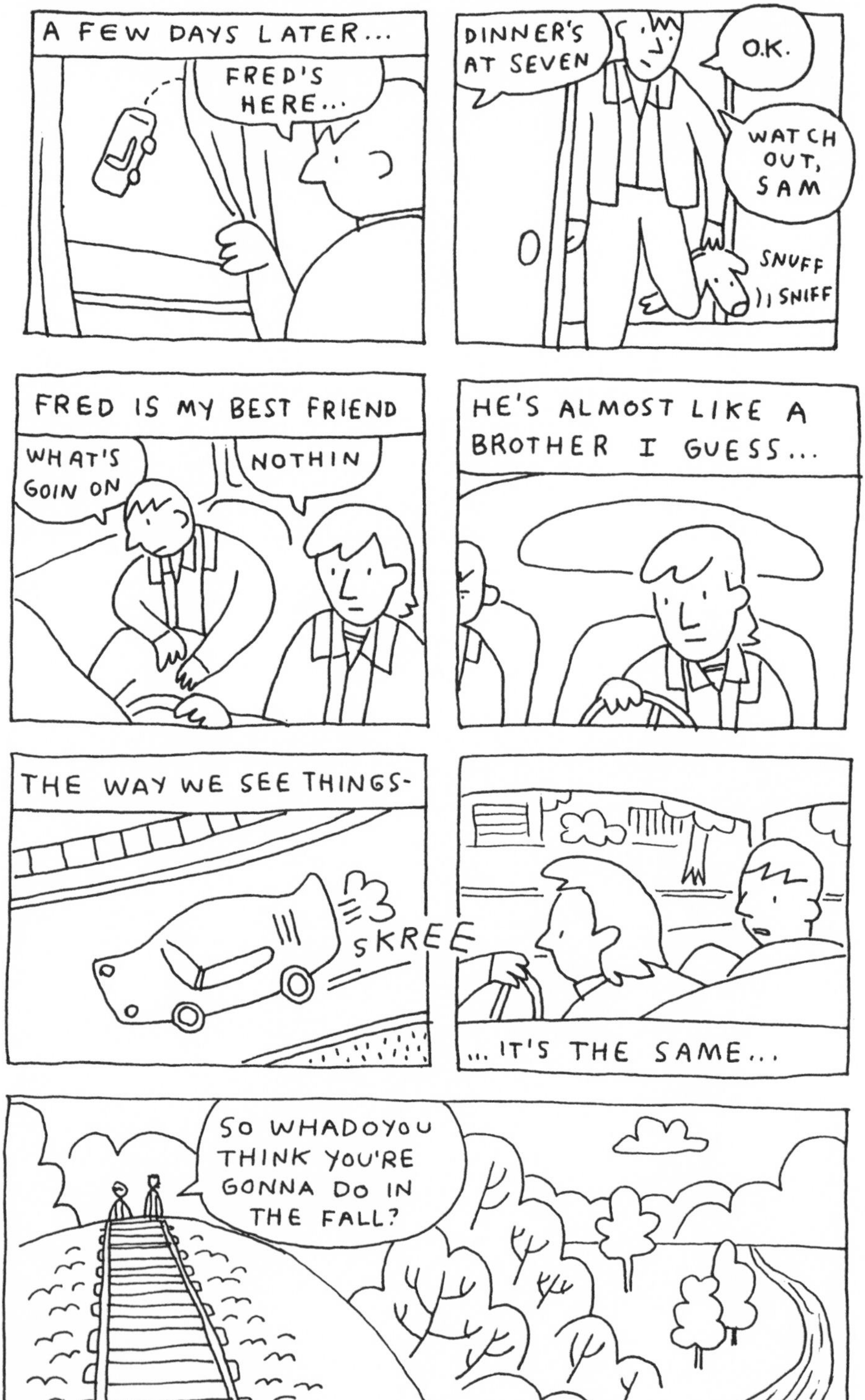
A FEW DAYS LATER...
FRED'S HERE...
DINNER'S AT SEVEN
O.K.
WATCH OUT, SAM
SNUFF
SNIFF
FRED IS MY BEST FRIEND
WHAT'S GOIN ON
NOTHIN
HE'S ALMOST LIKE A BROTHER I GUESS...
THE WAY WE SEE THINGS-
SKREE
...IT'S THE SAME...
SO WHADOYOU THINK YOU'RE GONNA DO IN THE FALL?

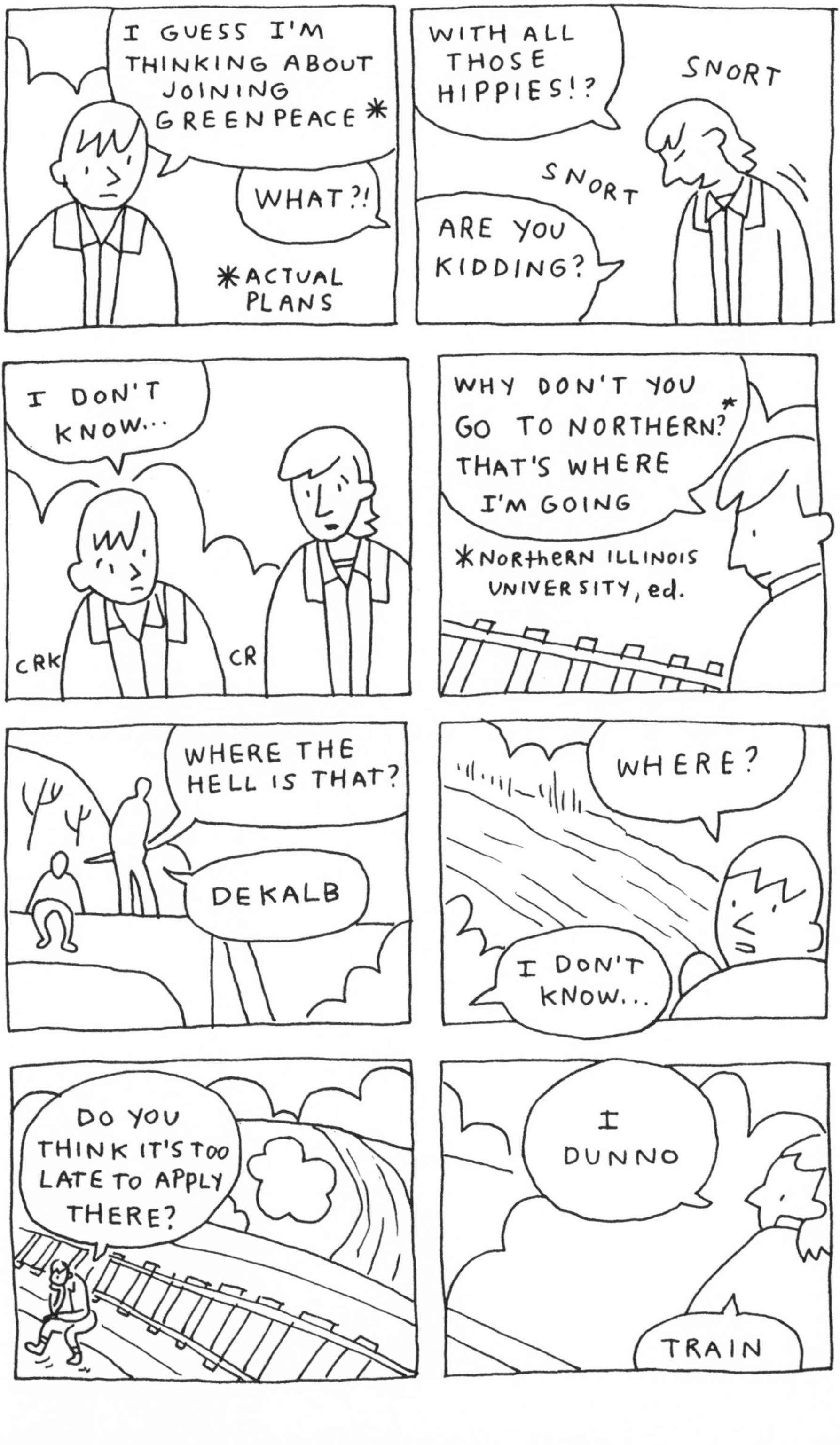
I GUESS I'M THINKING ABOUT JOINING GREENPEACE *
WHAT?!
* ACTUAL PLANS
WITH ALL THOSE HIPPIES!?
SNORT
SNORT
ARE YOU KIDDING?
I DON'T KNOW...
CRK
CR
WHY DON'T YOU GO TO NORTHERN?* THAT'S WHERE I'M GOING
* Northern ILLINOIS UNIVERSITY, ed.
WHERE THE HELL IS THAT?
DEKALB
WHERE?
I DON'T KNOW...
DO YOU THINK IT'S TOO LATE TO APPLY THERE?
I DUNNO
TRAIN

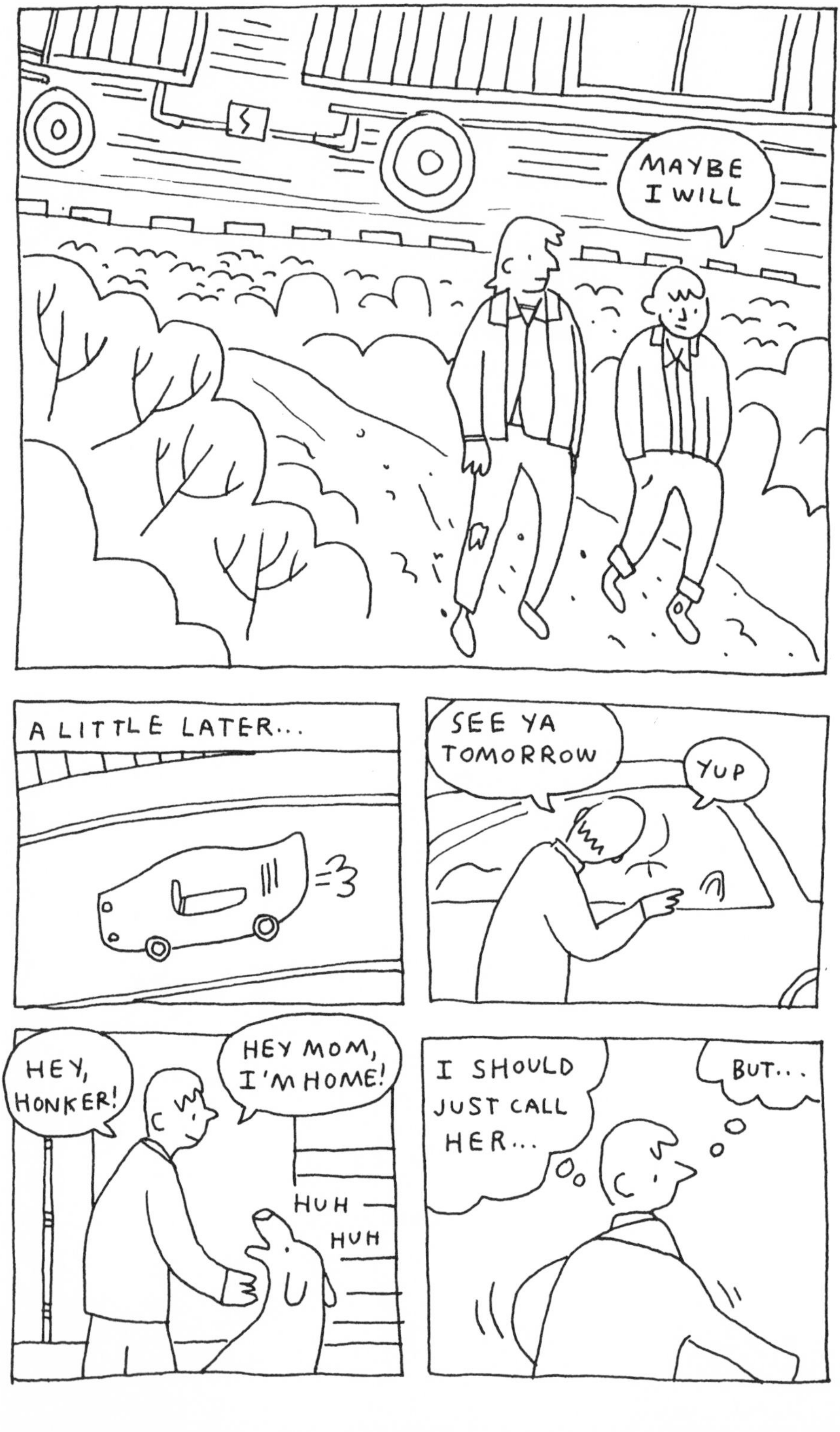
MAYBE I WILL
A LITTLE LATER...
SEE YA TOMORROW
YUP
HEY, HONKER!
HEY MOM, I'M HOME!
HUH
HUH
I SHOULD JUST CALL HER...
BUT...

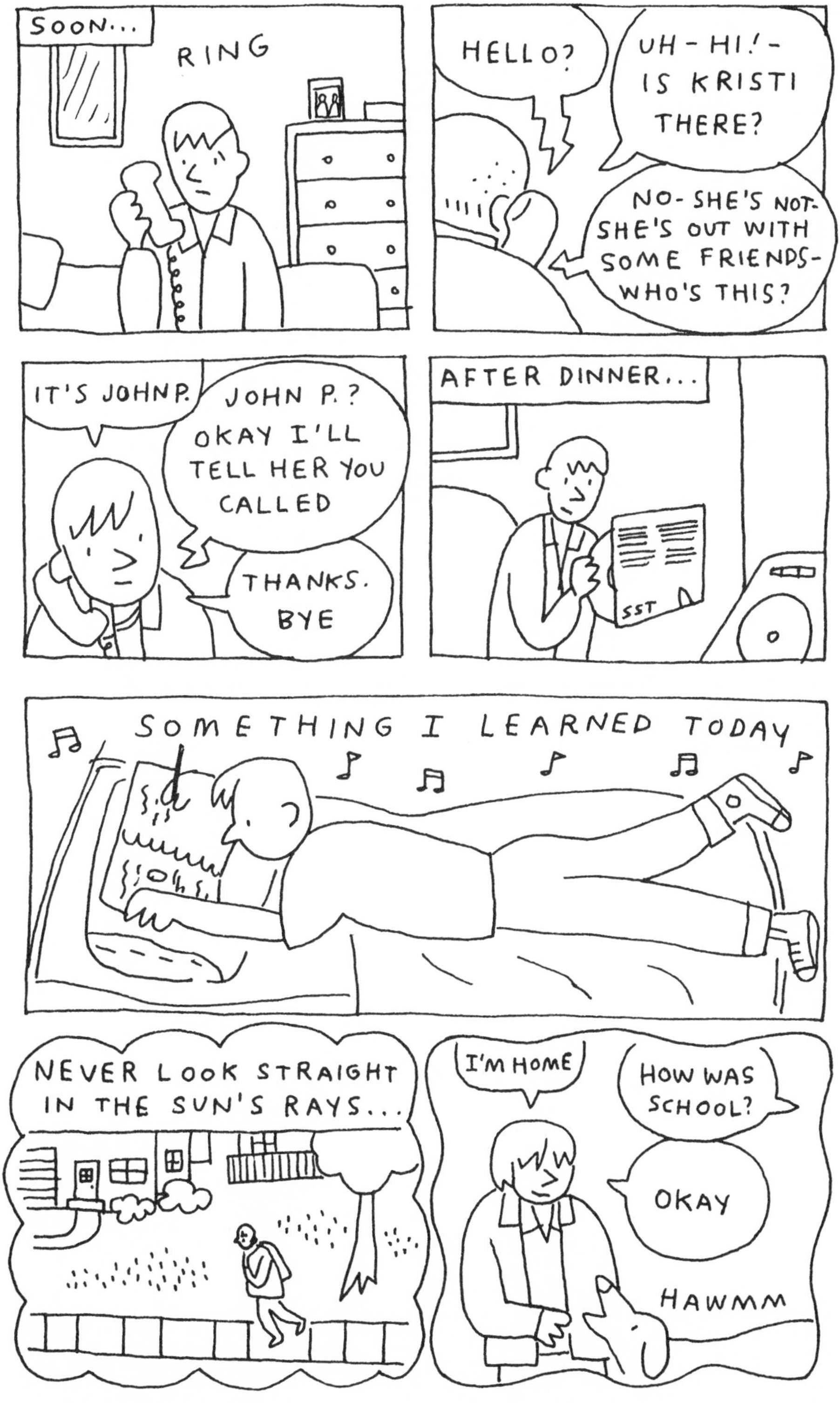
SOON...
RING
HELLO?
UH-HI!- IS KRISTI THERE?
NO-SHE'S NOT-SHE'S OUT WITH SOME FRIENDS-WHO'S THIS?
IT'S JOHN P.
JOHN P.? OKAY I'LL TELL HER YOU CALLED
THANKS. BYE
AFTER DINNER...
SST
SOMETHING I LEARNED TODAY
NEVER LOOK STRAIGHT IN THE SUN'S RAYS...
I'M HOME
HOW WAS SCHOOL?
OKAY
HAWMM

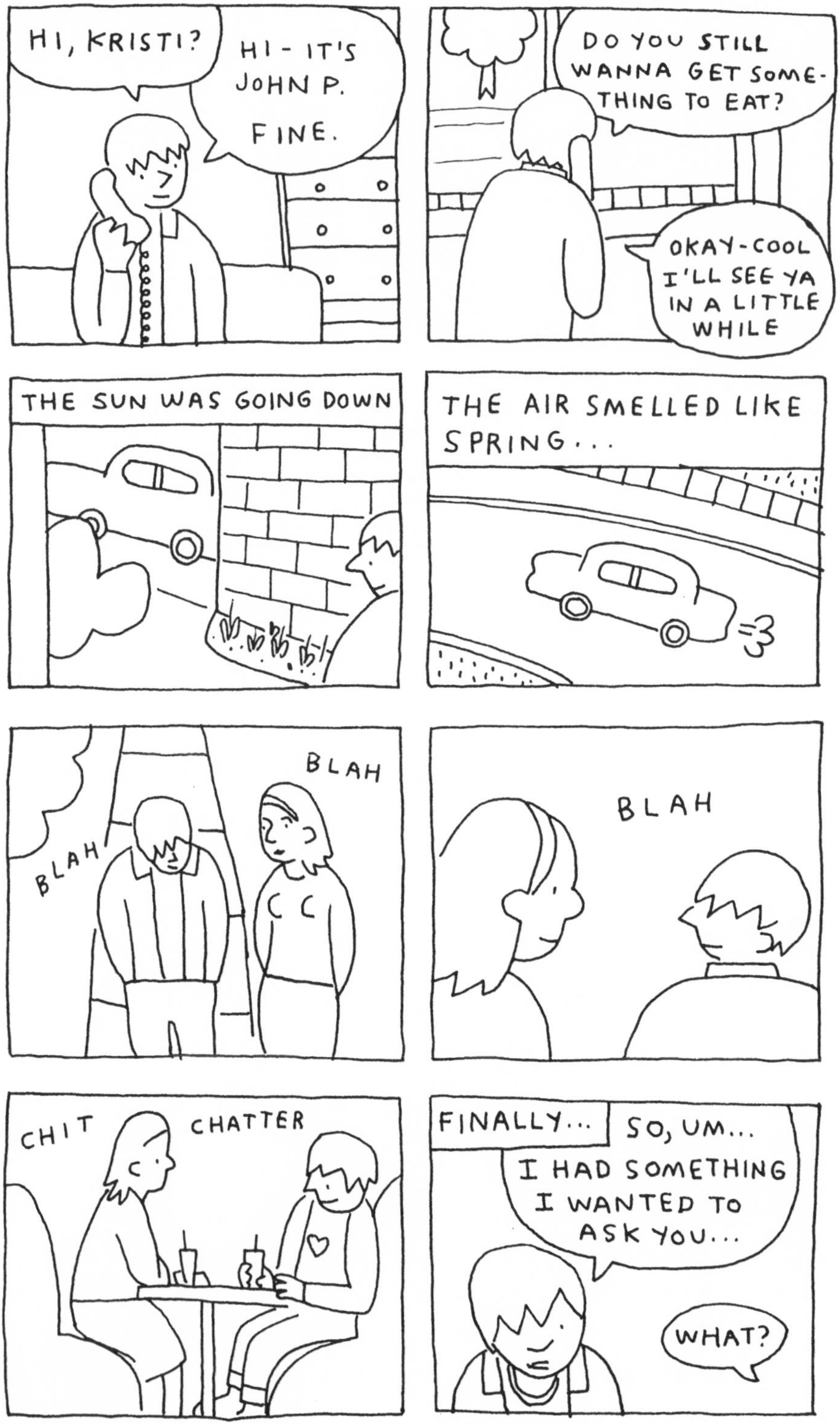
HI, KRISTI?
HI - IT'S JOHN P.
FINE.
DO YOU STILL WANNA GET SOME-THING TO EAT?
OKAY - COOL I'LL SEE YA IN A LITTLE WHILE
THE SUN WAS GOING DOWN
THE AIR SMELLED LIKE SPRING...
BLAH
BLAH
BLAH
CHIT
CHATTER
FINALLY...
SO, UM... I HAD SOMETHING I WANTED TO ASK YOU...
WHAT?

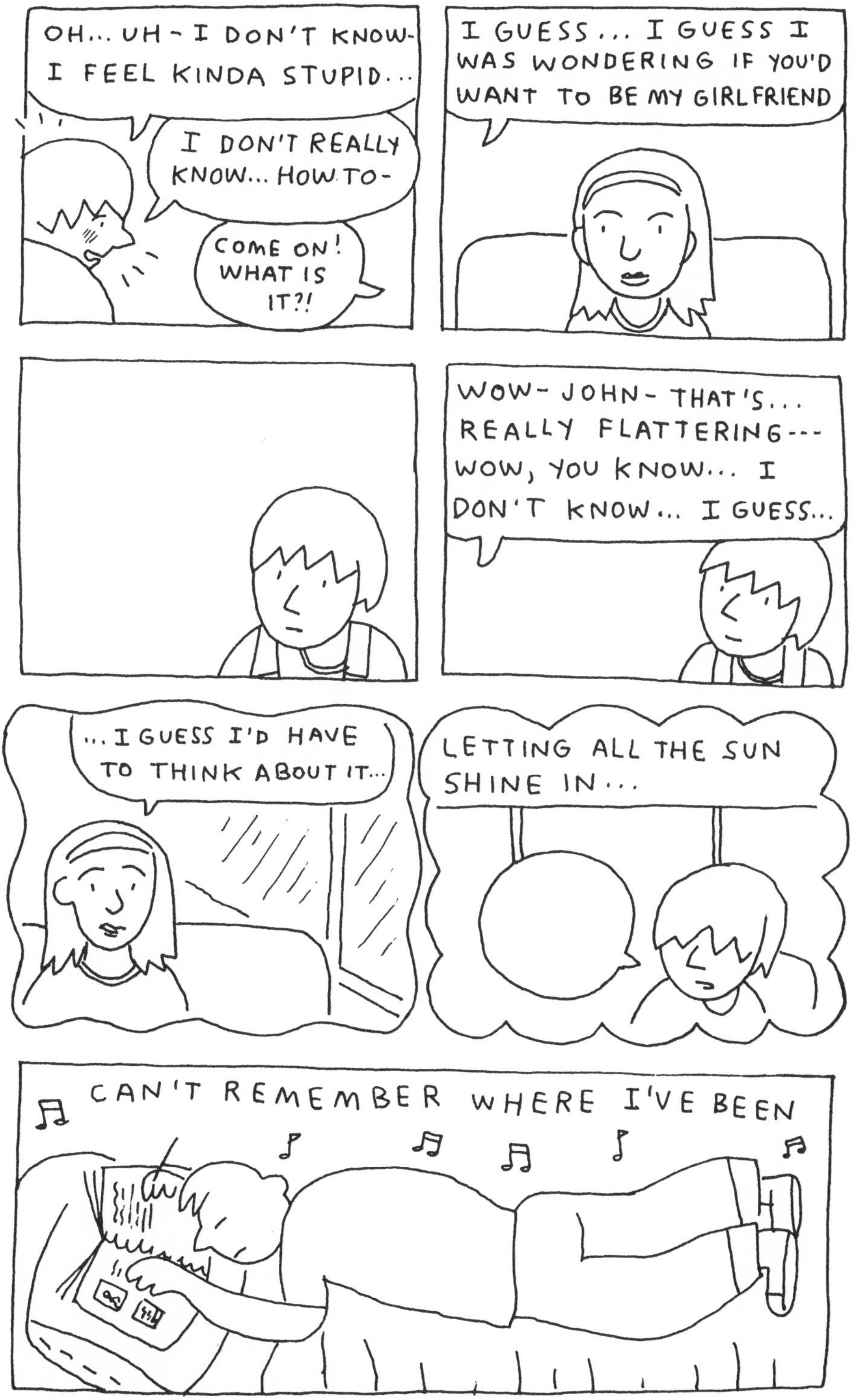
OH... UH - I DON'T KNOW - I FEEL KINDA STUPID...
I DON'T REALLY KNOW... HOW TO-
COME ON! WHAT IS IT?!
I GUESS... I GUESS I WAS WONDERING IF YOU'D WANT TO BE MY GIRLFRIEND
WOW - JOHN - THAT'S... REALLY FLATTERING--- WOW, YOU KNOW... I DON'T KNOW... I GUESS...
...I GUESS I'D HAVE TO THINK ABOUT IT...
LETTING ALL THE SUN SHINE IN...
CAN'T REMEMBER WHERE I'VE BEEN

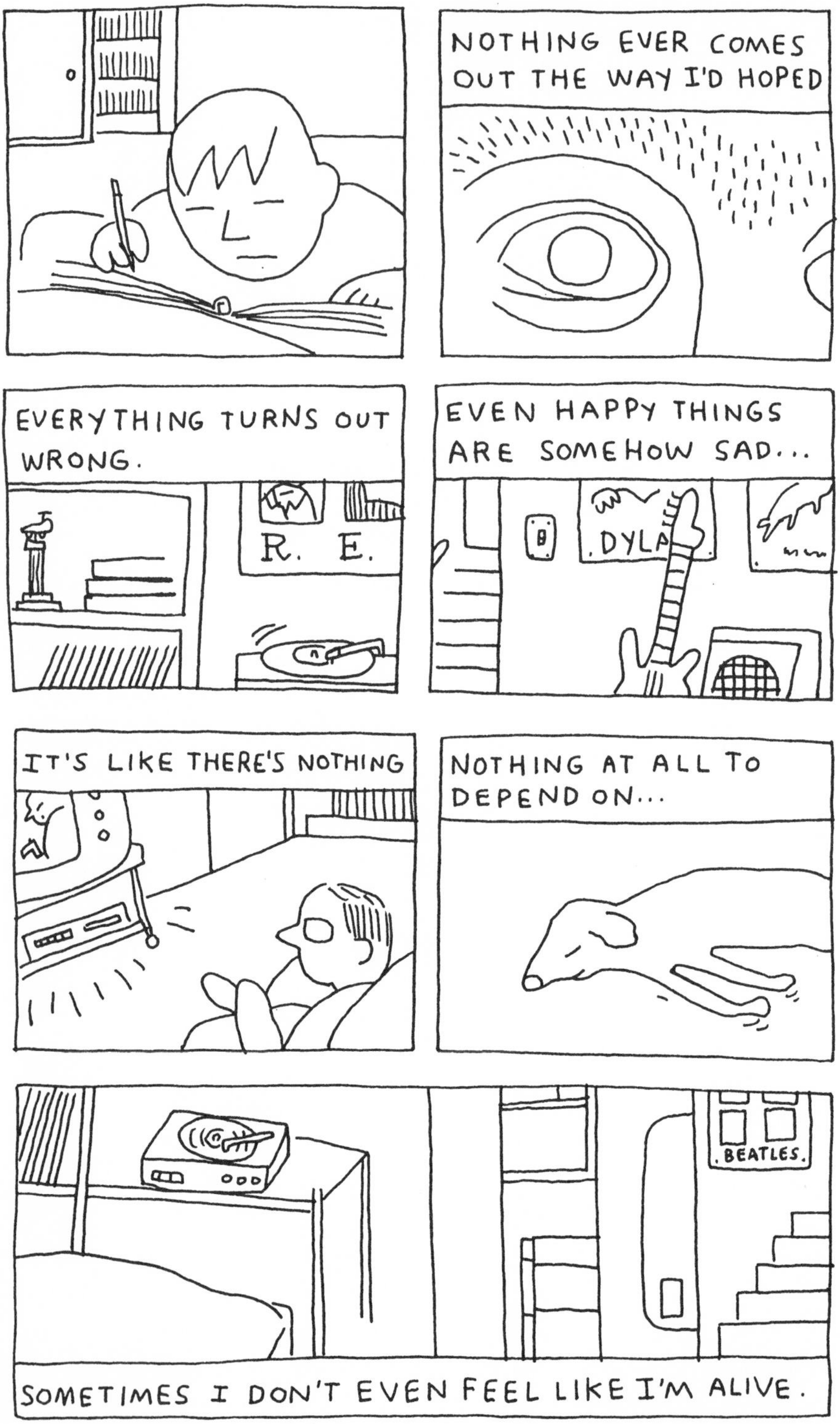

NOTHING EVER COMES OUT THE WAY I'D HOPED
EVERYTHING TURNS OUT WRONG.
R. E.
EVEN HAPPY THINGS ARE SOMEHOW SAD...
DYLA
IT'S LIKE THERE'S NOTHING
NOTHING AT ALL TO DEPEND ON...
BEATLES
SOMETIMES I DON'T EVEN FEEL LIKE I'M ALIVE.

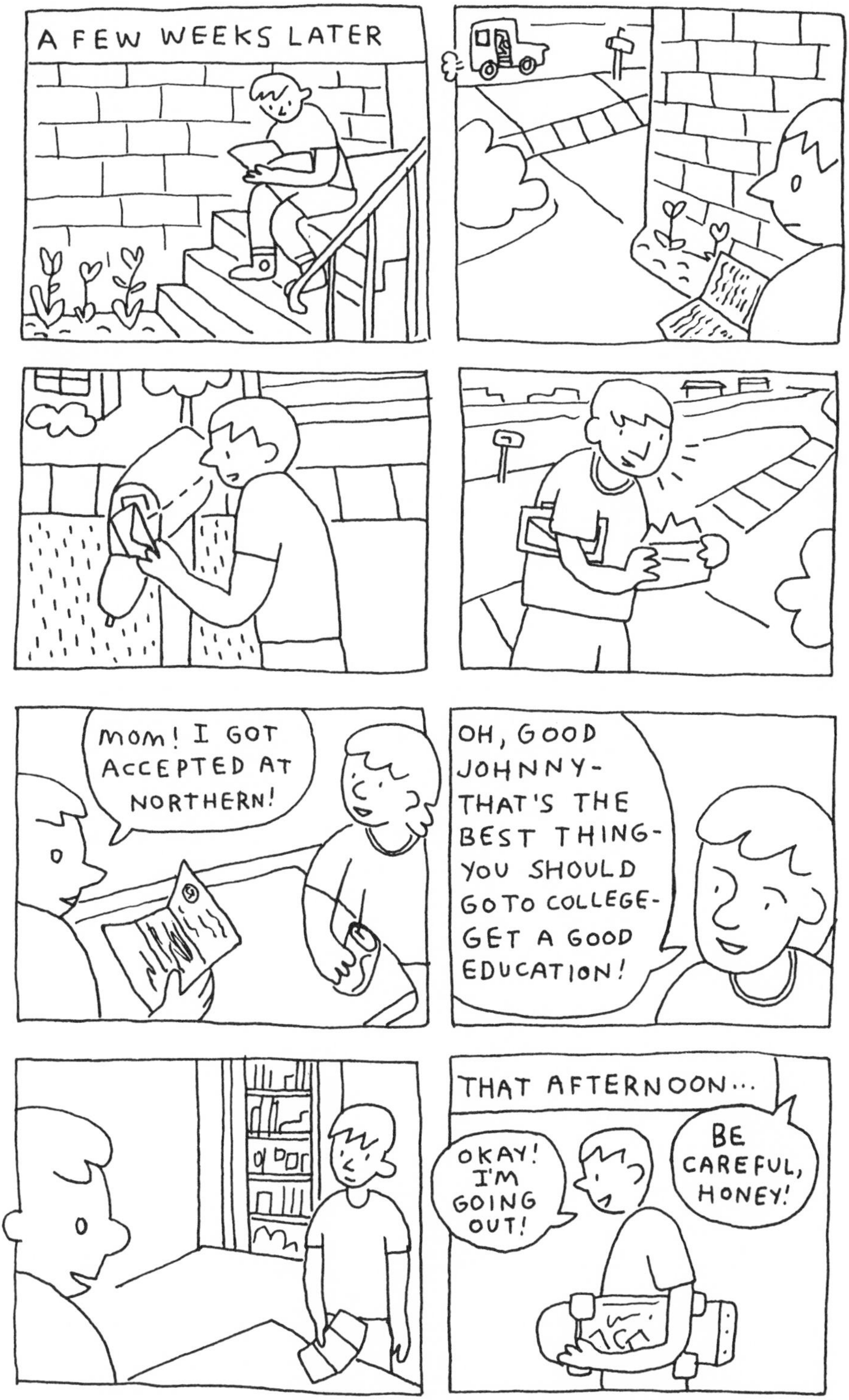
A FEW WEEKS LATER
MOM! I GOT ACCEPTED AT NORTHERN!
OH, GOOD JOHNNY- THAT'S THE BEST THING- YOU SHOULD GO TO COLLEGE- GET A GOOD EDUCATION!
THAT AFTERNOON...
OKAY! I'M GOING OUT!
BE CAREFUL, HONEY!

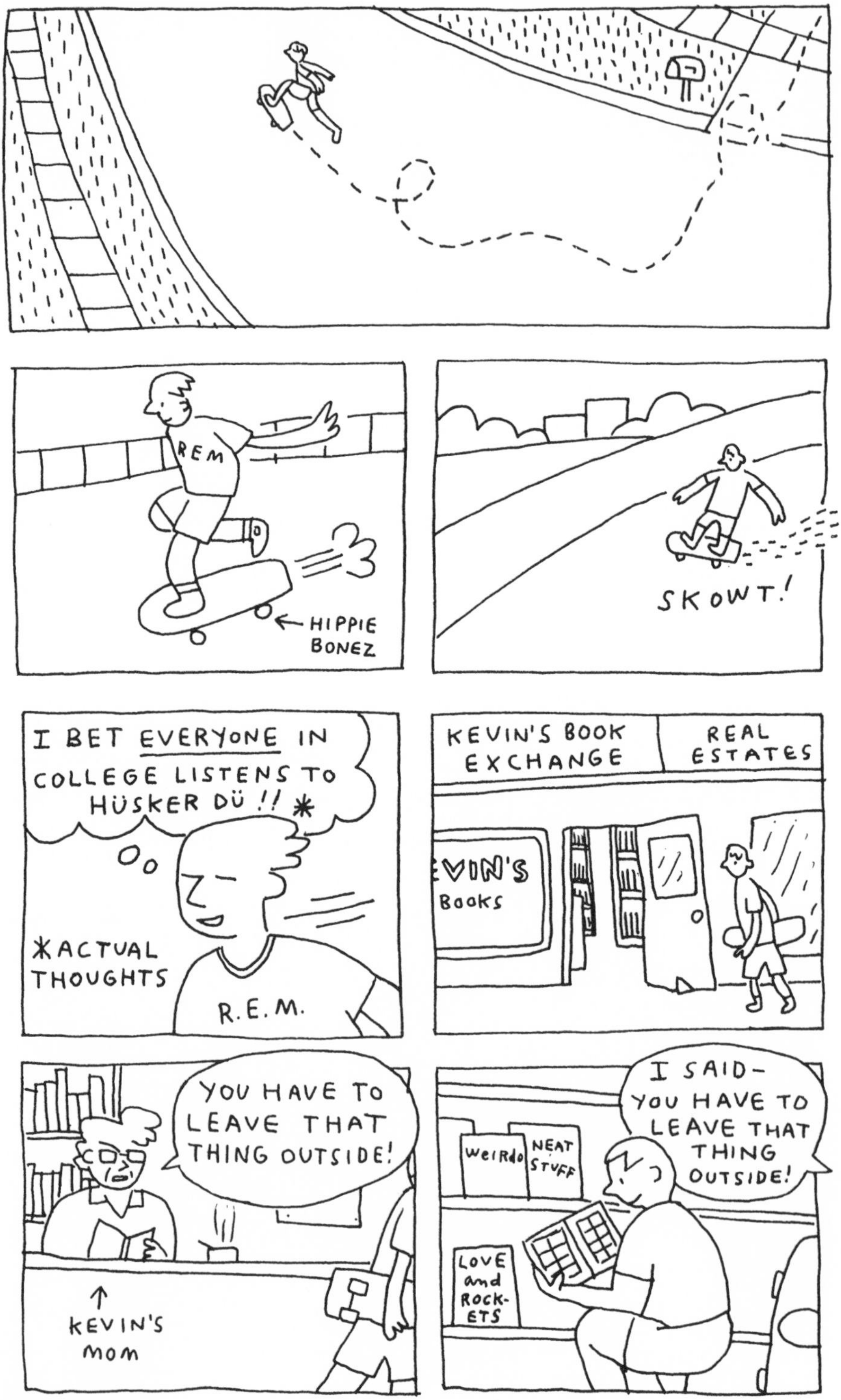
REM
HIPPIE BONEZ
SKOWT!
I BET EVERYONE IN COLLEGE LISTENS TO HÜSKER DÜ!! *
*ACTUAL THOUGHTS
R.E.M.
KEVIN'S BOOK EXCHANGE
REAL ESTATES
EVIN'S Books
YOU HAVE TO LEAVE THAT THING OUTSIDE!
KEVIN'S MOM
I SAID- YOU HAVE TO LEAVE THAT THING OUTSIDE!
WEIRDO
NEAT STUFF
LOVE and ROCK-ETS

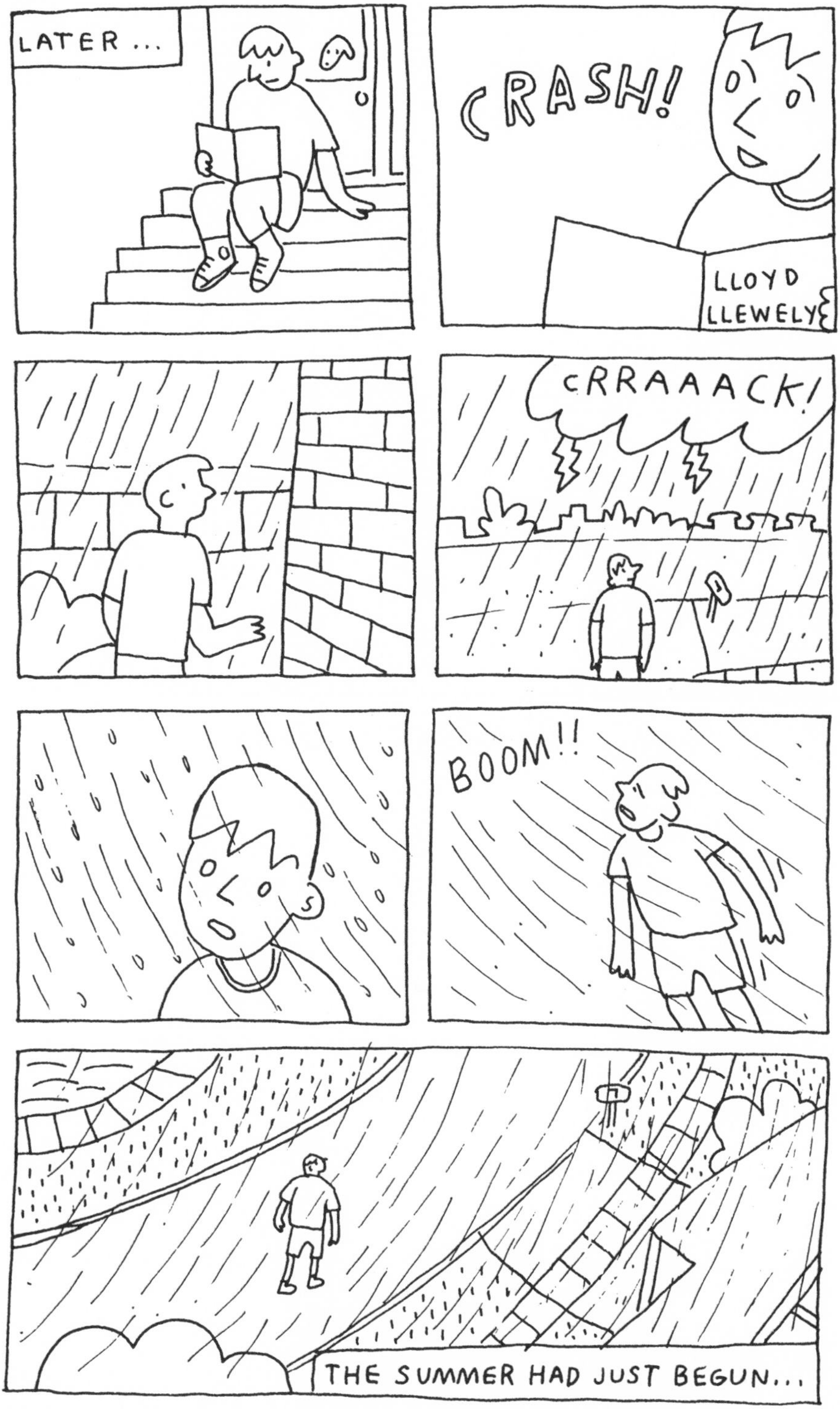
LATER ...
CRASH!
LLOYD
LLEWELY
CRRAAACK!
BOOM!!
THE SUMMER HAD JUST BEGUN...

Part Two
IN-BETWEEN DAYS

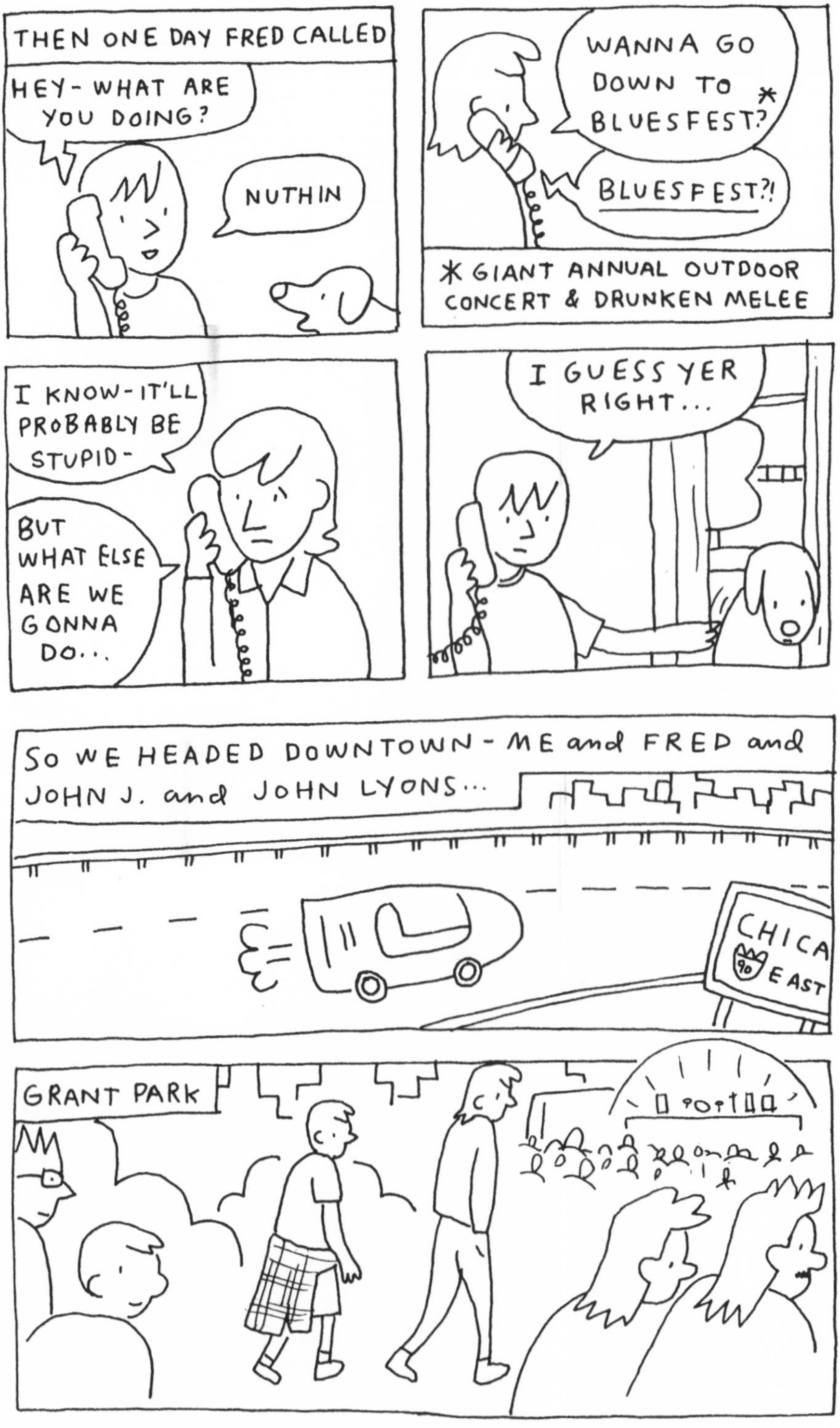
THEN ONE DAY FRED CALLED
HEY- WHAT ARE YOU DOING?
NUTHIN
WANNA GO DOWN TO BLUESFEST?*
BLUESFEST?!
* GIANT ANNUAL OUTDOOR CONCERT & DRUNKEN MELEE
I KNOW- IT'LL PROBABLY BE STUPID-
BUT WHAT ELSE ARE WE GONNA DO...
I GUESS YER RIGHT...
SO WE HEADED DOWNTOWN - ME and FRED and JOHN J. and JOHN LYONS...
CHICA
90
EAST
GRANT PARK

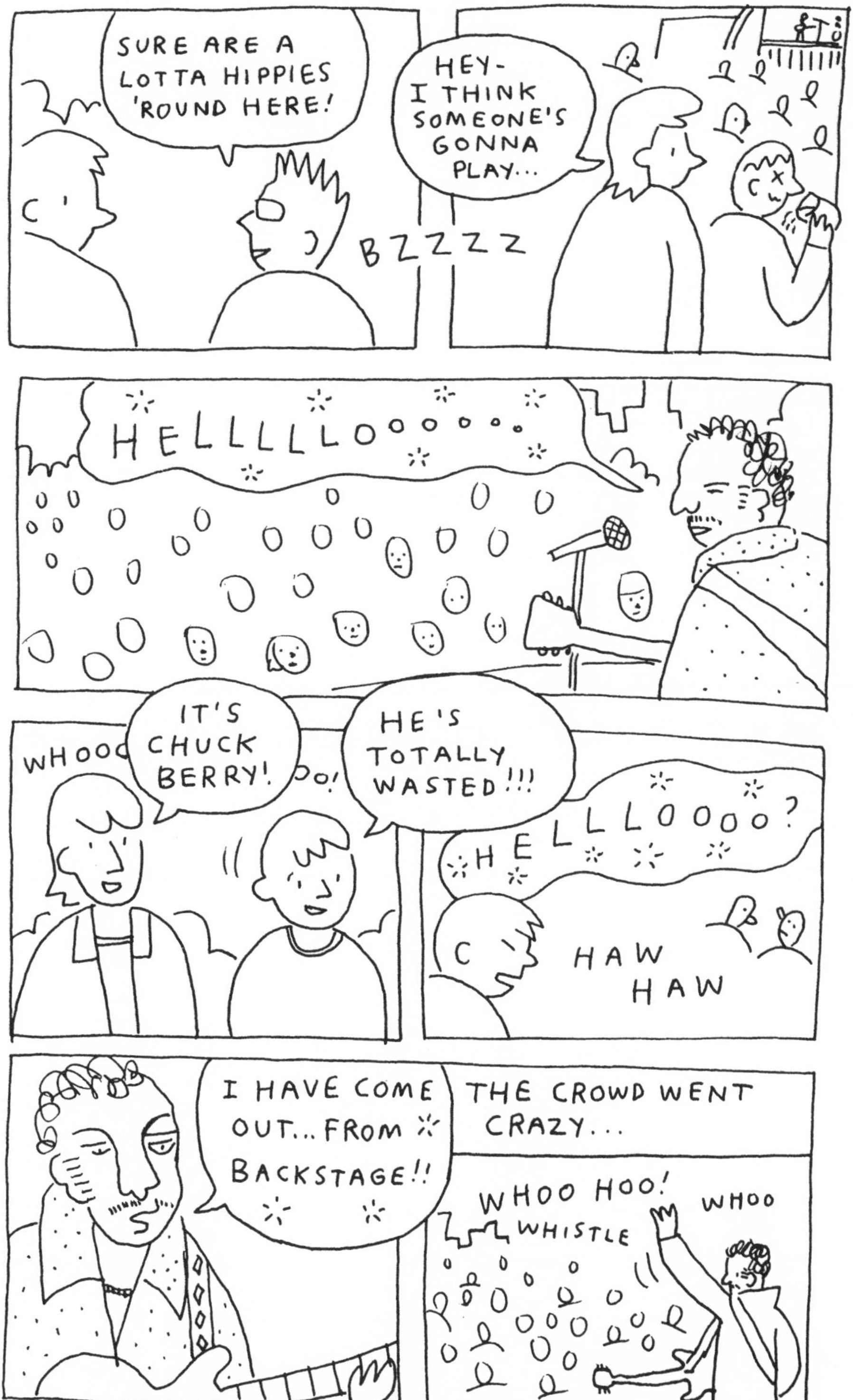
SURE ARE A LOTTA HIPPIES 'ROUND HERE!
BZZZZ
HEY- I THINK SOMEONE'S GONNA PLAY...
HELLLLLOooooo.
WHOOO
IT'S CHUCK BERRY!
OO!
HE'S TOTALLY WASTED!!!
HELLLOOOOO?
HAW HAW
I HAVE COME OUT... FROM BACKSTAGE!!
THE CROWD WENT CRAZY...
WHOO HOO!
WHISTLE
WHOO

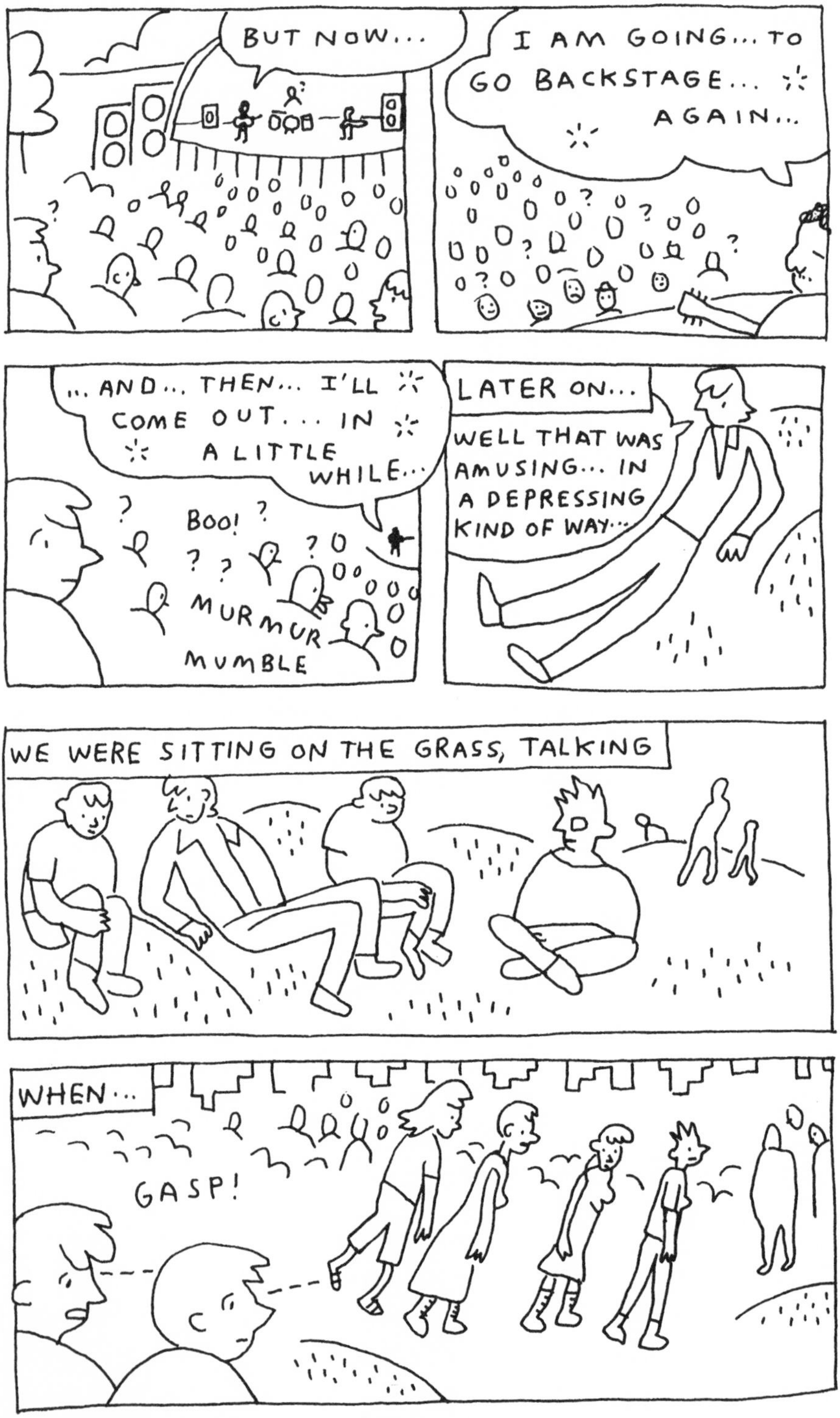
BUT NOW...
I AM GOING... TO GO BACKSTAGE... AGAIN...
... AND... THEN... I'LL COME OUT... IN A LITTLE WHILE...
BOO!
MURMUR
MUMBLE
LATER ON...
WELL THAT WAS AMUSING... IN A DEPRESSING KIND OF WAY...
WE WERE SITTING ON THE GRASS, TALKING
WHEN...
GASP!

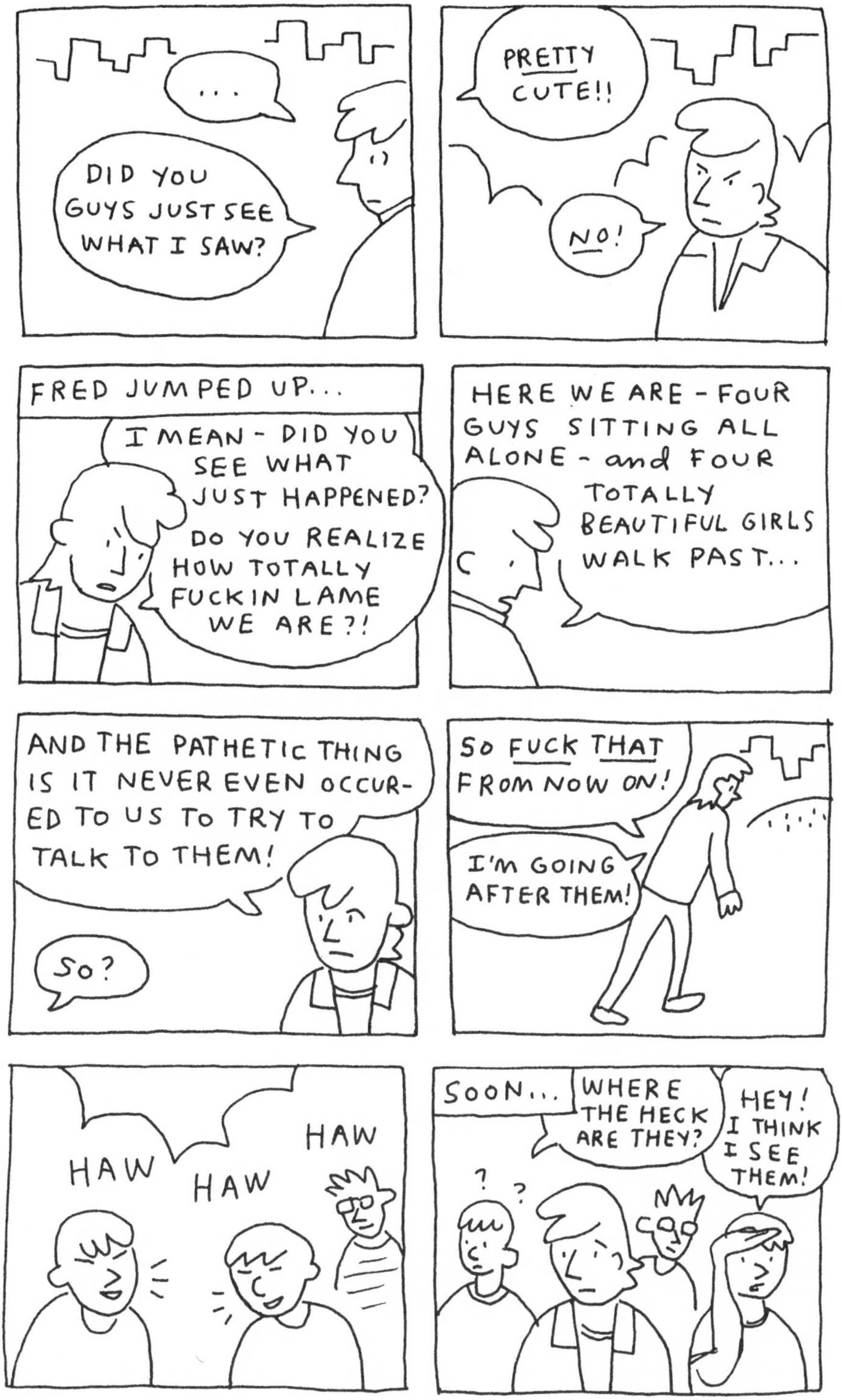
...
DID YOU GUYS JUST SEE WHAT I SAW?
PRETTY CUTE!!
NO!
FRED JUMPED UP...
I MEAN - DID YOU SEE WHAT JUST HAPPENED?
DO YOU REALIZE HOW TOTALLY FUCKIN LAME WE ARE?!
HERE WE ARE - FOUR GUYS SITTING ALL ALONE - and FOUR TOTALLY BEAUTIFUL GIRLS WALK PAST...
AND THE PATHETIC THING IS IT NEVER EVEN OCCUR-ED TO US TO TRY TO TALK TO THEM!
SO?
SO FUCK THAT FROM NOW ON!
I'M GOING AFTER THEM!
HAW
HAW
HAW
SOON...
WHERE THE HECK ARE THEY?
HEY! I THINK I SEE THEM!
? ?

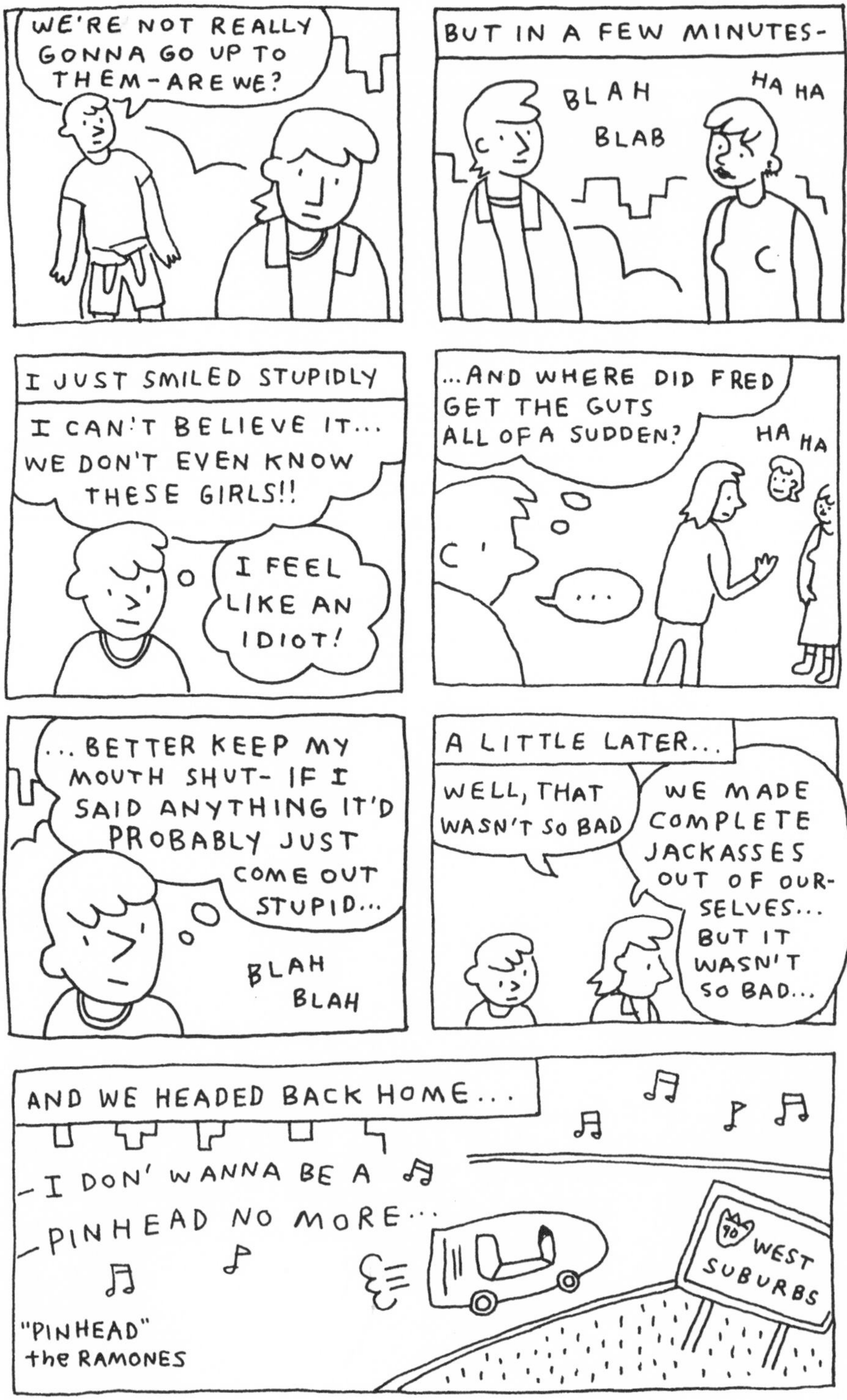
WE'RE NOT REALLY GONNA GO UP TO THEM-ARE WE?
BUT IN A FEW MINUTES-
BLAH BLAB
HA HA
I JUST SMILED STUPIDLY
I CAN'T BELIEVE IT... WE DON'T EVEN KNOW THESE GIRLS!!
I FEEL LIKE AN IDIOT!
...AND WHERE DID FRED GET THE GUTS ALL OF A SUDDEN?
HA HA
...
...BETTER KEEP MY MOUTH SHUT- IF I SAID ANYTHING IT'D PROBABLY JUST COME OUT STUPID...
BLAH BLAH
A LITTLE LATER...
WELL, THAT WASN'T SO BAD
WE MADE COMPLETE JACKASSES OUT OF OURSELVES... BUT IT WASN'T SO BAD...
AND WE HEADED BACK HOME...
-I DON' WANNA BE A
-PINHEAD NO MORE...
"PINHEAD" the RAMONES
90
WEST SUBURBS

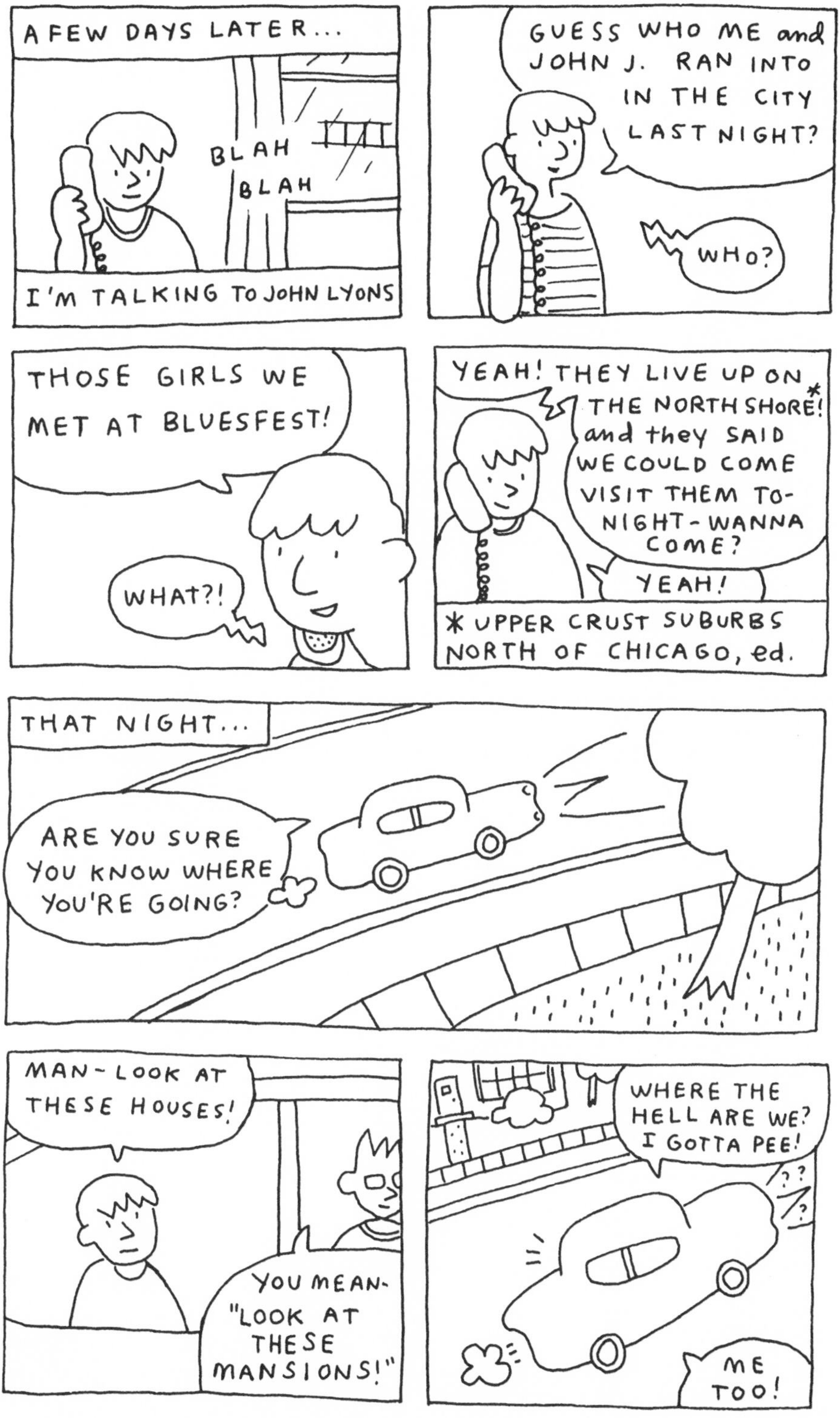
A FEW DAYS LATER...
BLAH
BLAH
I'M TALKING TO JOHN LYONS
GUESS WHO ME and JOHN J. RAN INTO IN THE CITY LAST NIGHT?
WHO?
THOSE GIRLS WE MET AT BLUESFEST!
WHAT?!
YEAH! THEY LIVE UP ON THE NORTH SHORE!* and they SAID WE COULD COME VISIT THEM TO-NIGHT - WANNA COME?
YEAH!
* UPPER CRUST SUBURBS NORTH OF CHICAGO, ed.
THAT NIGHT...
ARE YOU SURE YOU KNOW WHERE YOU'RE GOING?
MAN - LOOK AT THESE HOUSES!
YOU MEAN- "LOOK AT THESE MANSIONS!"
WHERE THE HELL ARE WE? I GOTTA PEE!
???
ME TOO!

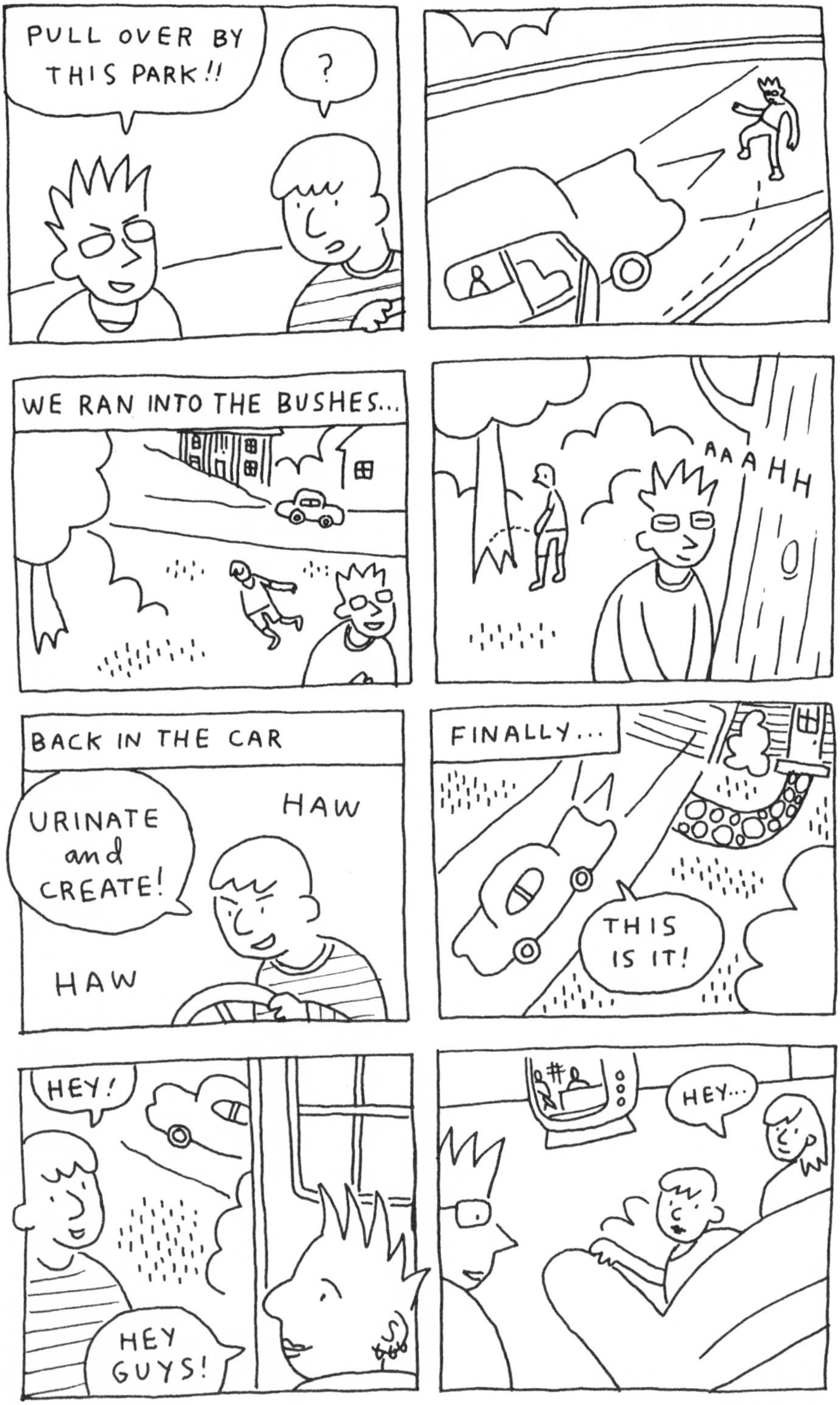
PULL OVER BY THIS PARK!!
?
WE RAN INTO THE BUSHES...
AAAHHH
BACK IN THE CAR
URINATE and CREATE!
HAW
HAW
FINALLY...
THIS IS IT!
HEY!
HEY GUYS!
HEY...

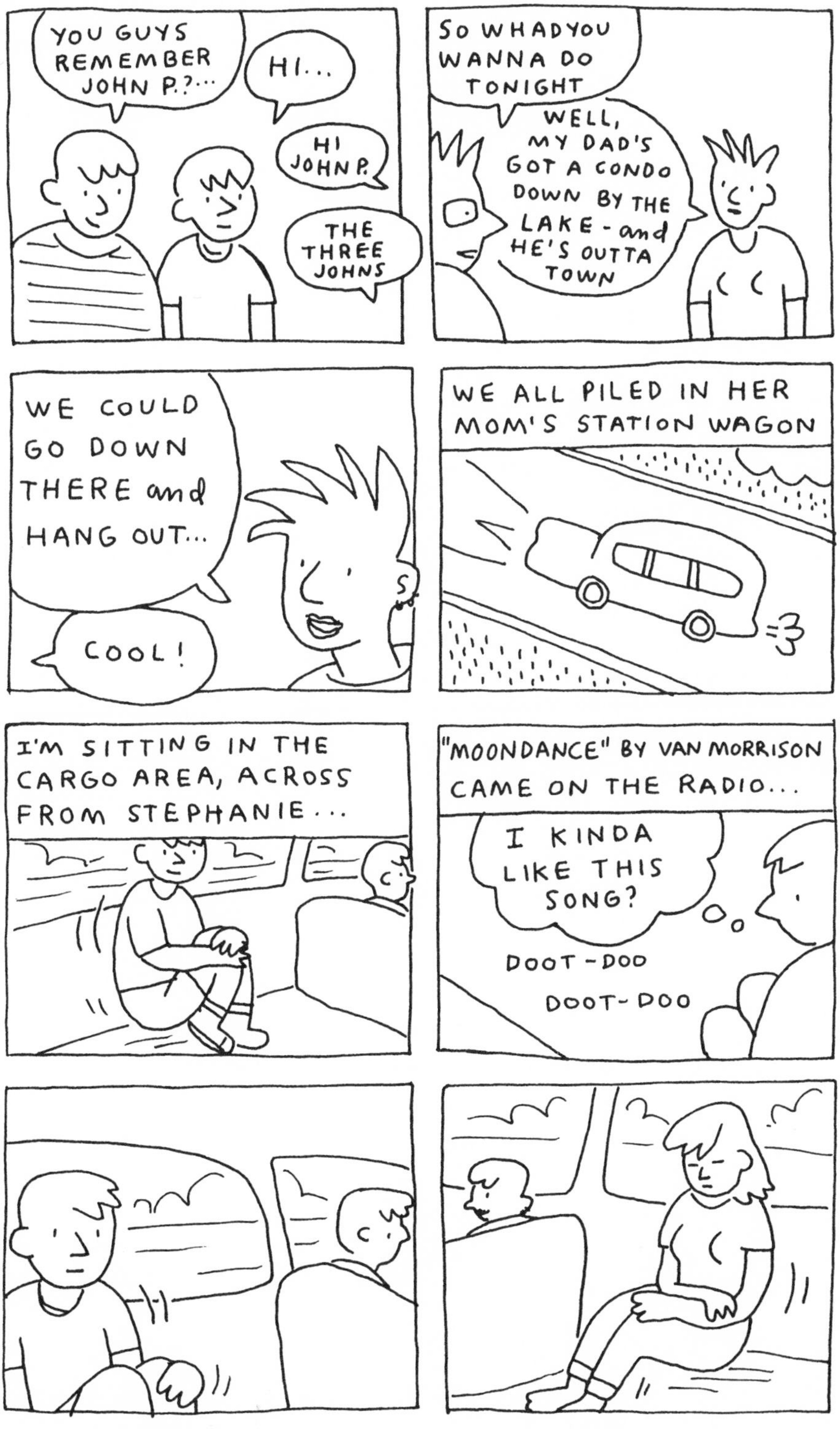
YOU GUYS REMEMBER JOHN P.?...
HI...
HI JOHN P.
THE THREE JOHNS
SO WHADYOU WANNA DO TONIGHT
WELL, MY DAD'S GOT A CONDO DOWN BY THE LAKE - and HE'S OUTTA TOWN
WE COULD GO DOWN THERE and HANG OUT...
COOL!
WE ALL PILED IN HER MOM'S STATION WAGON
I'M SITTING IN THE CARGO AREA, ACROSS FROM STEPHANIE...
"MOONDANCE" BY VAN MORRISON CAME ON THE RADIO...
I KINDA LIKE THIS SONG?
DOOT-DOO
DOOT-DOO

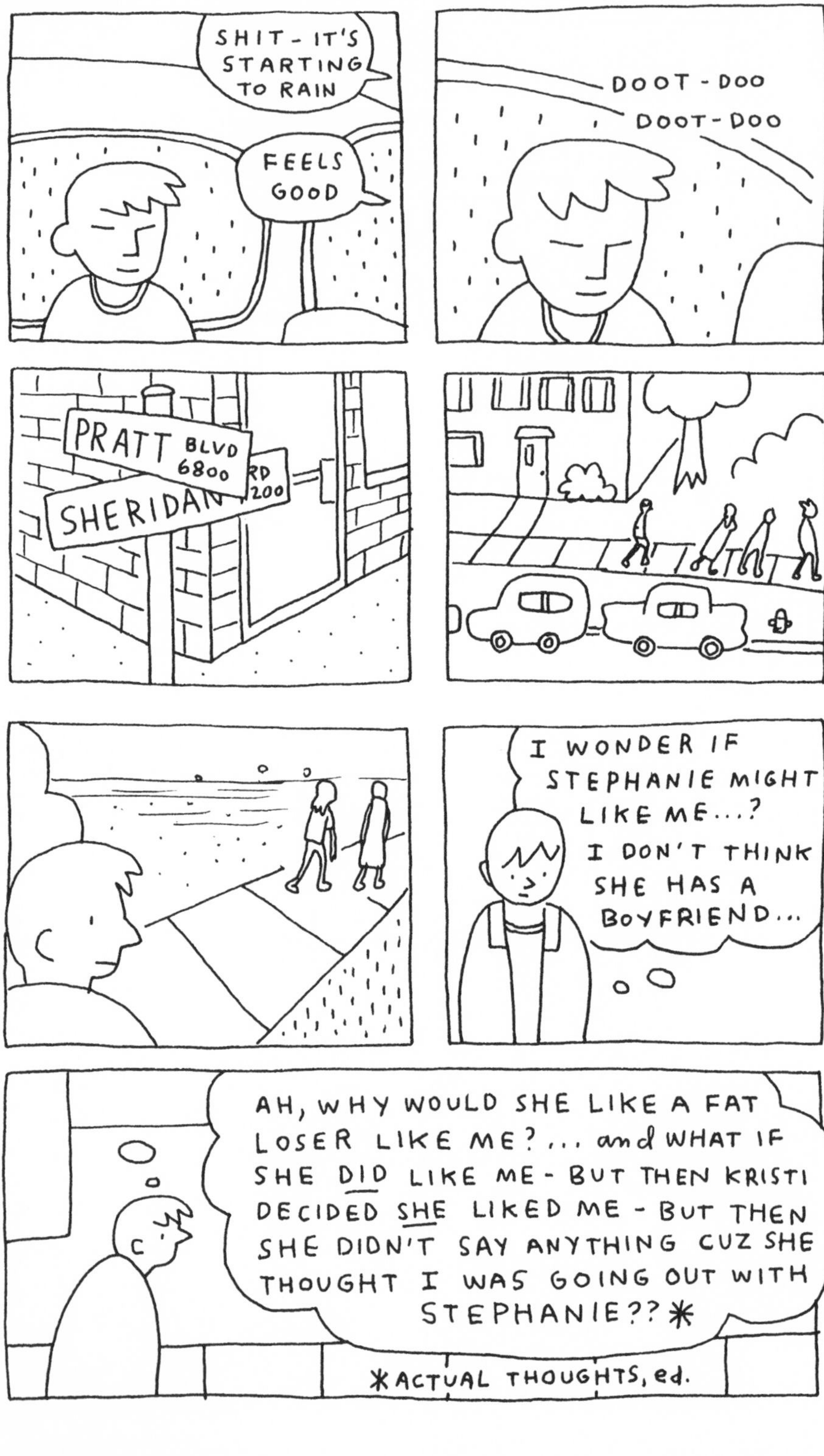
SHIT - IT'S STARTING TO RAIN
FEELS GOOD
DOOT - DOO
DOOT - DOO
PRATT BLVD 6800
SHERIDAN RD 1200
I WONDER IF STEPHANIE MIGHT LIKE ME...?
I DON'T THINK SHE HAS A BOYFRIEND...
AH, WHY WOULD SHE LIKE A FAT LOSER LIKE ME?... and WHAT IF SHE DID LIKE ME - BUT THEN KRISTI DECIDED SHE LIKED ME - BUT THEN SHE DIDN'T SAY ANYTHING CUZ SHE THOUGHT I WAS GOING OUT WITH STEPHANIE??*
*ACTUAL THOUGHTS, ed.

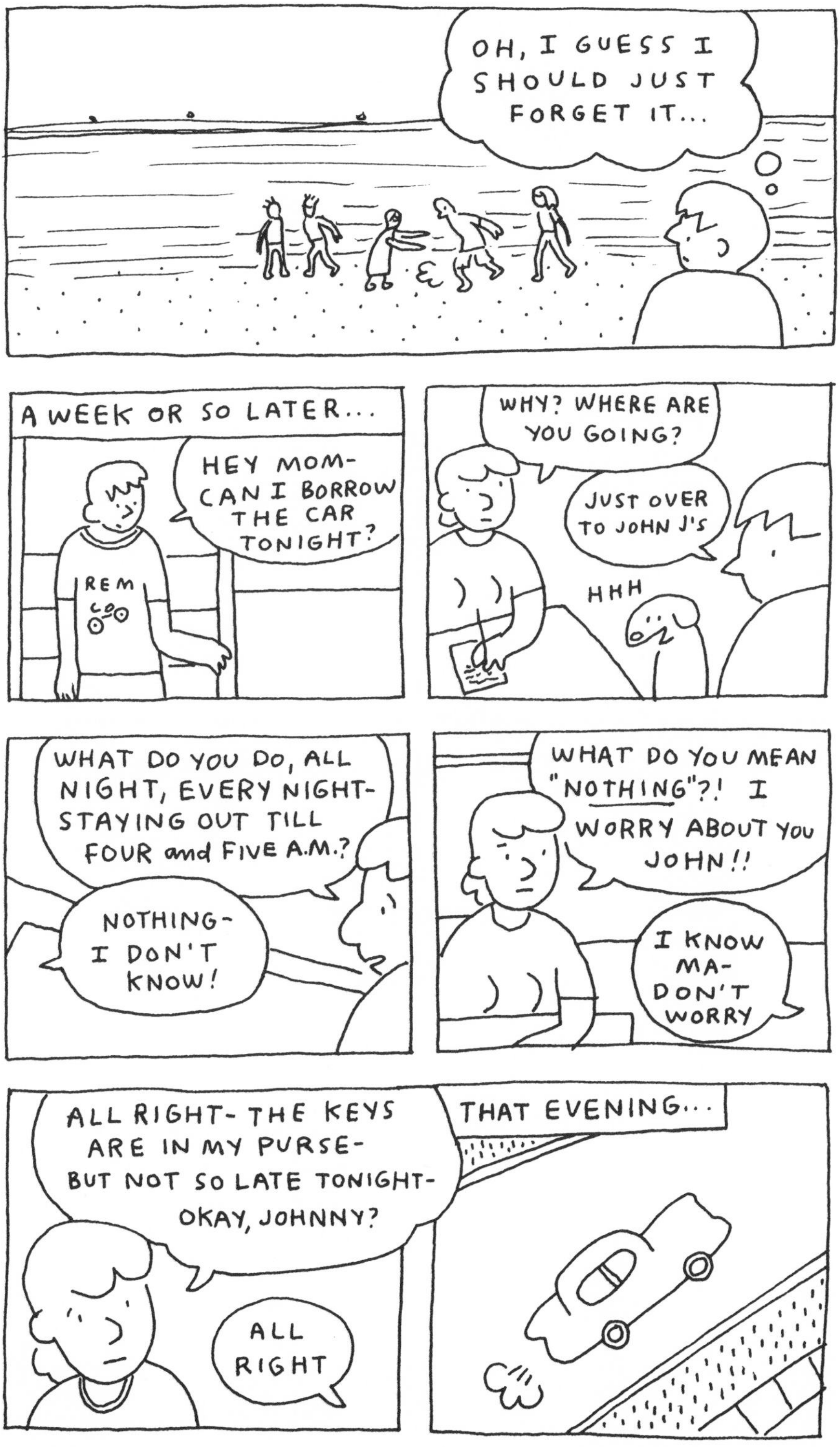
OH, I GUESS I SHOULD JUST FORGET IT...
A WEEK OR SO LATER...
HEY MOM- CAN I BORROW THE CAR TONIGHT?
REM
WHY? WHERE ARE YOU GOING?
JUST OVER TO JOHN J'S
HHH
WHAT DO YOU DO, ALL NIGHT, EVERY NIGHT- STAYING OUT TILL FOUR and FIVE A.M.?
NOTHING- I DON'T KNOW!
WHAT DO YOU MEAN "NOTHING"?! I WORRY ABOUT YOU JOHN!!
I KNOW MA- DON'T WORRY
ALL RIGHT- THE KEYS ARE IN MY PURSE- BUT NOT SO LATE TONIGHT- OKAY, JOHNNY?
ALL RIGHT
THAT EVENING...

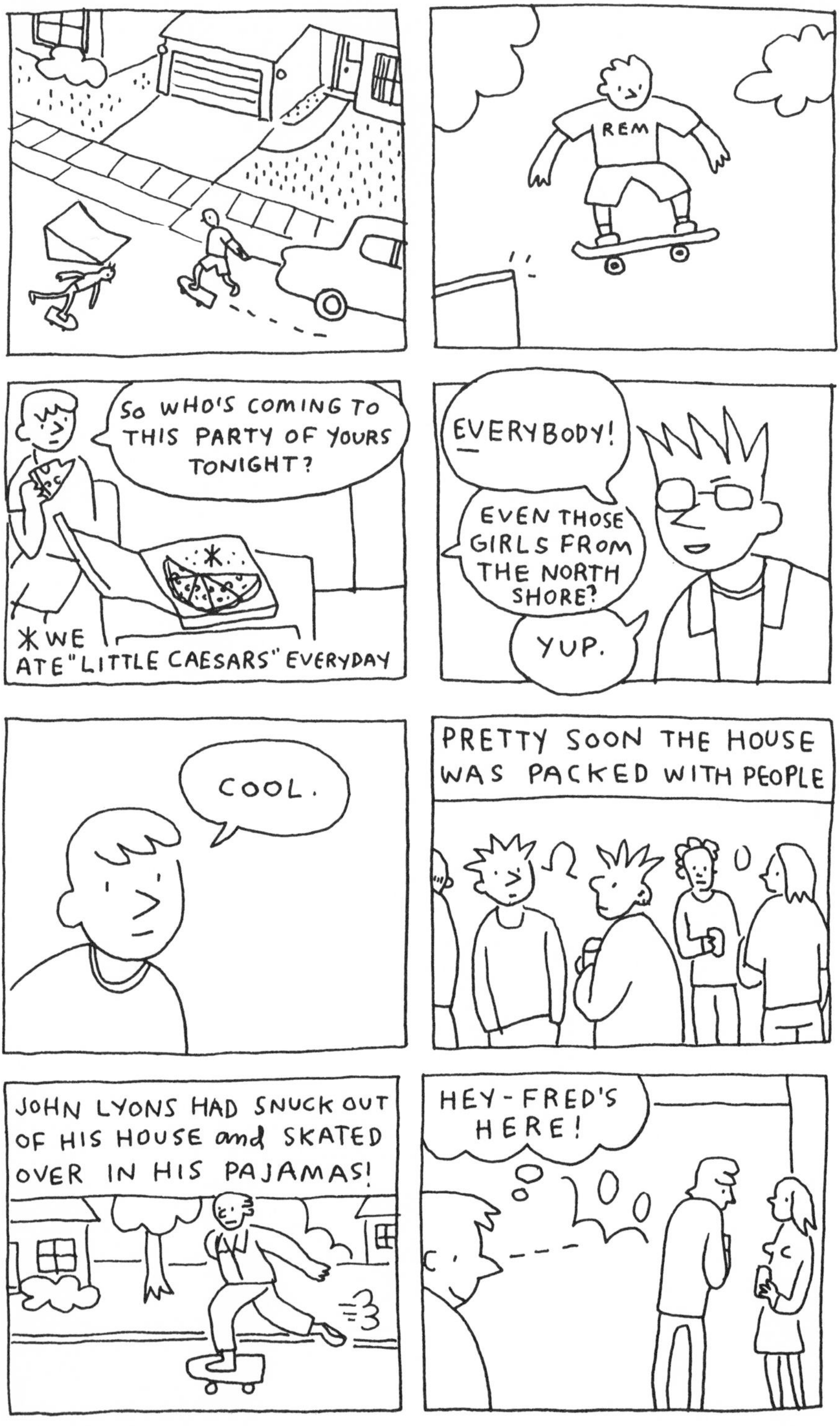
REM
SO WHO'S COMING TO THIS PARTY OF YOURS TONIGHT?
* WE ATE "LITTLE CAESARS" EVERYDAY
EVERYBODY!
EVEN THOSE GIRLS FROM THE NORTH SHORE?
YUP.
COOL.
PRETTY SOON THE HOUSE WAS PACKED WITH PEOPLE
JOHN LYONS HAD SNUCK OUT OF HIS HOUSE and SKATED OVER IN HIS PAJAMAS!
HEY - FRED'S HERE!

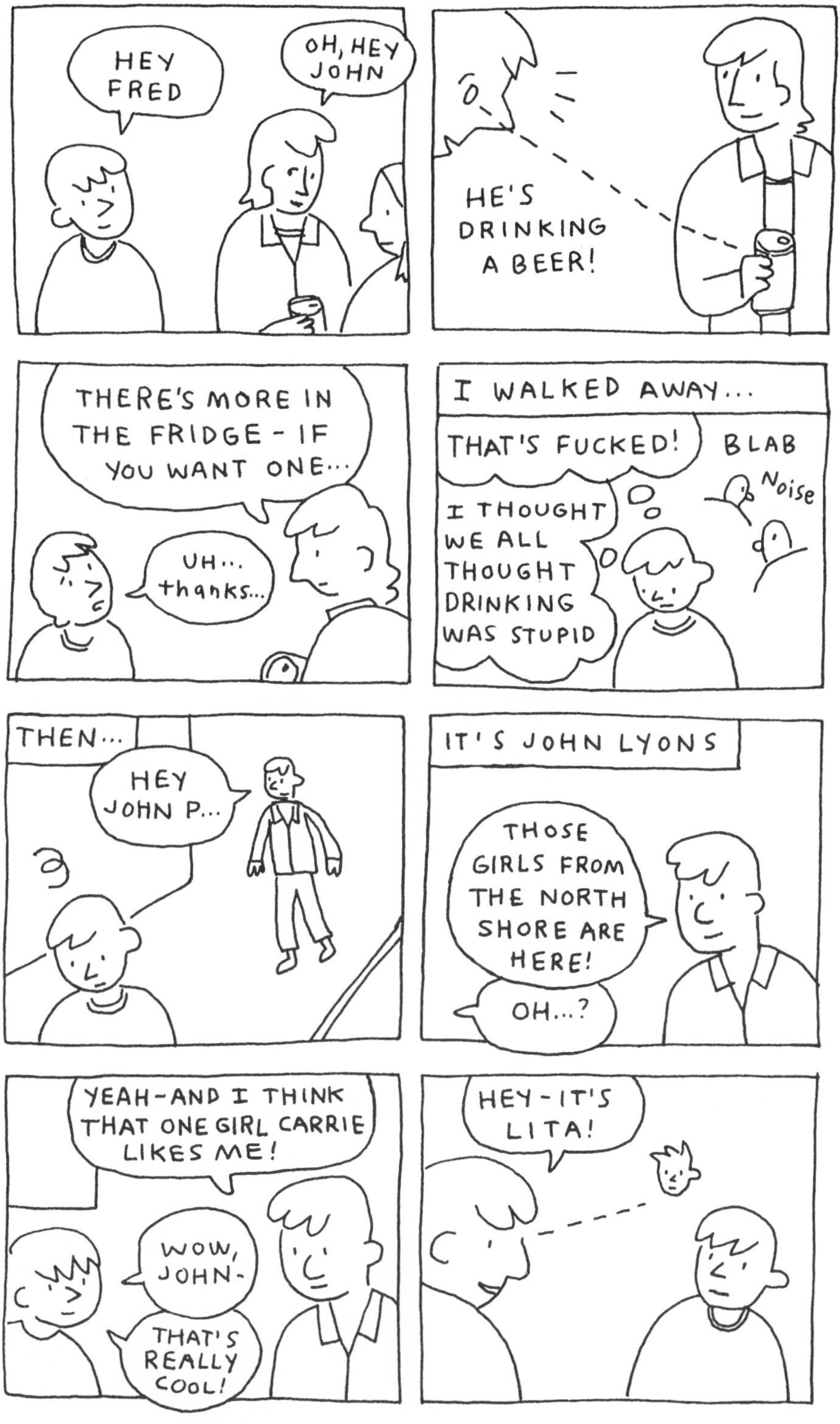
HEY FRED
OH, HEY JOHN
HE'S DRINKING A BEER!
THERE'S MORE IN THE FRIDGE - IF YOU WANT ONE...
UH... thanks...
I WALKED AWAY...
THAT'S FUCKED!
I THOUGHT WE ALL THOUGHT DRINKING WAS STUPID
BLAB
Noise
THEN...
HEY JOHN P...
IT'S JOHN LYONS
THOSE GIRLS FROM THE NORTH SHORE ARE HERE!
OH...?
YEAH - AND I THINK THAT ONE GIRL CARRIE LIKES ME!
WOW, JOHN-
THAT'S REALLY COOL!
HEY - IT'S LITA!

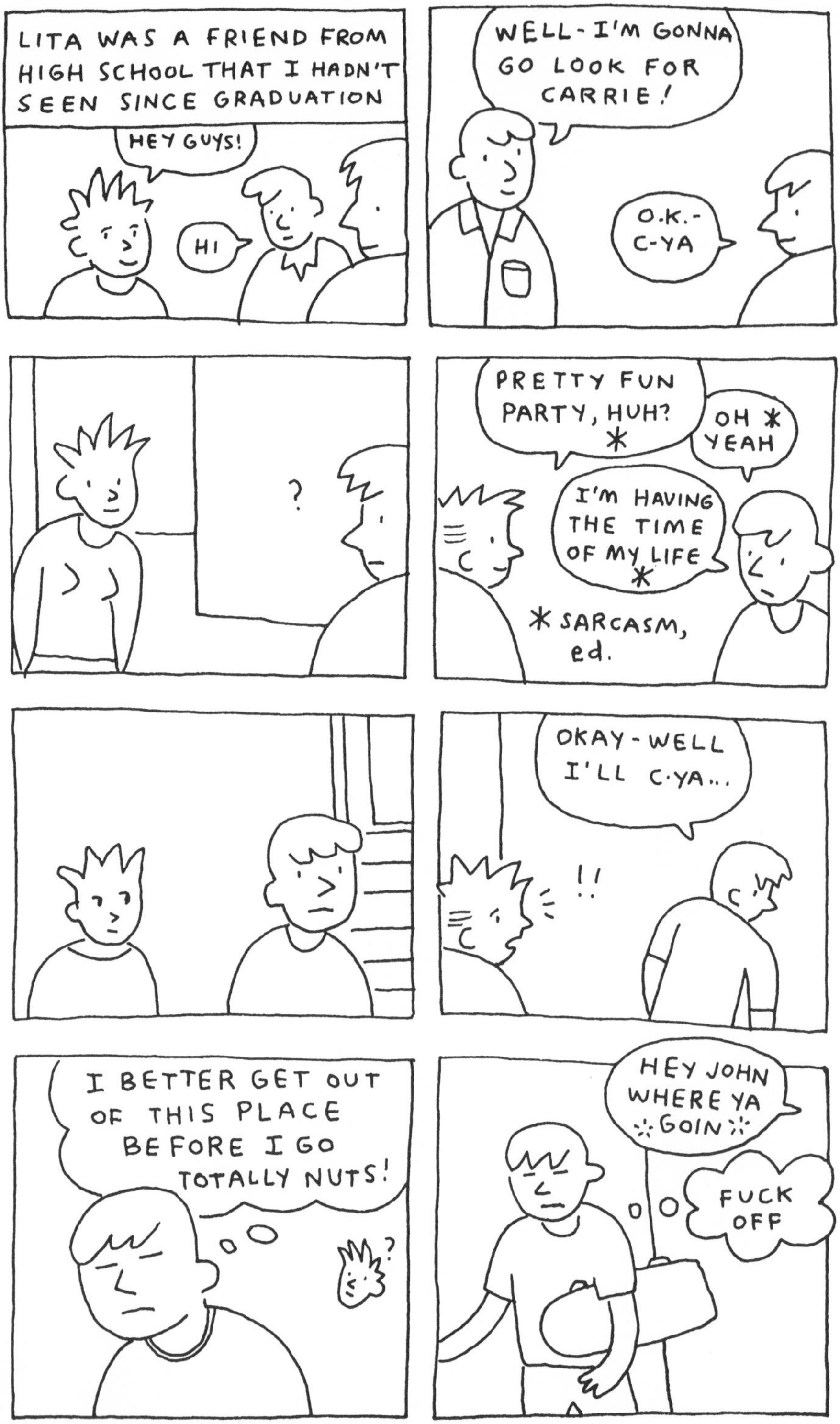
LITA WAS A FRIEND FROM HIGH SCHOOL THAT I HADN'T SEEN SINCE GRADUATION
HEY GUYS!
HI
WELL - I'M GONNA GO LOOK FOR CARRIE!
O.K. - C-YA
?
PRETTY FUN PARTY, HUH? *
OH * YEAH
I'M HAVING THE TIME OF MY LIFE *
* SARCASM, ed.
OKAY - WELL I'LL C·YA...
!!
I BETTER GET OUT OF THIS PLACE BEFORE I GO TOTALLY NUTS!
?
HEY JOHN WHERE YA GOIN
FUCK OFF

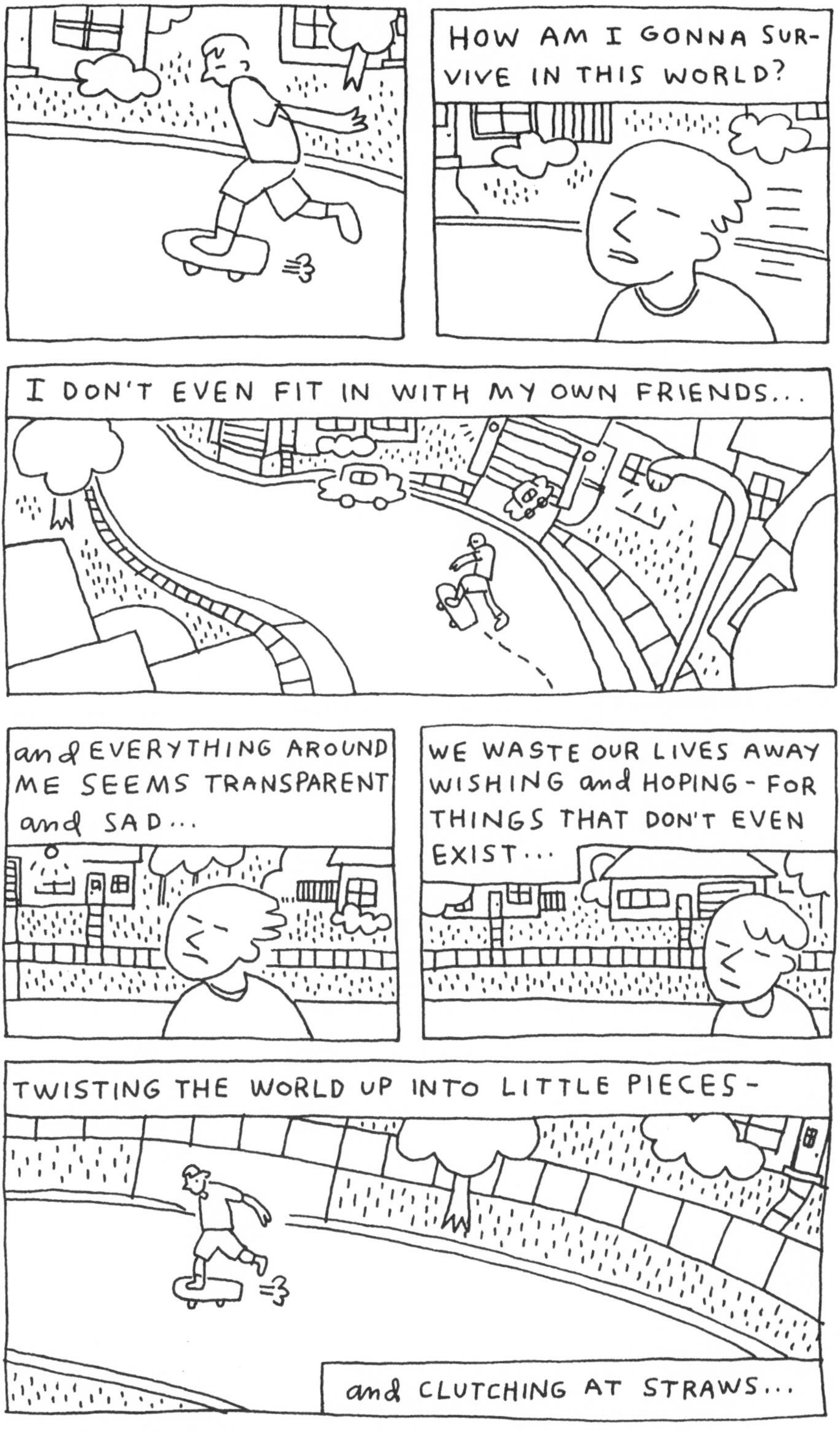
HOW AM I GONNA SURVIVE IN THIS WORLD?
I DON'T EVEN FIT IN WITH MY OWN FRIENDS...
and EVERYTHING AROUND ME SEEMS TRANSPARENT and SAD...
WE WASTE OUR LIVES AWAY WISHING and HOPING - FOR THINGS THAT DON'T EVEN EXIST...
TWISTING THE WORLD UP INTO LITTLE PIECES -
and CLUTCHING AT STRAWS...

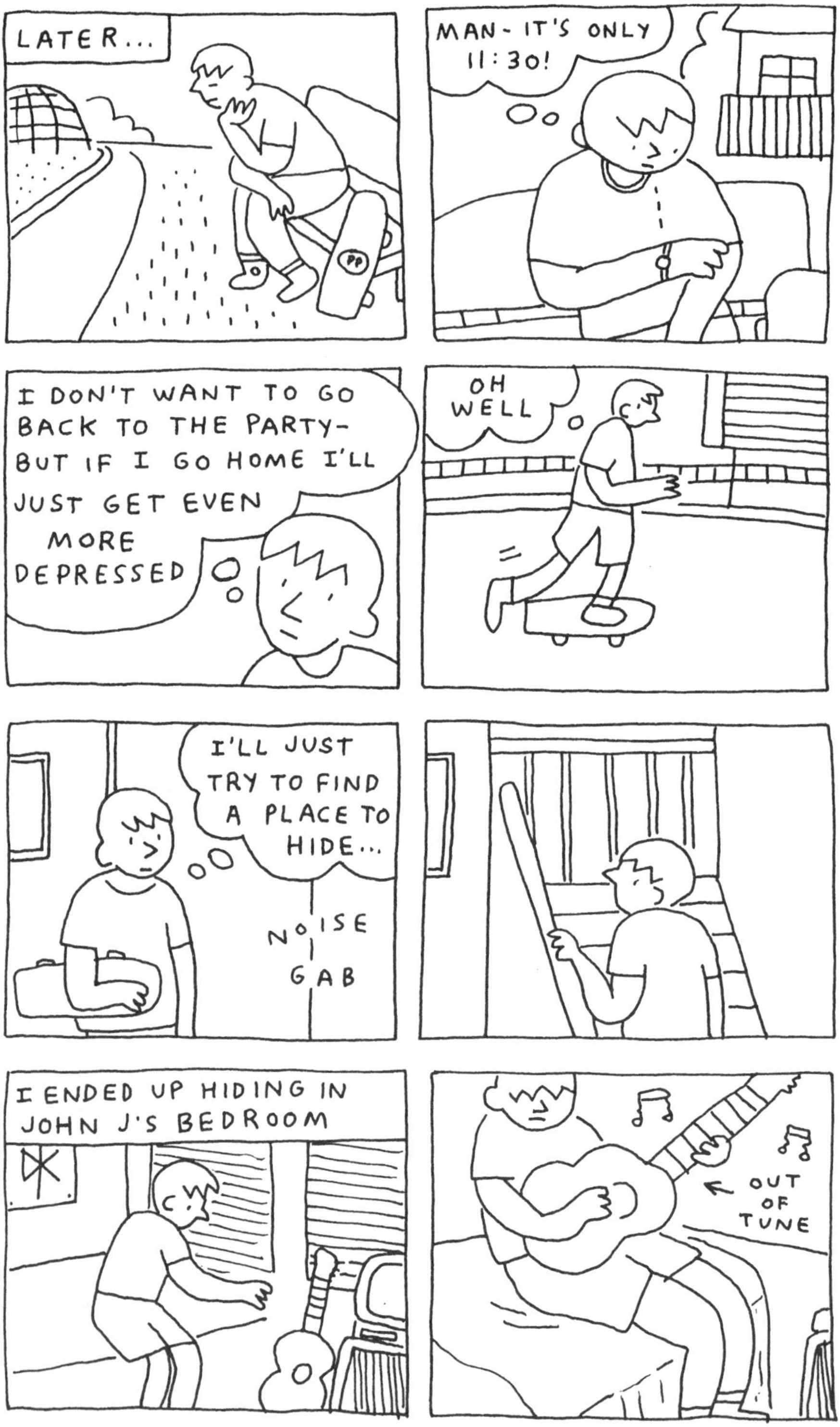
LATER...
MAN- IT'S ONLY 11:30!
I DON'T WANT TO GO BACK TO THE PARTY- BUT IF I GO HOME I'LL JUST GET EVEN MORE DEPRESSED
OH WELL
I'LL JUST TRY TO FIND A PLACE TO HIDE...
NOISE
GAB
I ENDED UP HIDING IN JOHN J'S BEDROOM
OUT OF TUNE

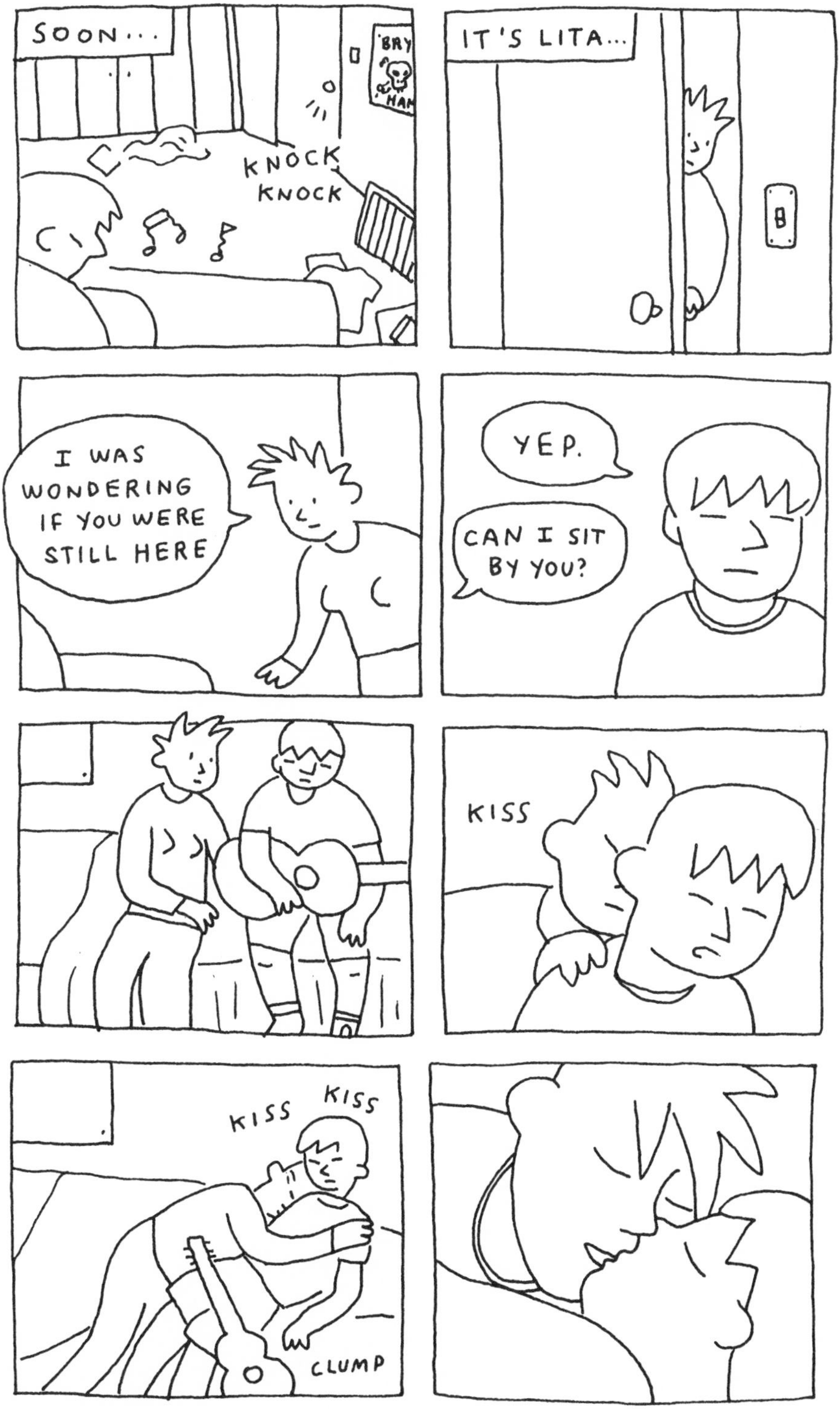
SOON...
BRY
HAM
KNOCK KNOCK
IT'S LITA...
I WAS WONDERING IF YOU WERE STILL HERE
YEP.
CAN I SIT BY YOU?
KISS
KISS KISS
CLUMP

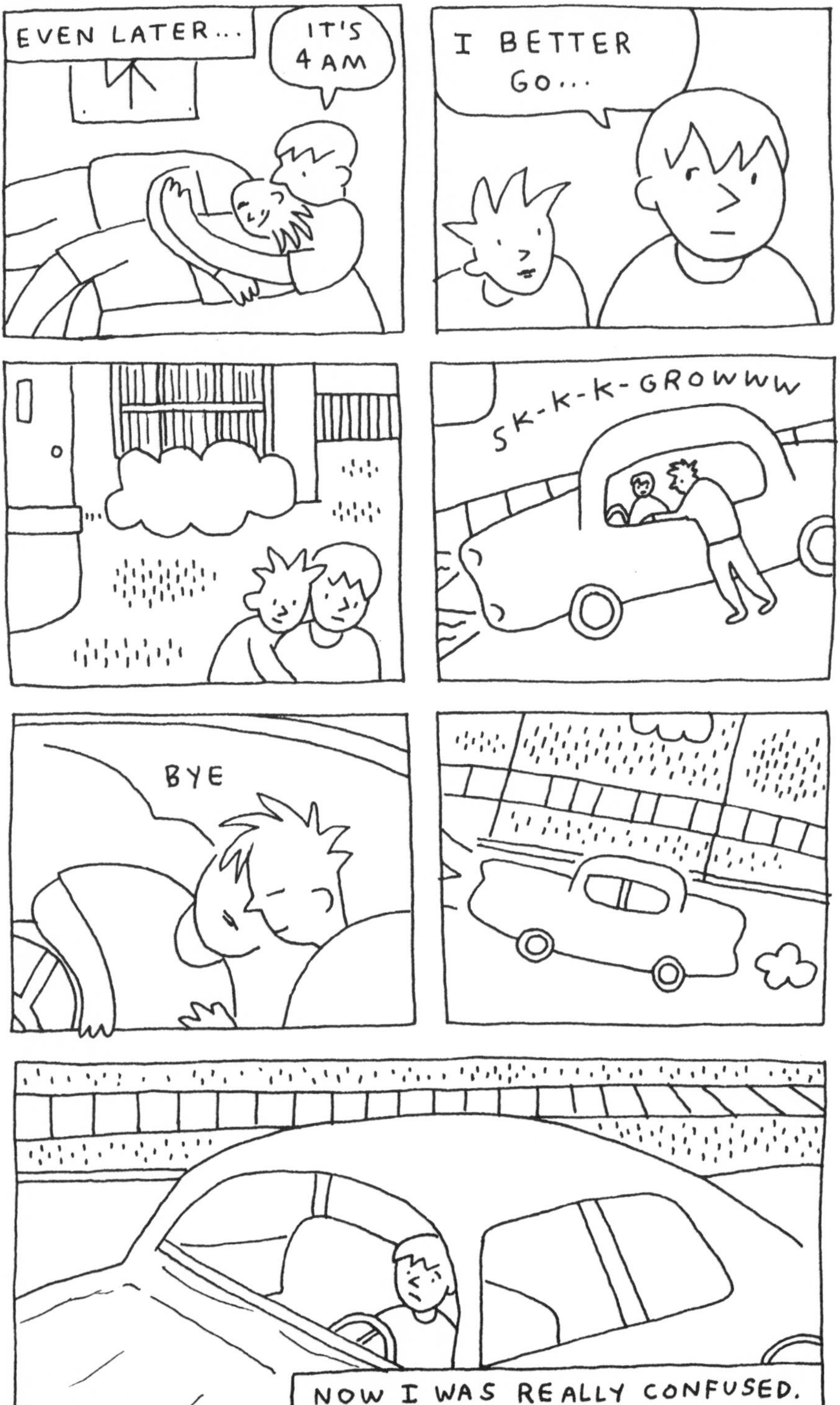
EVEN LATER...
IT'S 4 AM
I BETTER GO...
SK-K-K-GROWWW
BYE
NOW I WAS REALLY CONFUSED.

Part Three
THE FOURTH OF JULY

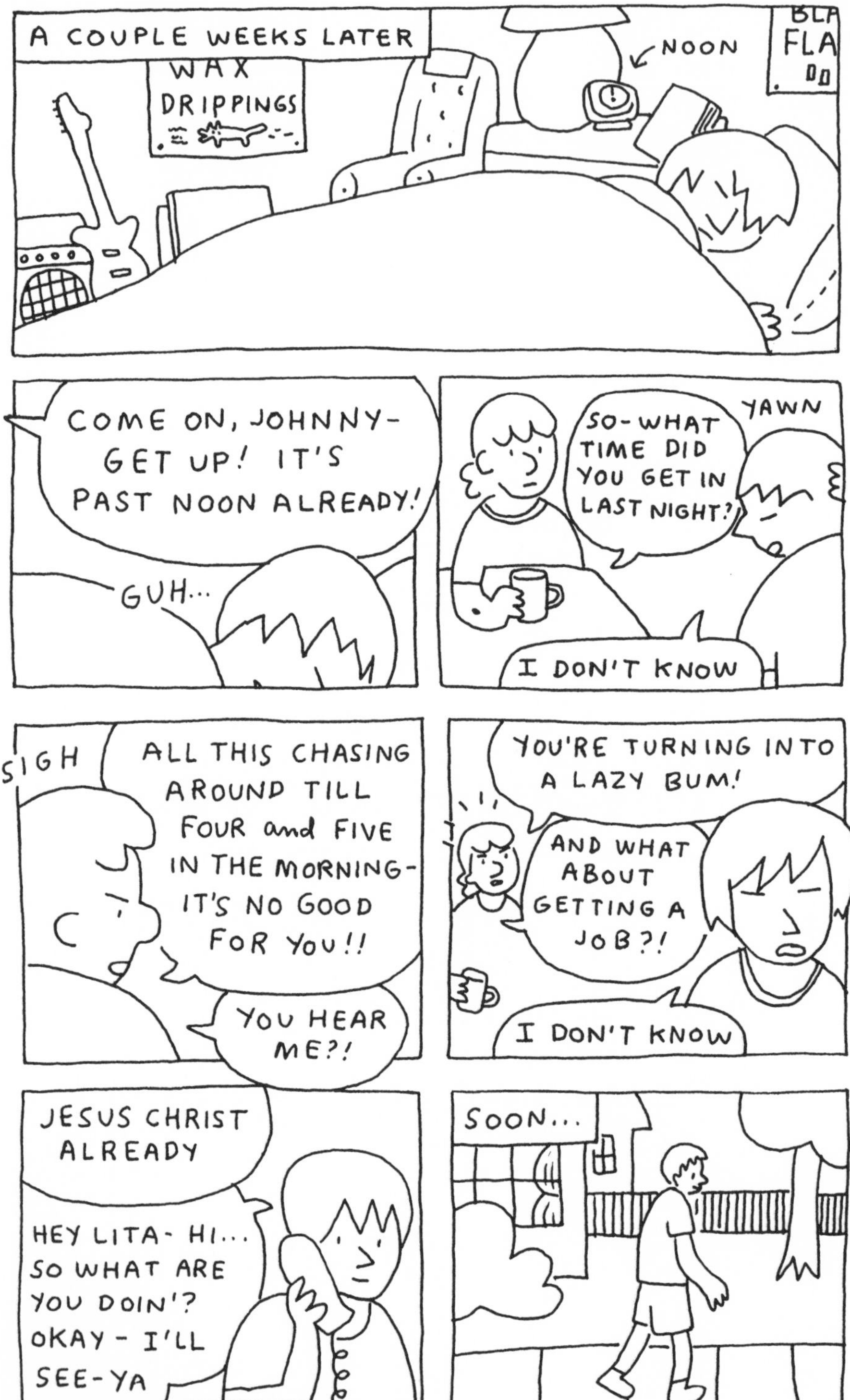
A COUPLE WEEKS LATER
WAX DRIPPINGS
NOON
BLA FLA
COME ON, JOHNNY- GET UP! IT'S PAST NOON ALREADY!
GUH...
SO- WHAT TIME DID YOU GET IN LAST NIGHT?
YAWN
I DON'T KNOW
SIGH
ALL THIS CHASING AROUND TILL FOUR and FIVE IN THE MORNING- IT'S NO GOOD FOR YOU!!
YOU HEAR ME?!
YOU'RE TURNING INTO A LAZY BUM!
AND WHAT ABOUT GETTING A JOB?!
I DON'T KNOW
JESUS CHRIST ALREADY
HEY LITA- HI... SO WHAT ARE YOU DOIN'? OKAY - I'LL SEE-YA
SOON...

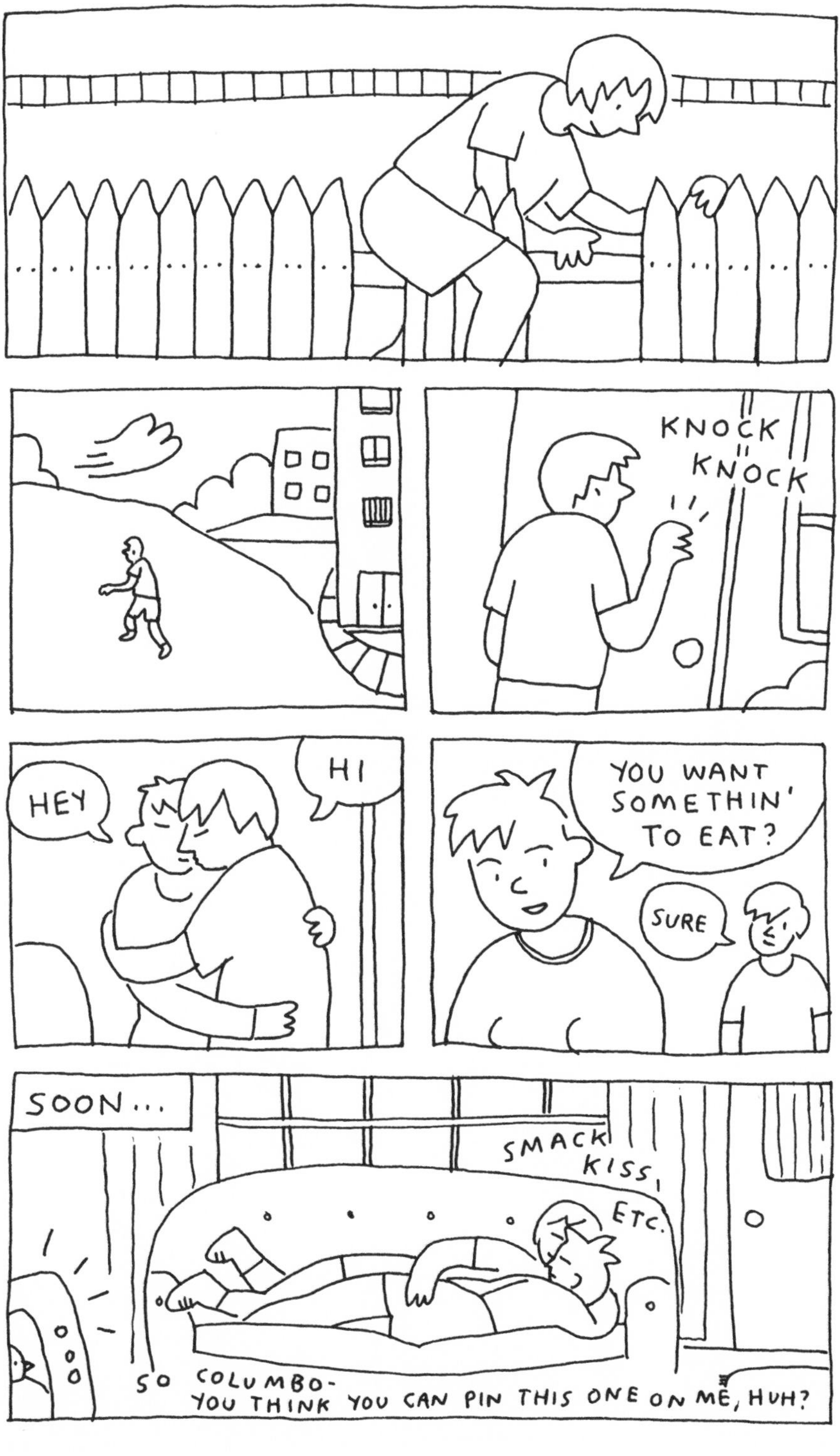
KNOCK KNOCK
HEY
HI
YOU WANT SOMETHIN' TO EAT?
SURE
SOON...
SMACK KISS, ETC.
SO COLUMBO-
YOU THINK YOU CAN PIN THIS ONE ON ME, HUH?

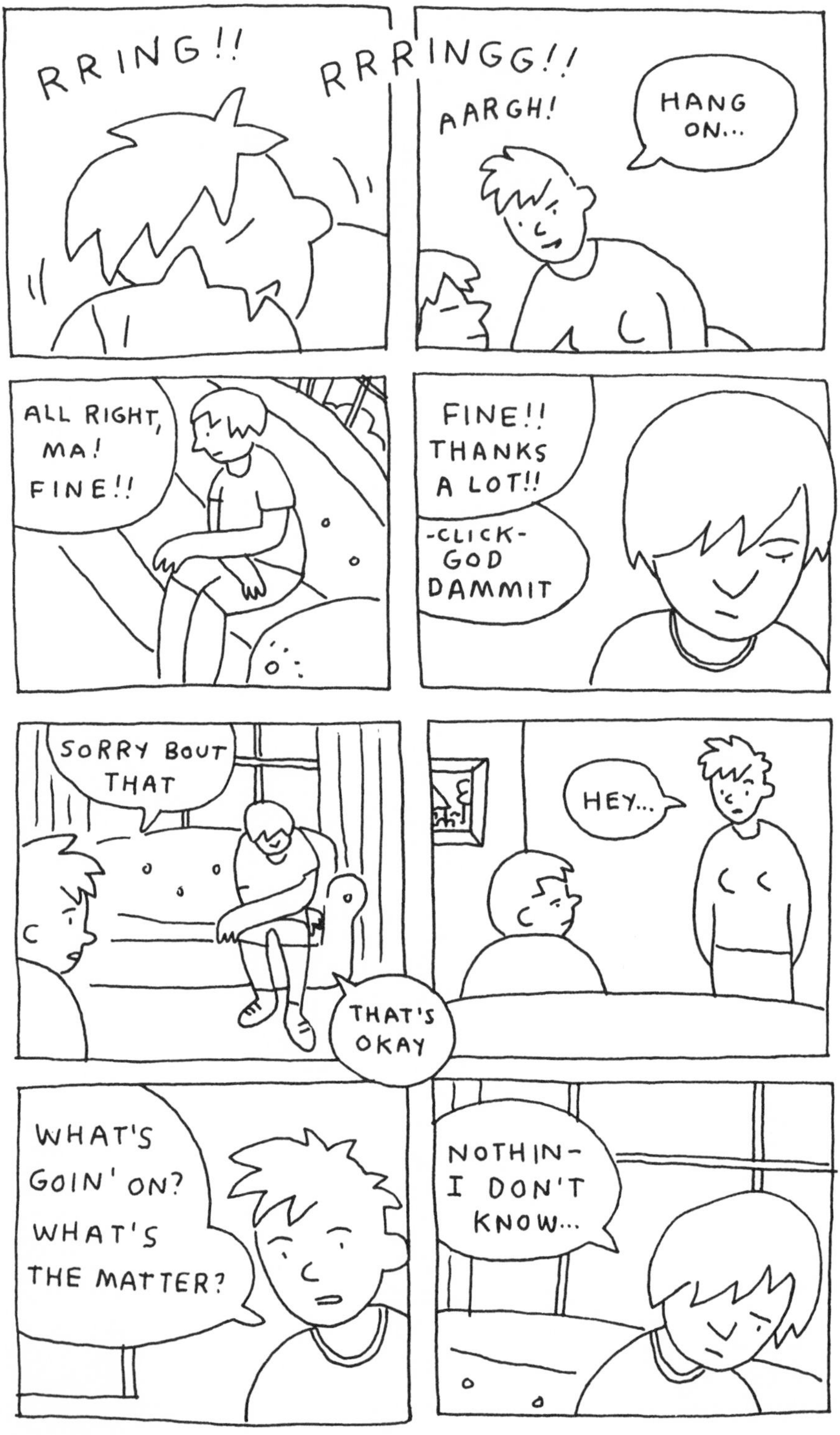
RRING!!
RRRINGG!!
AARGH!
HANG ON...
ALL RIGHT, MA! FINE!!
FINE!! THANKS A LOT!!
-CLICK- GOD DAMMIT
SORRY BOUT THAT
THAT'S OKAY
HEY...
WHAT'S GOIN' ON? WHAT'S THE MATTER?
NOTHIN- I DON'T KNOW...

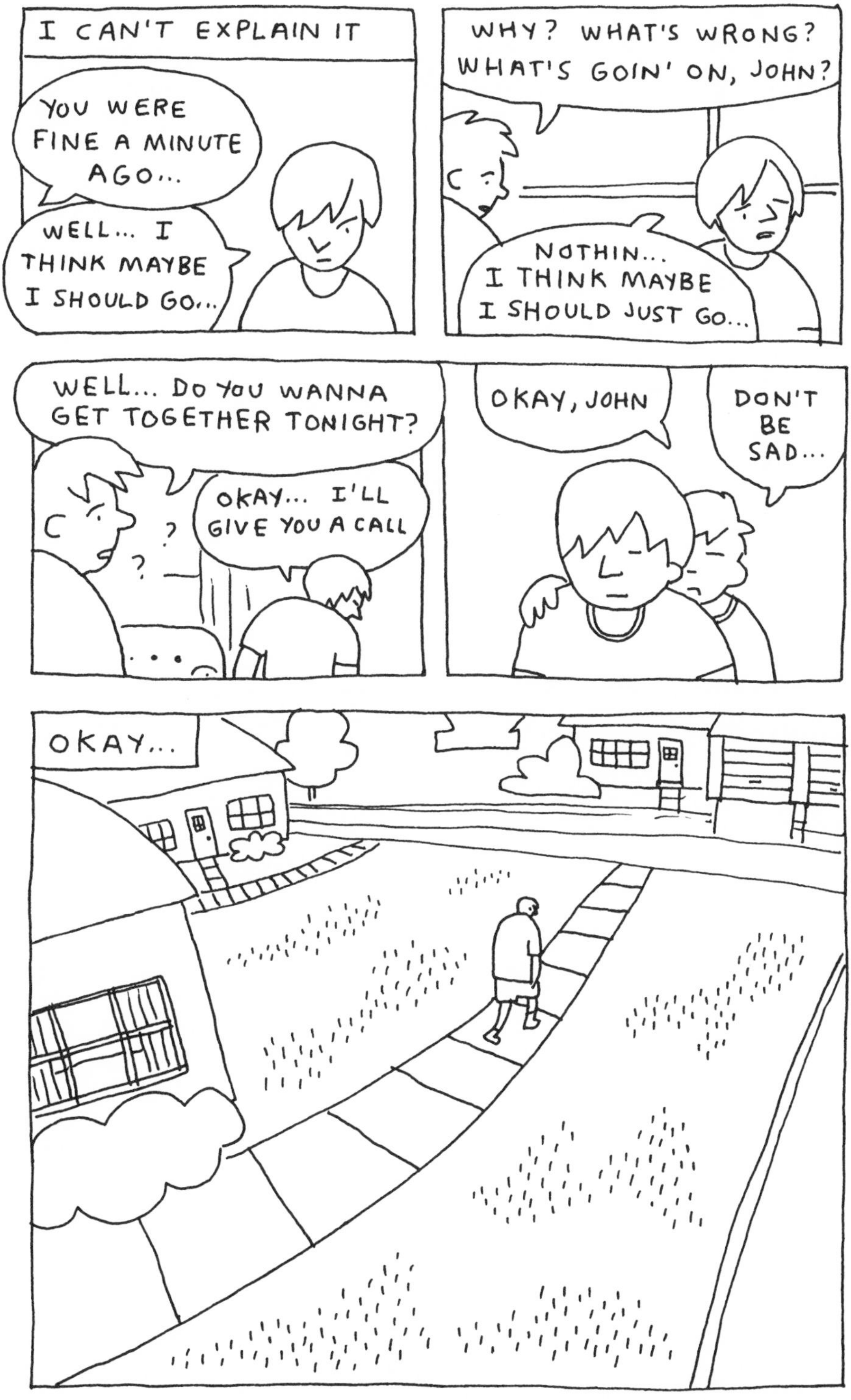
I CAN'T EXPLAIN IT
YOU WERE FINE A MINUTE AGO...
WELL... I THINK MAYBE I SHOULD GO...
WHY? WHAT'S WRONG? WHAT'S GOIN' ON, JOHN?
NOTHIN... I THINK MAYBE I SHOULD JUST GO...
WELL... DO YOU WANNA GET TOGETHER TONIGHT?
OKAY... I'LL GIVE YOU A CALL
? ?
...
OKAY, JOHN
DON'T BE SAD...
OKAY...

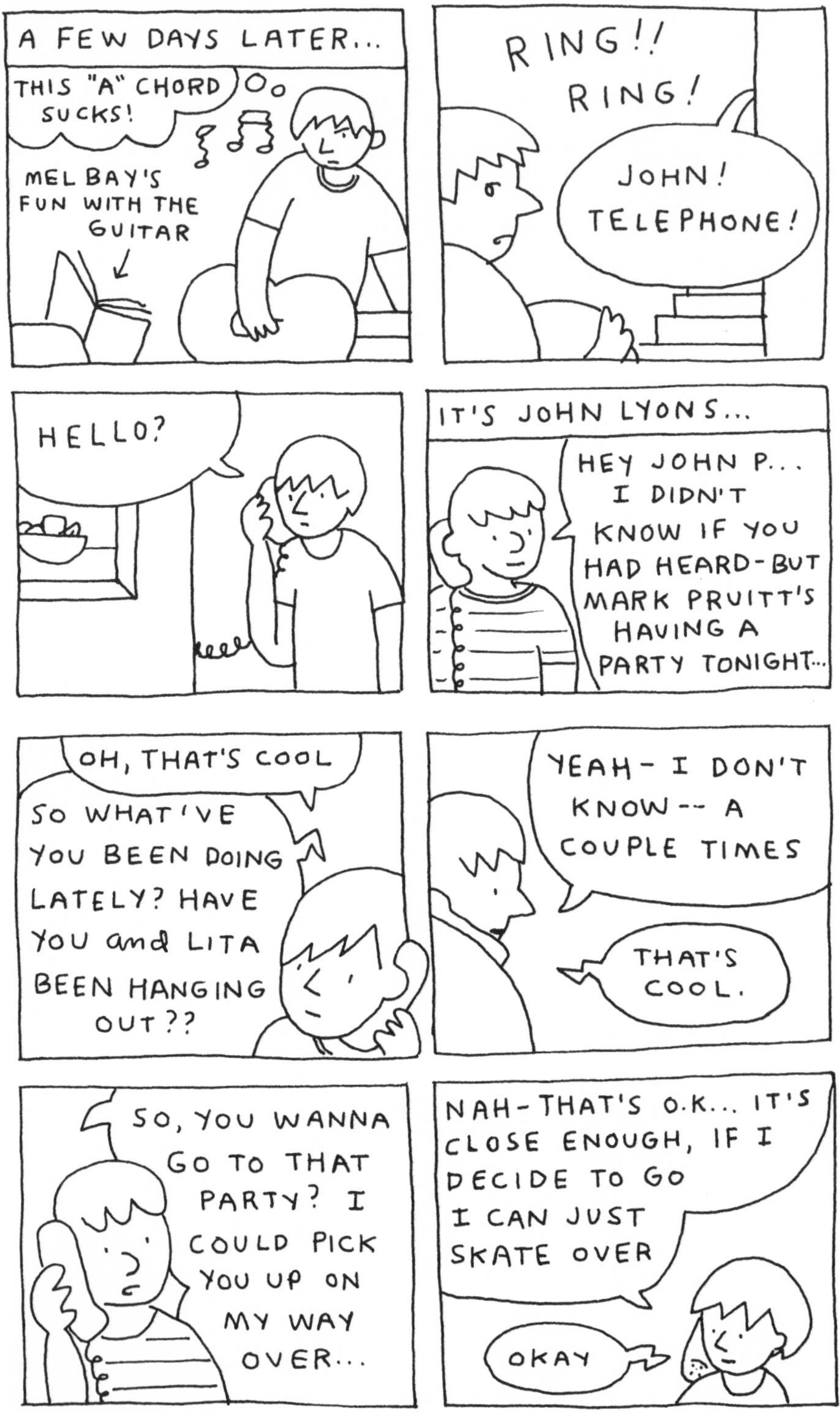
A FEW DAYS LATER...
THIS "A" CHORD SUCKS!
MEL BAY'S FUN WITH THE GUITAR
RING!! RING!
JOHN! TELEPHONE!
HELLO?
IT'S JOHN LYONS...
HEY JOHN P... I DIDN'T KNOW IF YOU HAD HEARD - BUT MARK PRUITT'S HAVING A PARTY TONIGHT...
OH, THAT'S COOL
SO WHAT'VE YOU BEEN DOING LATELY? HAVE YOU and LITA BEEN HANGING OUT??
YEAH - I DON'T KNOW -- A COUPLE TIMES
THAT'S COOL.
SO, YOU WANNA GO TO THAT PARTY? I COULD PICK YOU UP ON MY WAY OVER...
NAH - THAT'S O.K... IT'S CLOSE ENOUGH, IF I DECIDE TO GO I CAN JUST SKATE OVER
OKAY

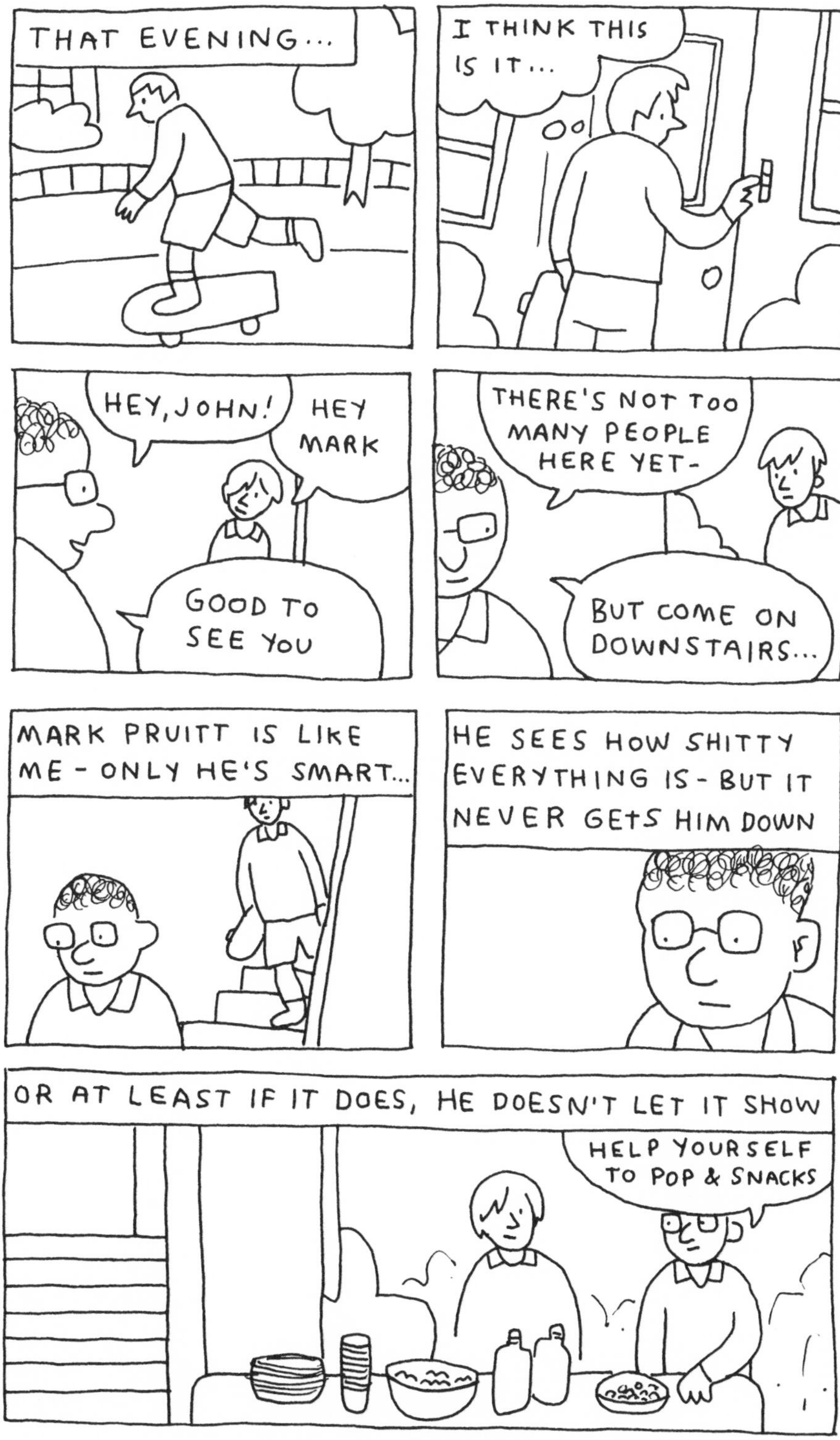
THAT EVENING...
I THINK THIS IS IT...
HEY, JOHN!
HEY MARK
GOOD TO SEE YOU
THERE'S NOT TOO MANY PEOPLE HERE YET-
BUT COME ON DOWNSTAIRS...
MARK PRUITT IS LIKE ME - ONLY HE'S SMART...
HE SEES HOW SHITTY EVERYTHING IS - BUT IT NEVER GETS HIM DOWN
OR AT LEAST IF IT DOES, HE DOESN'T LET IT SHOW
HELP YOURSELF TO POP & SNACKS

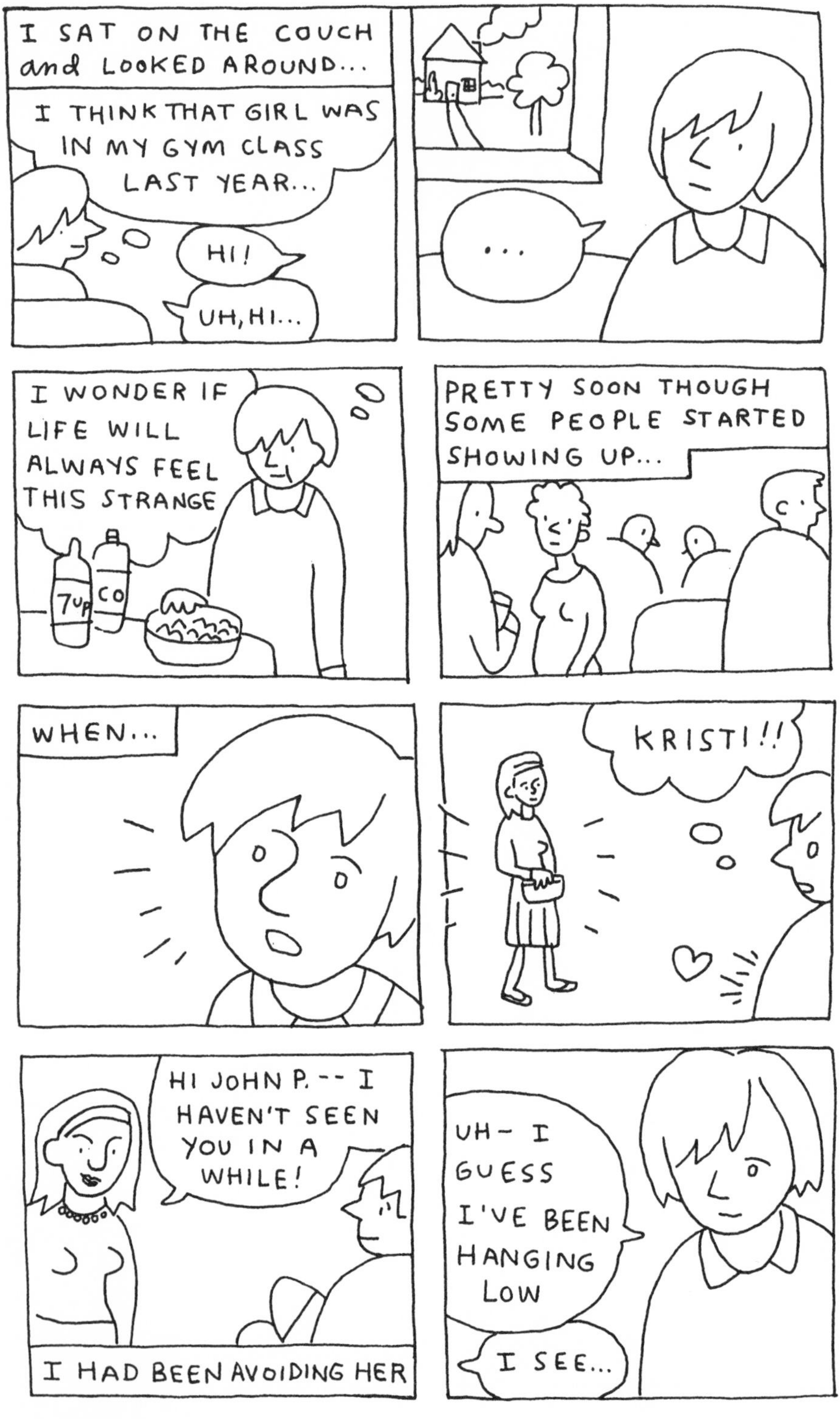
I SAT ON THE COUCH and LOOKED AROUND...
I THINK THAT GIRL WAS IN MY GYM CLASS LAST YEAR...
HI!
UH, HI...
...
I WONDER IF LIFE WILL ALWAYS FEEL THIS STRANGE
7UP
CO
PRETTY SOON THOUGH SOME PEOPLE STARTED SHOWING UP...
WHEN...
KRISTI!!
HI JOHN P. -- I HAVEN'T SEEN YOU IN A WHILE!
I HAD BEEN AVOIDING HER
UH- I GUESS I'VE BEEN HANGING LOW
I SEE...

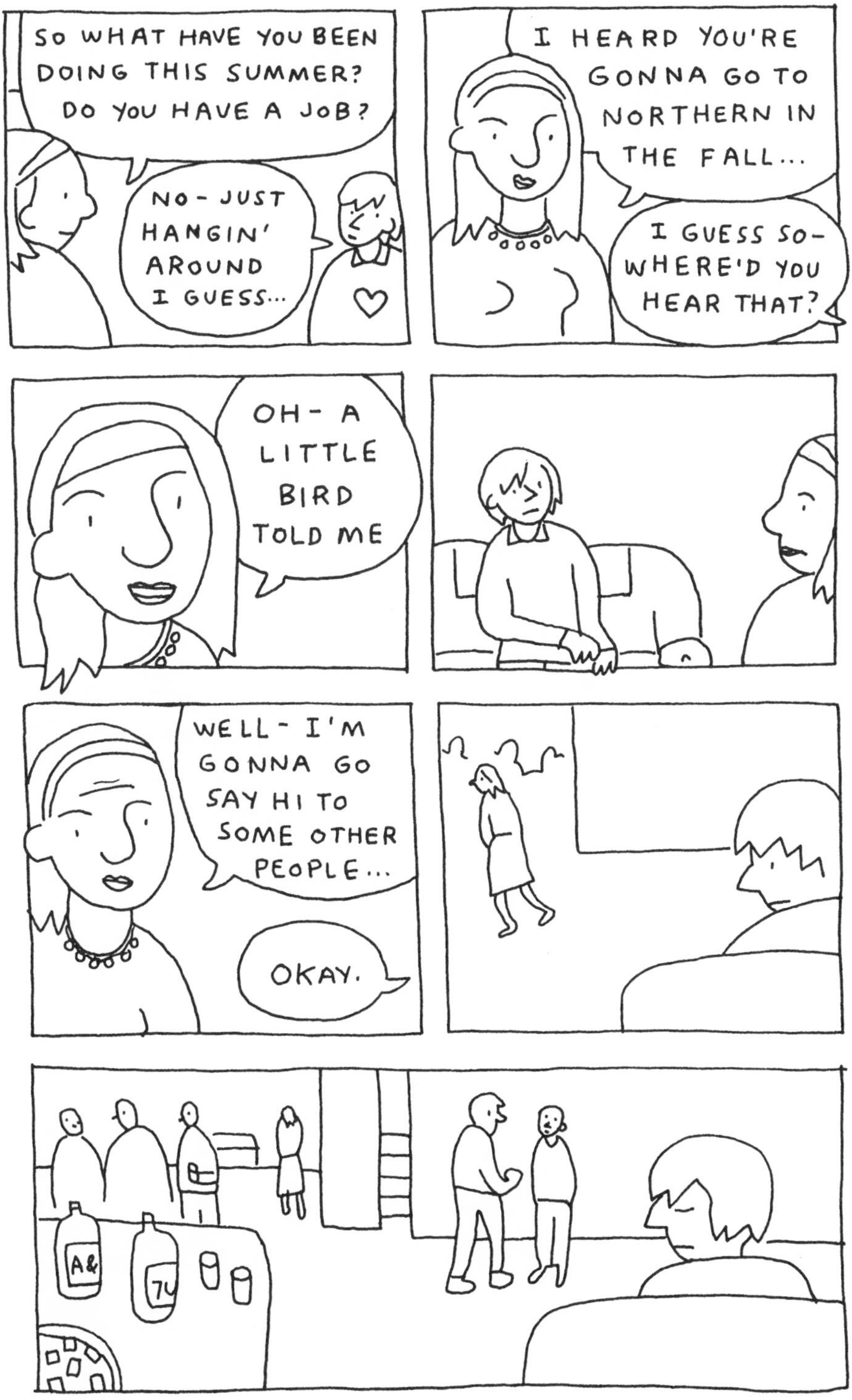
SO WHAT HAVE YOU BEEN DOING THIS SUMMER? DO YOU HAVE A JOB?
NO- JUST HANGIN' AROUND I GUESS...
I HEARD YOU'RE GONNA GO TO NORTHERN IN THE FALL...
I GUESS SO- WHERE'D YOU HEAR THAT?
OH- A LITTLE BIRD TOLD ME
WELL- I'M GONNA GO SAY HI TO SOME OTHER PEOPLE...
OKAY.

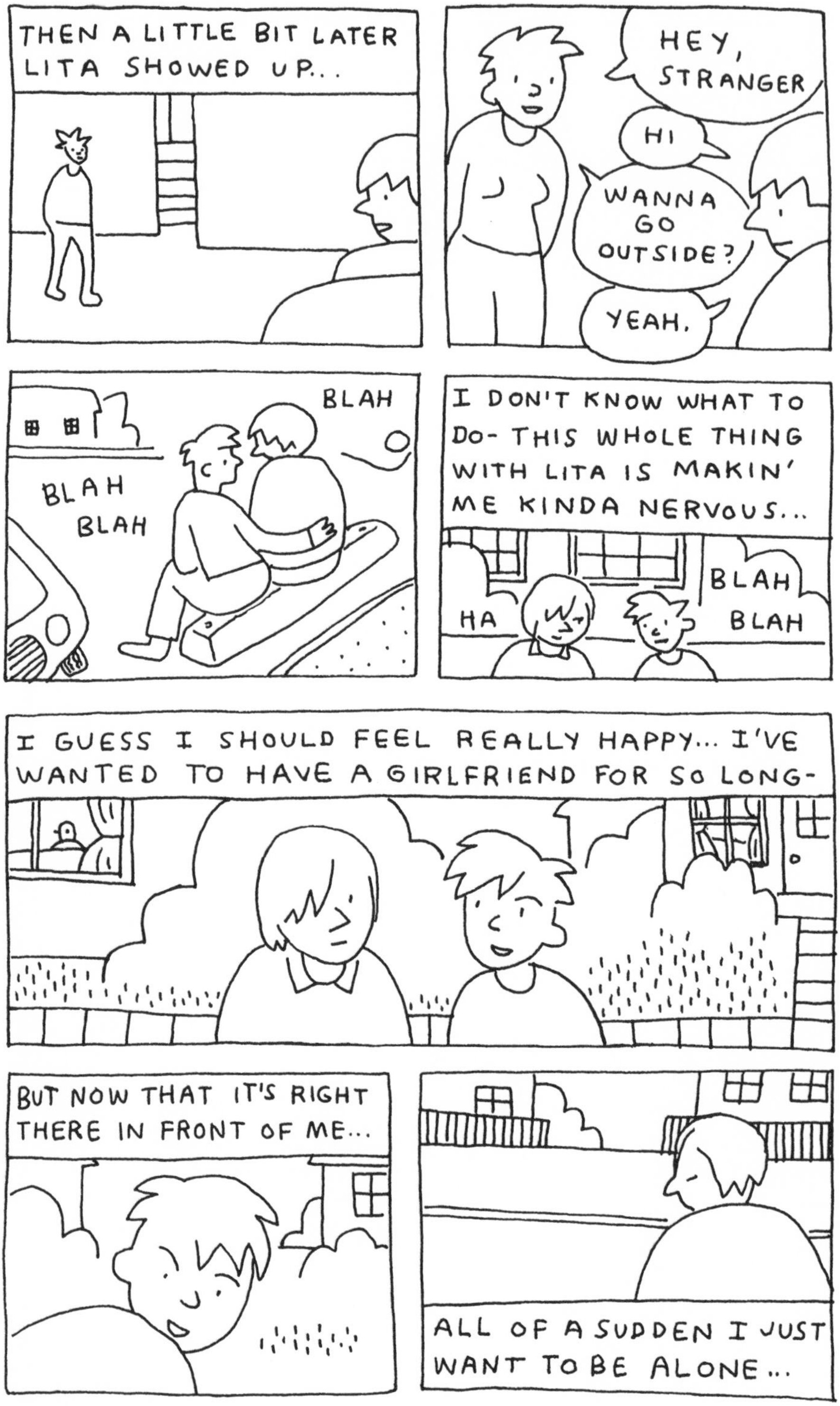
THEN A LITTLE BIT LATER LITA SHOWED UP...
HEY, STRANGER
HI
WANNA GO OUTSIDE?
YEAH.
BLAH
BLAH BLAH
I DON'T KNOW WHAT TO DO- THIS WHOLE THING WITH LITA IS MAKIN' ME KINDA NERVOUS...
BLAH BLAH
HA
I GUESS I SHOULD FEEL REALLY HAPPY... I'VE WANTED TO HAVE A GIRLFRIEND FOR SO LONG-
BUT NOW THAT IT'S RIGHT THERE IN FRONT OF ME...
ALL OF A SUDDEN I JUST WANT TO BE ALONE...

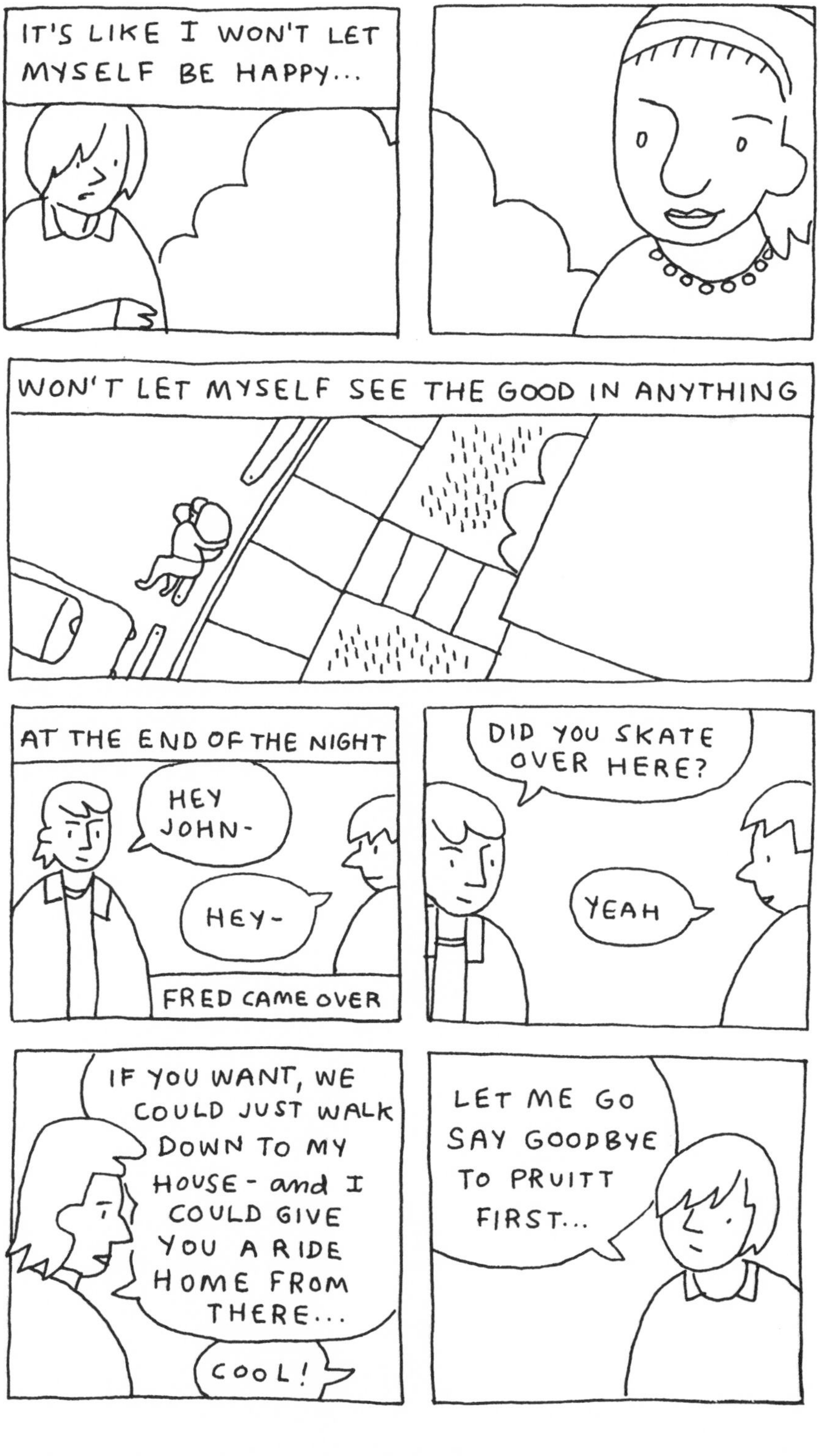
IT'S LIKE I WON'T LET MYSELF BE HAPPY...
WON'T LET MYSELF SEE THE GOOD IN ANYTHING
AT THE END OF THE NIGHT
HEY JOHN-
HEY-
FRED CAME OVER
DID YOU SKATE OVER HERE?
YEAH
IF YOU WANT, WE COULD JUST WALK DOWN TO MY HOUSE - and I COULD GIVE YOU A RIDE HOME FROM THERE...
COOL!
LET ME GO SAY GOODBYE TO PRUITT FIRST...

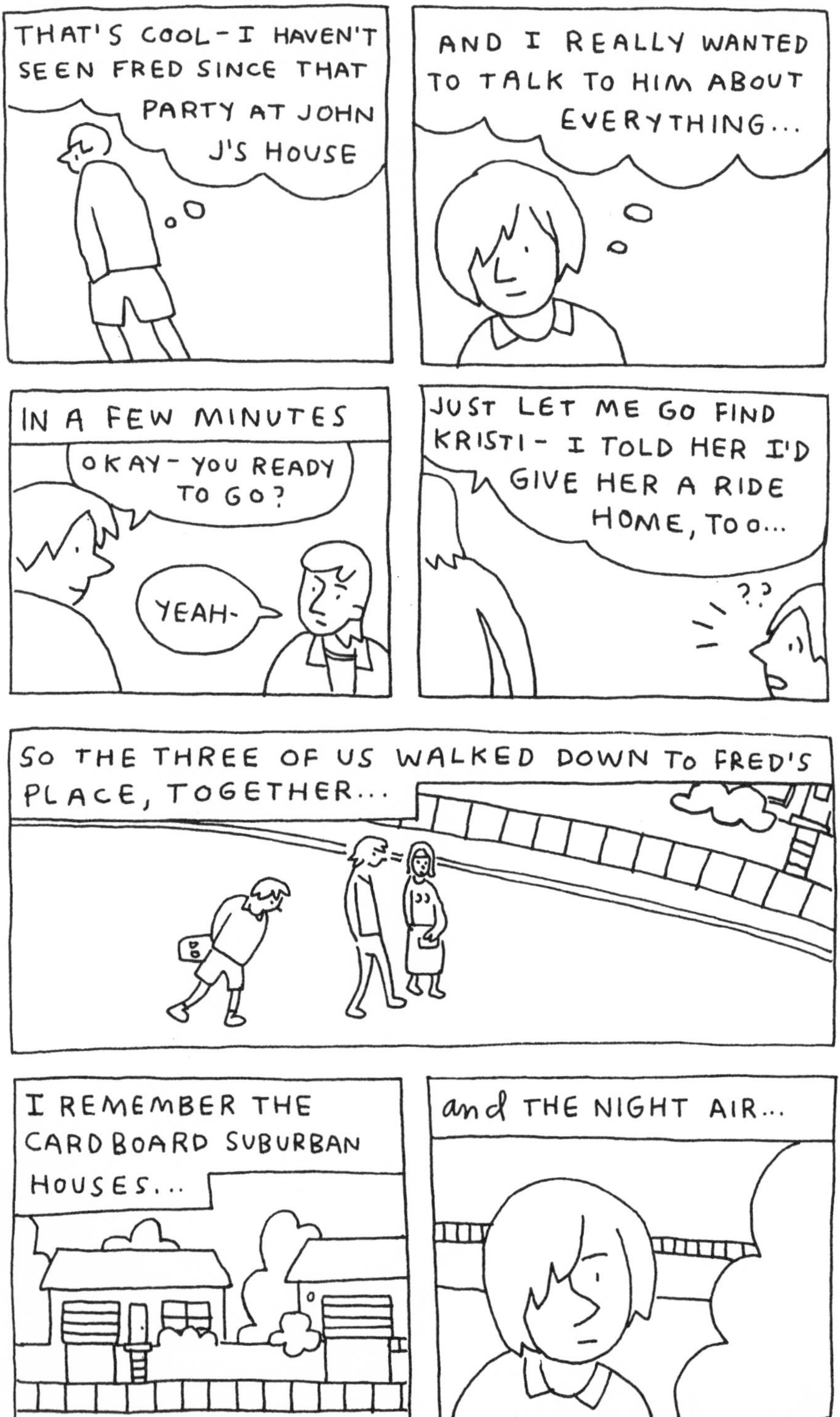
THAT'S COOL - I HAVEN'T SEEN FRED SINCE THAT PARTY AT JOHN J'S HOUSE
AND I REALLY WANTED TO TALK TO HIM ABOUT EVERYTHING...
IN A FEW MINUTES
OKAY - YOU READY TO GO?
YEAH-
JUST LET ME GO FIND KRISTI - I TOLD HER I'D GIVE HER A RIDE HOME, TOO...
??
SO THE THREE OF US WALKED DOWN TO FRED'S PLACE, TOGETHER...
I REMEMBER THE CARDBOARD SUBURBAN HOUSES...
and THE NIGHT AIR...

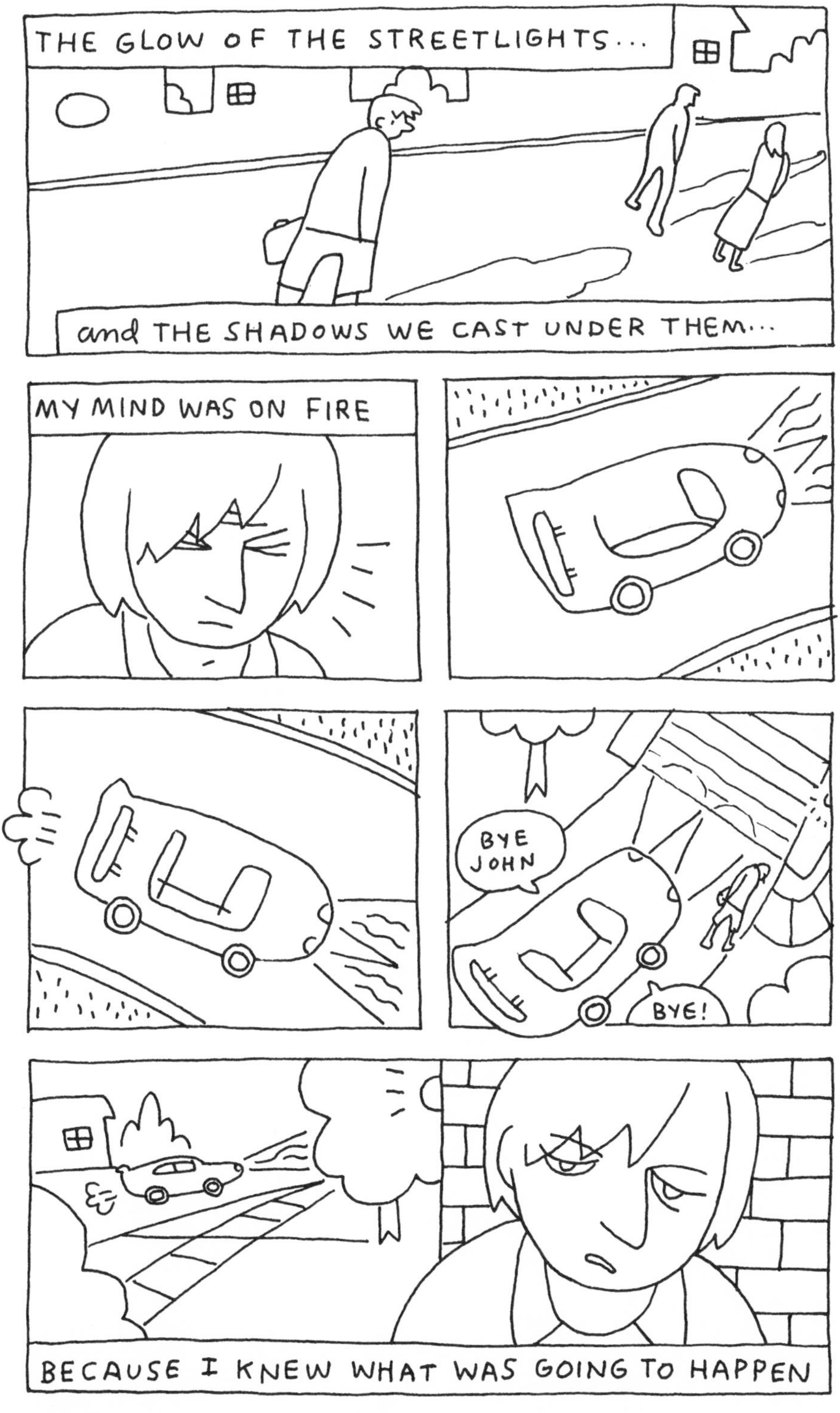
THE GLOW OF THE STREETLIGHTS...
and THE SHADOWS WE CAST UNDER THEM...
MY MIND WAS ON FIRE
BYE JOHN
BYE!
BECAUSE I KNEW WHAT WAS GOING TO HAPPEN

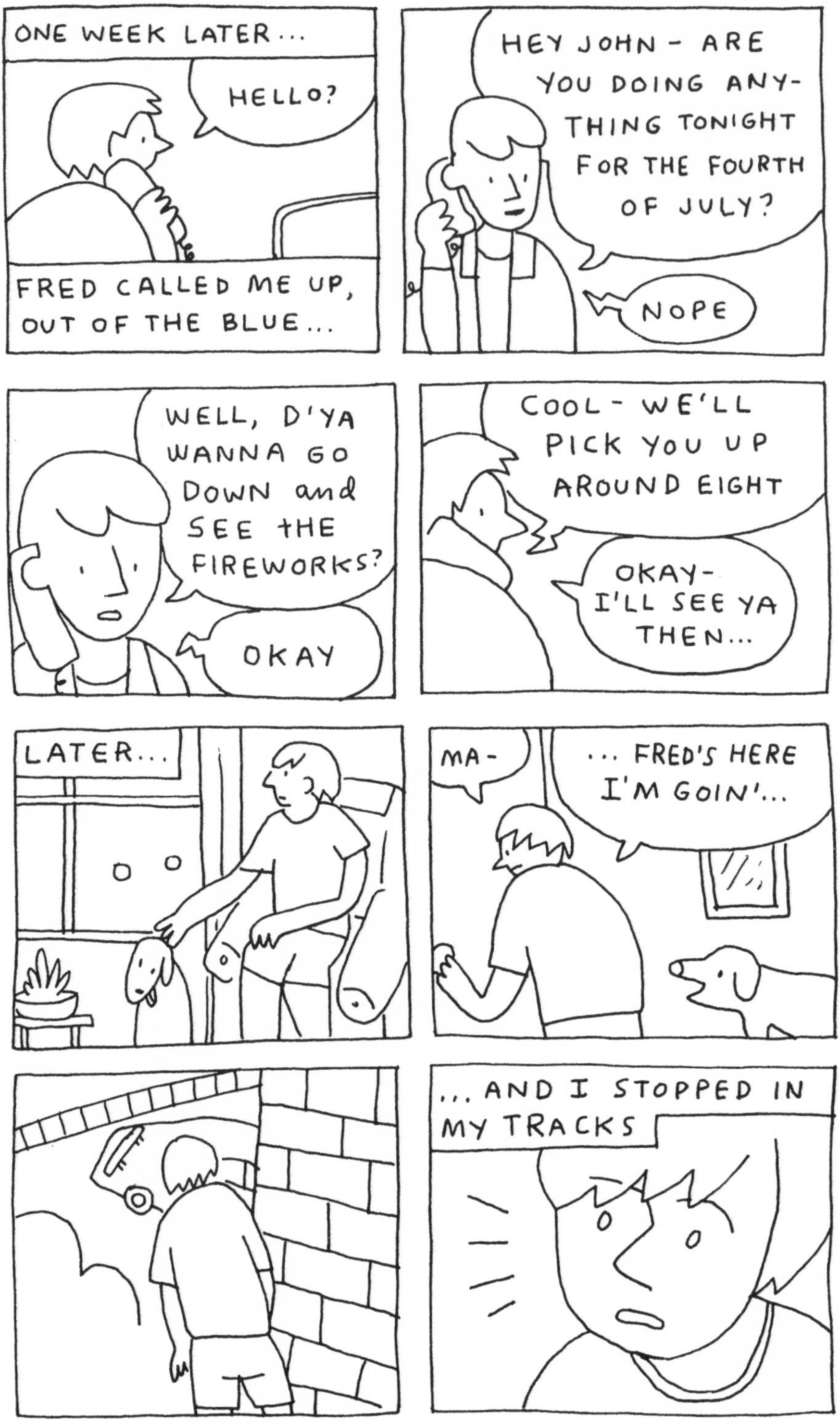
ONE WEEK LATER...
HELLO?
FRED CALLED ME UP, OUT OF THE BLUE...
HEY JOHN - ARE YOU DOING ANY-THING TONIGHT FOR THE FOURTH OF JULY?
NOPE
WELL, D'YA WANNA GO DOWN and SEE tHE FIREWORKS?
OKAY
COOL - WE'LL PICK YOU UP AROUND EIGHT
OKAY - I'LL SEE YA THEN...
LATER...
MA -
... FRED'S HERE I'M GOIN'...
... AND I STOPPED IN MY TRACKS

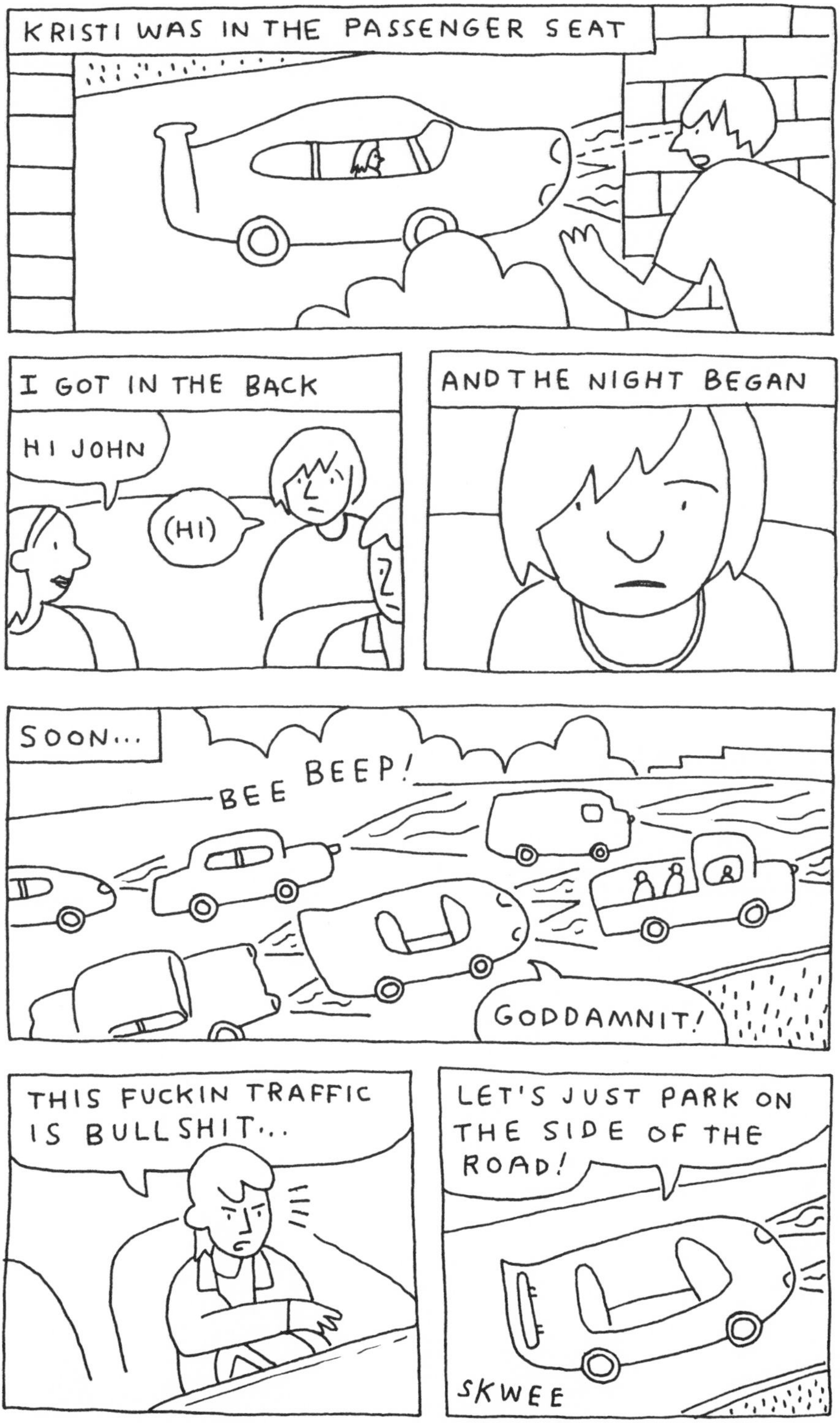
KRISTI WAS IN THE PASSENGER SEAT
I GOT IN THE BACK
HI JOHN
(HI)
AND THE NIGHT BEGAN
SOON...
BEE BEEP!
GODDAMNIT!
THIS FUCKIN TRAFFIC IS BULLSHIT...
LET'S JUST PARK ON THE SIDE OF THE ROAD!
SKWEE

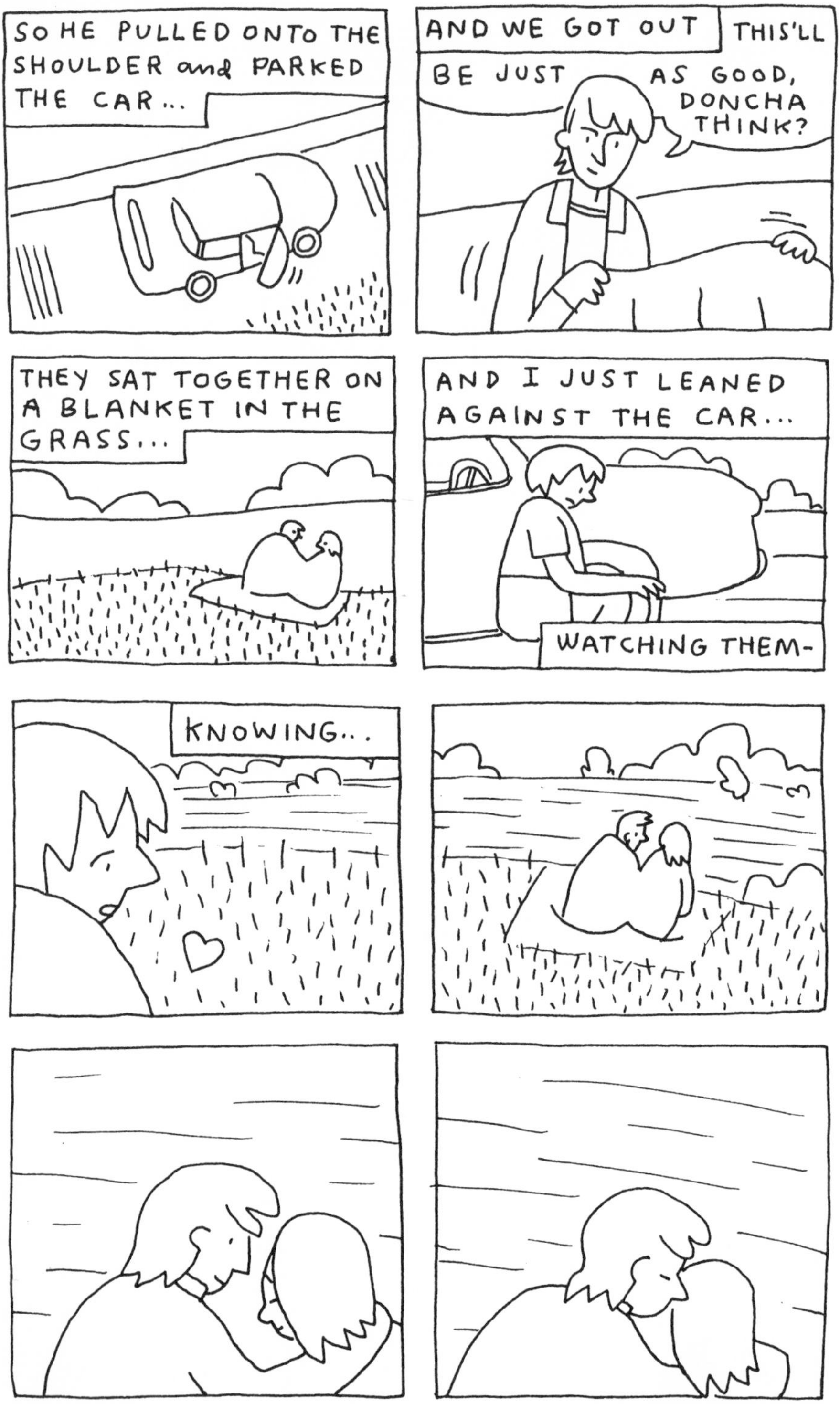
SO HE PULLED ONTO THE SHOULDER and PARKED THE CAR...
AND WE GOT OUT
THIS'LL BE JUST AS GOOD, DONCHA THINK?
THEY SAT TOGETHER ON A BLANKET IN THE GRASS...
AND I JUST LEANED AGAINST THE CAR...
WATCHING THEM-
KNOWING...

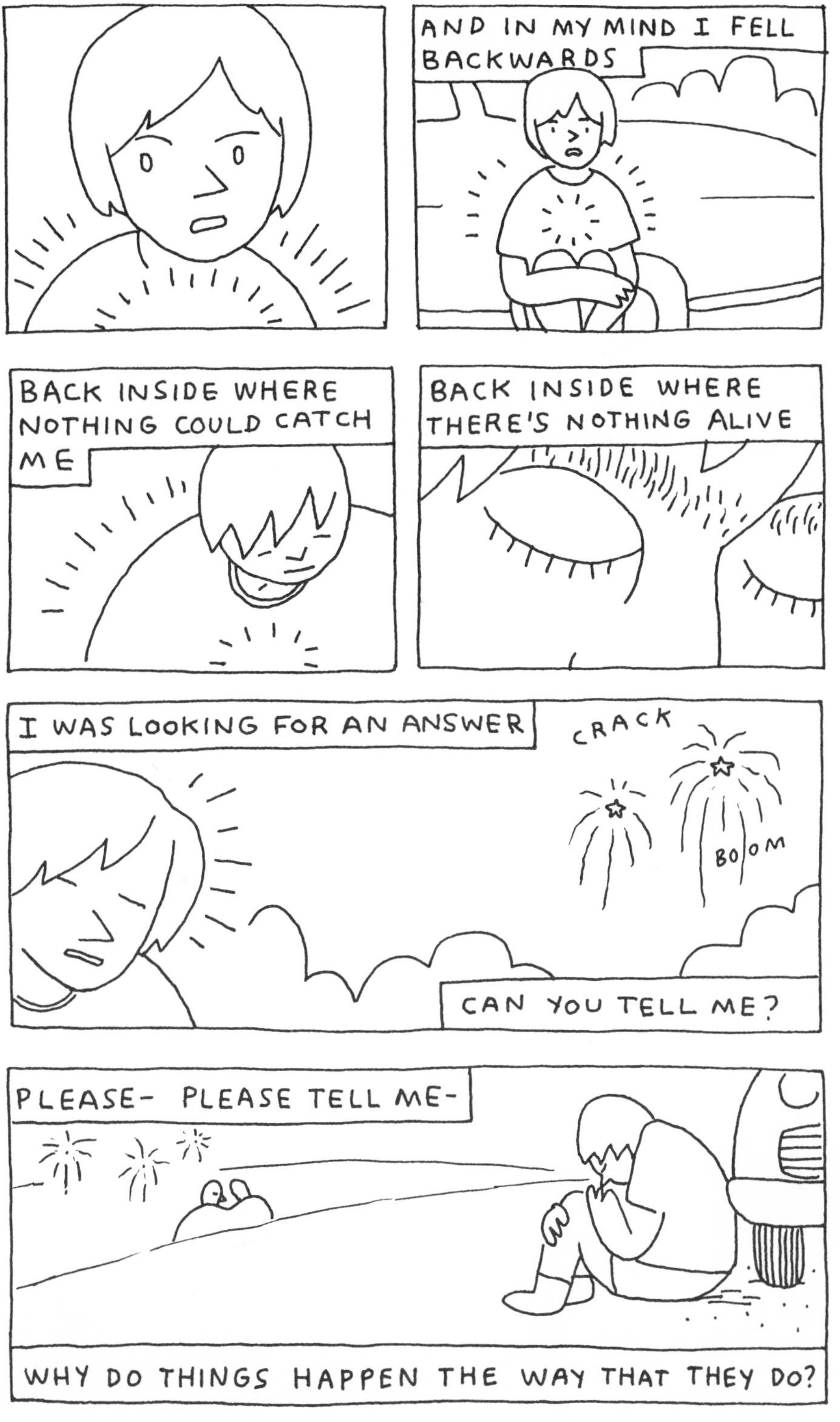
AND IN MY MIND I FELL BACKWARDS
BACK INSIDE WHERE NOTHING COULD CATCH ME
BACK INSIDE WHERE THERE'S NOTHING ALIVE
I WAS LOOKING FOR AN ANSWER
CRACK
BOOM
CAN YOU TELL ME?
PLEASE- PLEASE TELL ME-
WHY DO THINGS HAPPEN THE WAY THAT THEY DO?

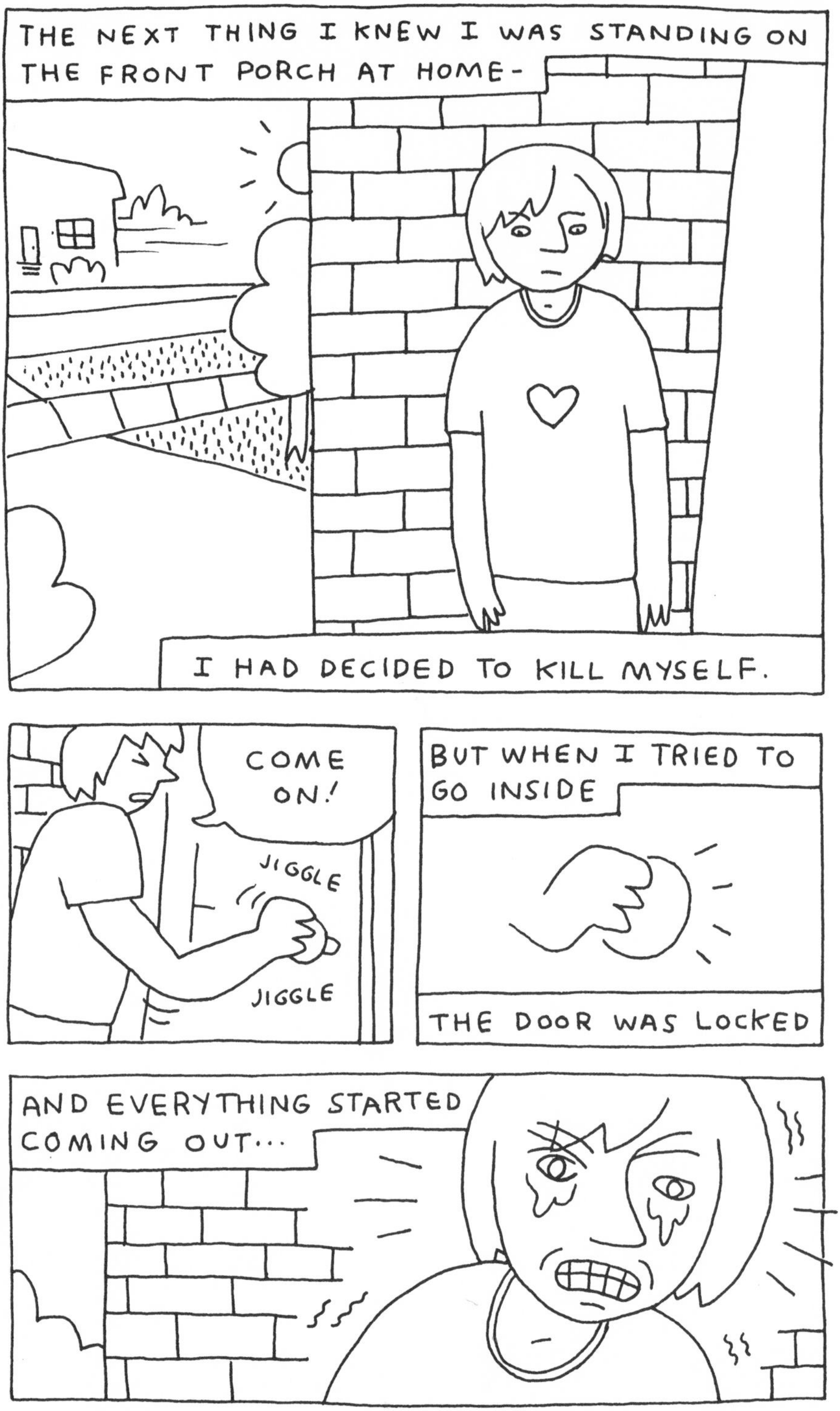
THE NEXT THING I KNEW I WAS STANDING ON THE FRONT PORCH AT HOME-
I HAD DECIDED TO KILL MYSELF.
COME ON!
JIGGLE
JIGGLE
BUT WHEN I TRIED TO GO INSIDE
THE DOOR WAS LOCKED
AND EVERYTHING STARTED COMING OUT...

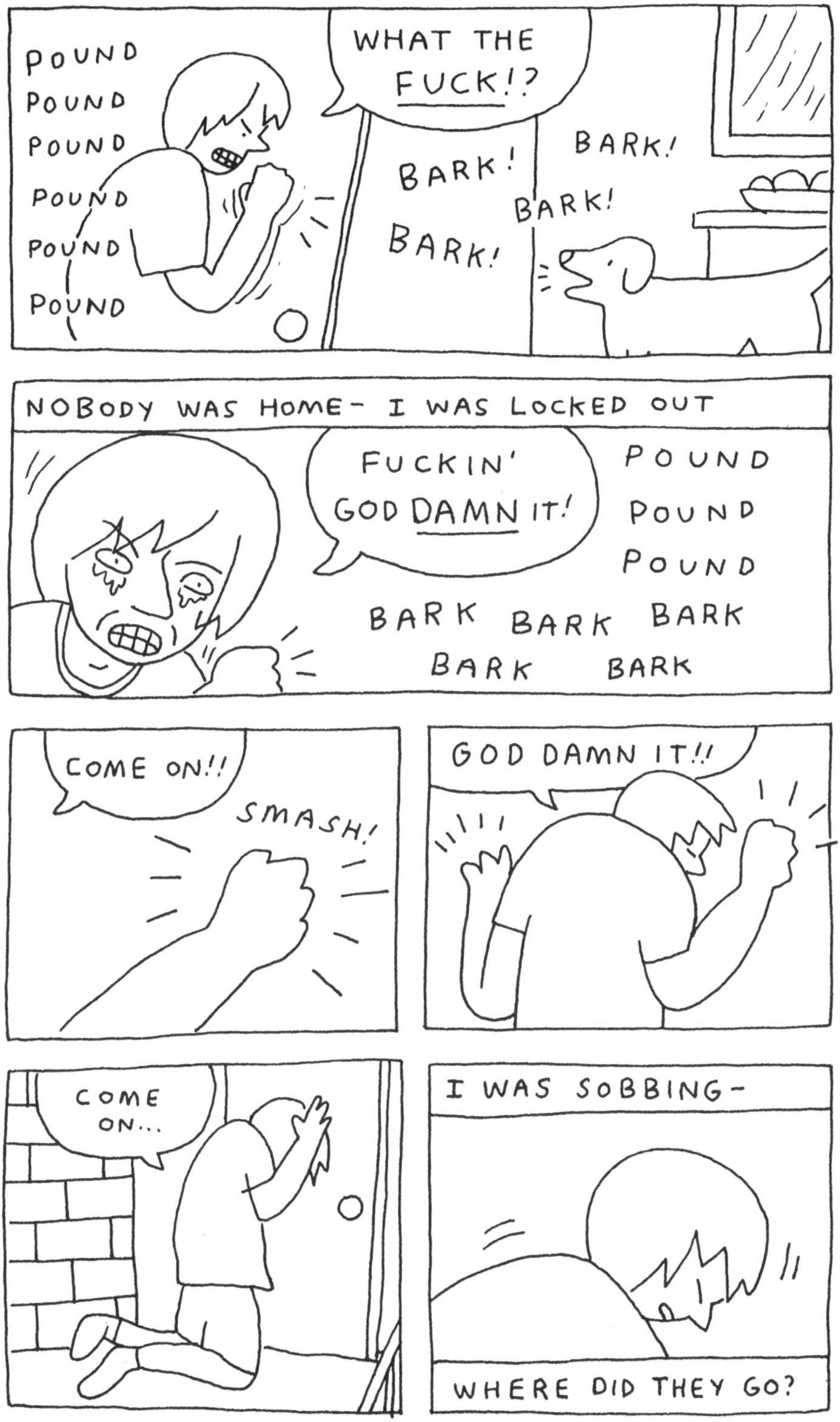
POUND
POUND
POUND
POUND
POUND
POUND
WHAT THE FUCK!?
BARK!
BARK!
BARK!
BARK!
BARK!
NOBODY WAS HOME- I WAS LOCKED OUT
FUCKIN' GOD DAMN IT!
POUND
POUND
POUND
BARK BARK BARK
BARK BARK
COME ON!!
SMASH!
GOD DAMN IT!!
COME ON...
I WAS SOBBING-
WHERE DID THEY GO?

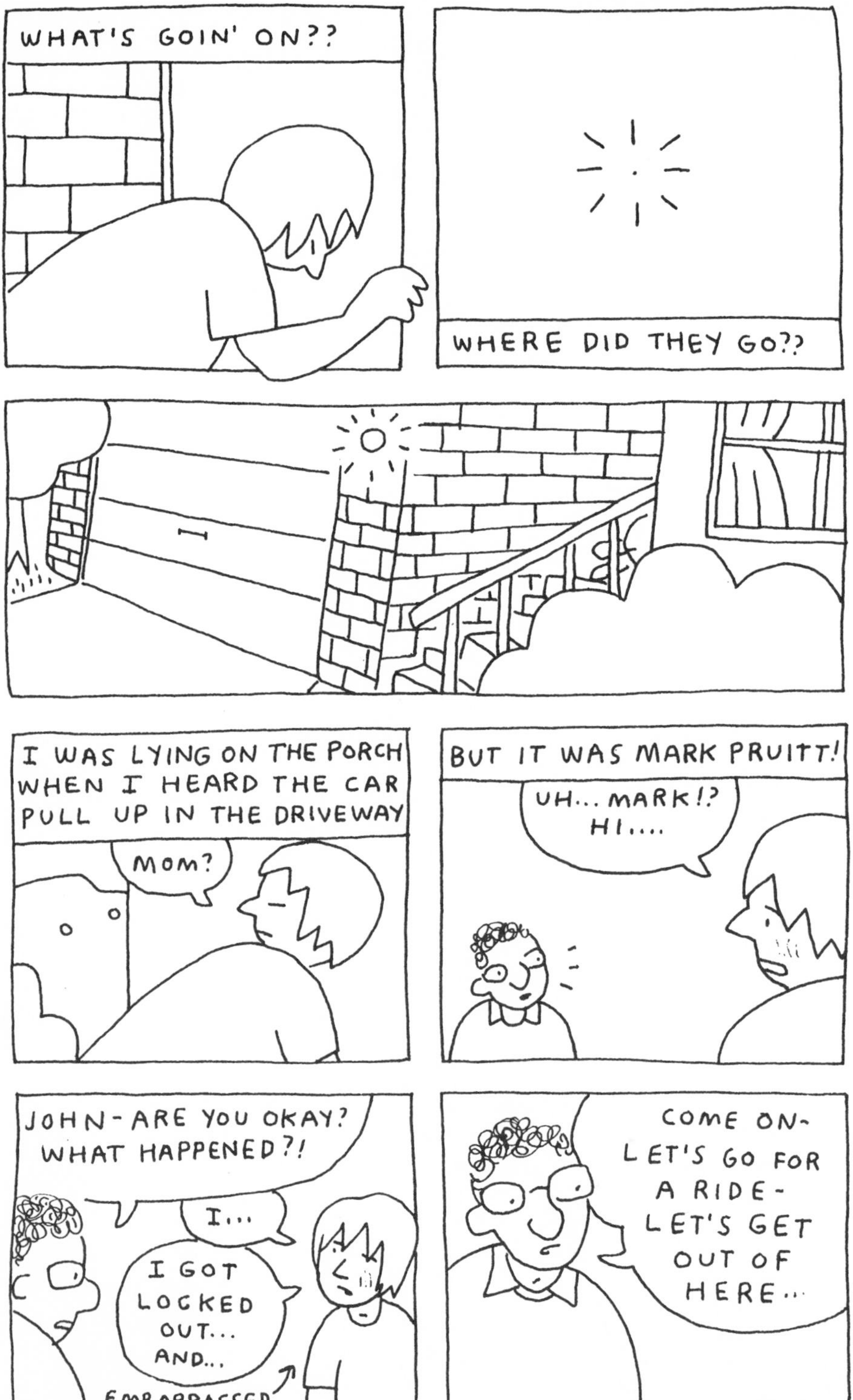

WHAT'S GOIN' ON??
WHERE DID THEY GO??
I WAS LYING ON THE PORCH WHEN I HEARD THE CAR PULL UP IN THE DRIVEWAY
MOM?
BUT IT WAS MARK PRUITT!
UH... MARK!? HI....
JOHN - ARE YOU OKAY? WHAT HAPPENED?!
I...
I GOT LOCKED OUT... AND...
EMBARRASSED
COME ON - LET'S GO FOR A RIDE - LET'S GET OUT OF HERE...

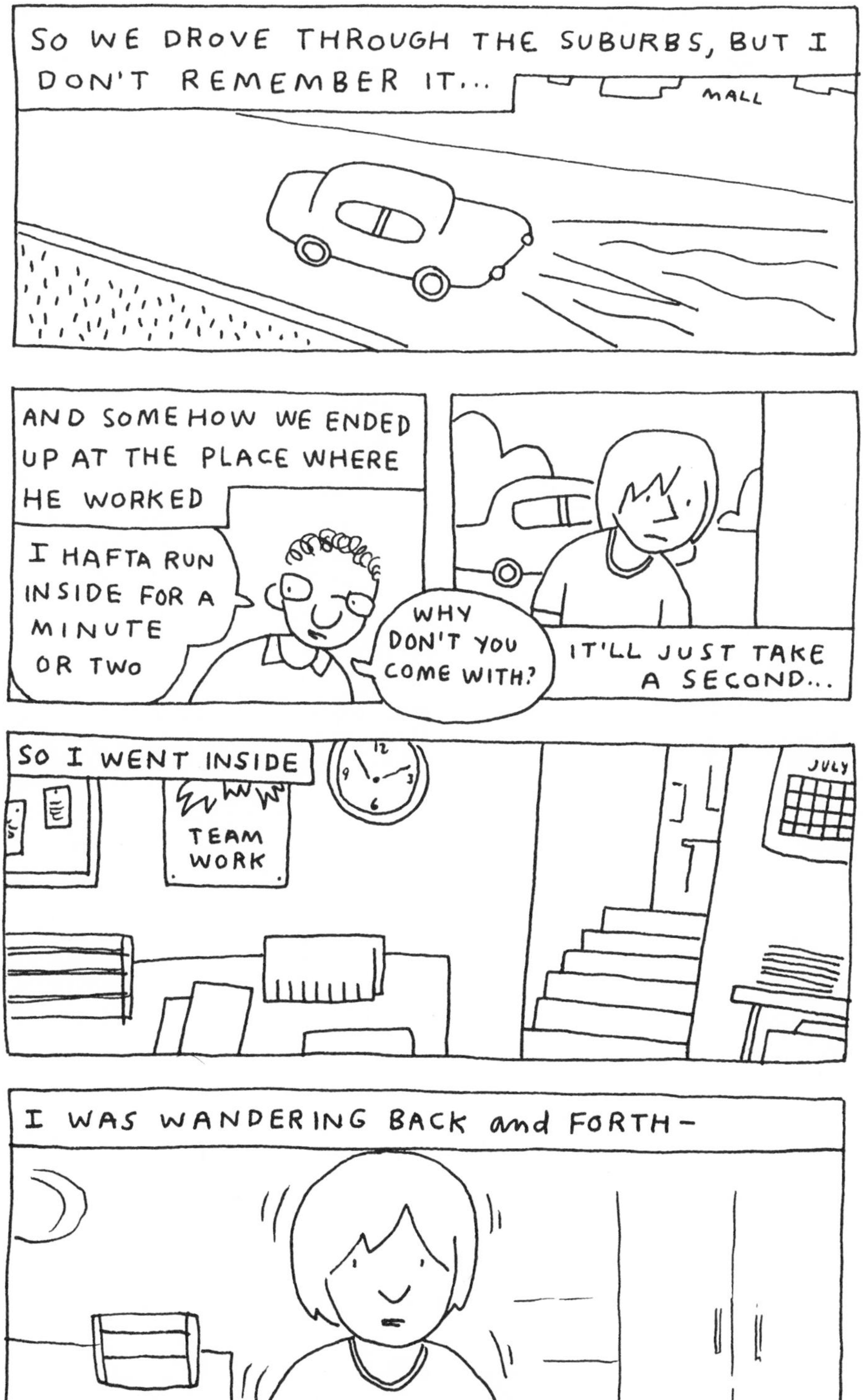
SO WE DROVE THROUGH THE SUBURBS, BUT I DON'T REMEMBER IT...
MALL
AND SOMEHOW WE ENDED UP AT THE PLACE WHERE HE WORKED
I HAFTA RUN INSIDE FOR A MINUTE OR TWO
WHY DON'T YOU COME WITH?
IT'LL JUST TAKE A SECOND...
SO I WENT INSIDE
TEAM WORK
JULY
I WAS WANDERING BACK and FORTH-

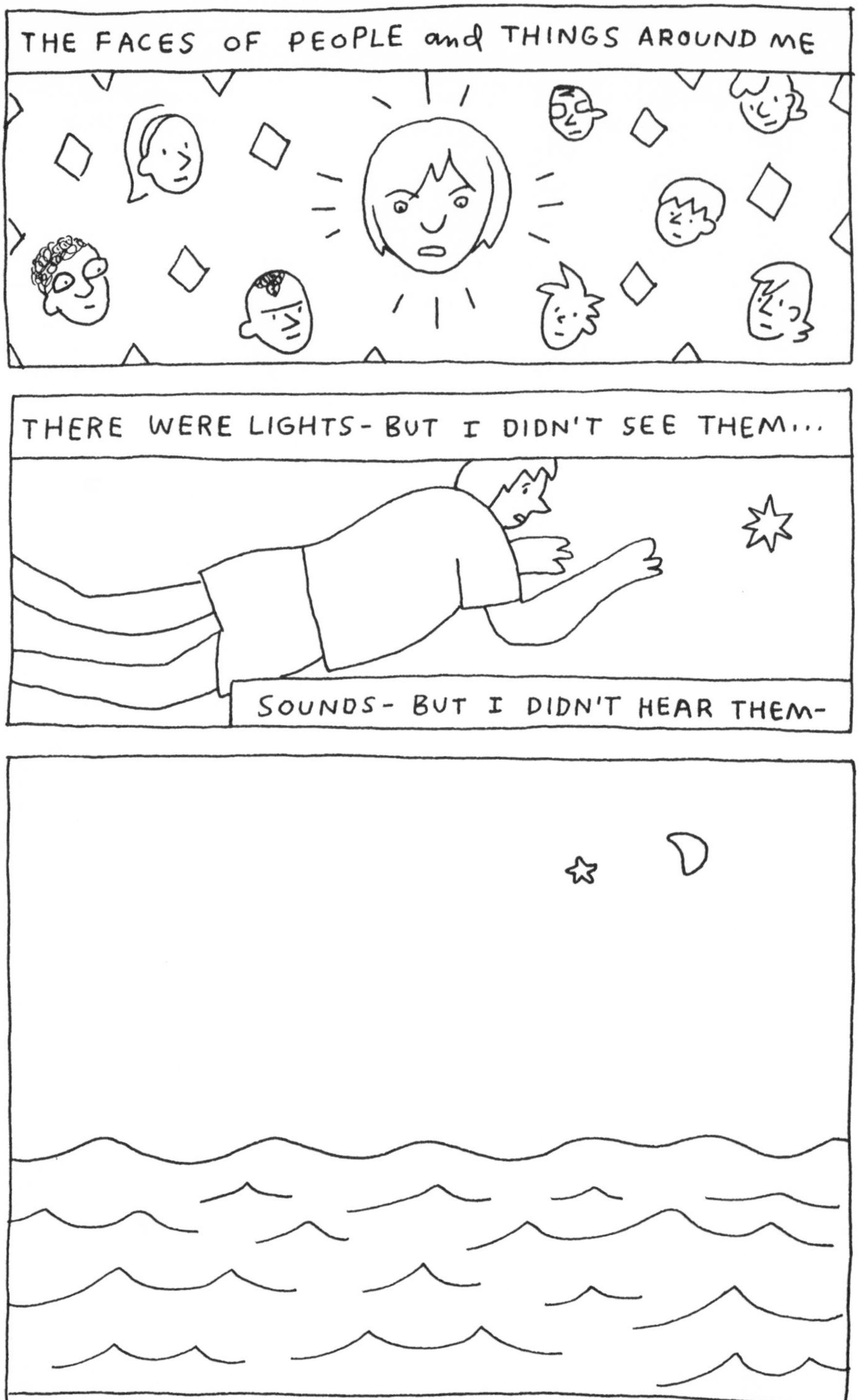
THE FACES OF PEOPLE and THINGS AROUND ME
THERE WERE LIGHTS - BUT I DIDN'T SEE THEM...
SOUNDS - BUT I DIDN'T HEAR THEM-
BECAUSE I SAW THEN THAT LIFE IS LIKE A DREAM

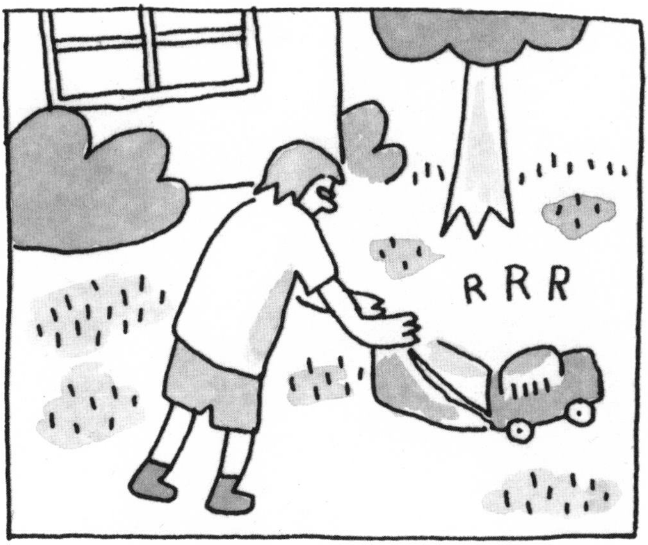
RRR

Part Four
CELEBRATED SUMMER

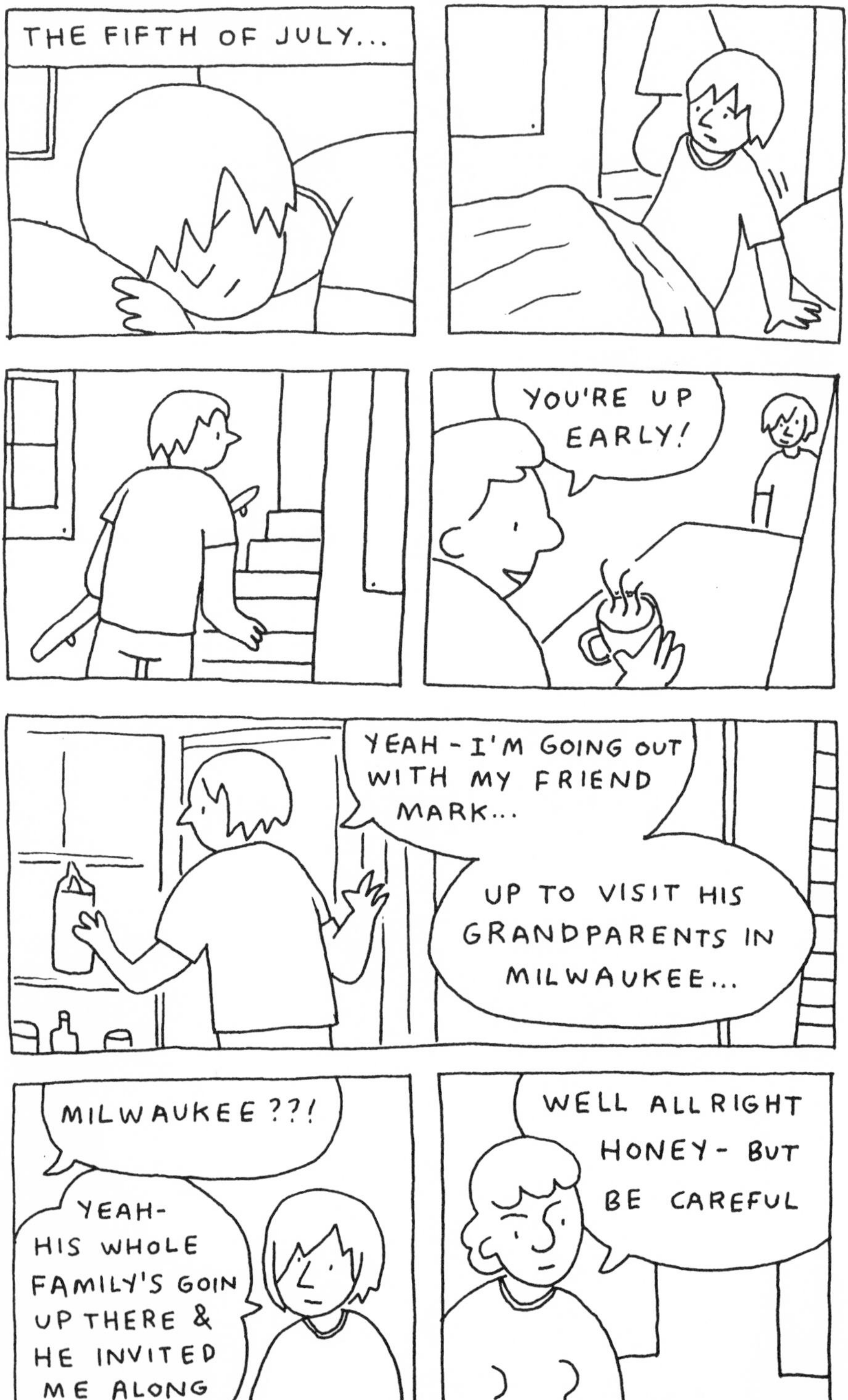
THE FIFTH OF JULY...
YOU'RE UP EARLY!
YEAH - I'M GOING OUT WITH MY FRIEND MARK...
UP TO VISIT HIS GRANDPARENTS IN MILWAUKEE...
MILWAUKEE??!
YEAH- HIS WHOLE FAMILY'S GOIN UP THERE & HE INVITED ME ALONG
WELL ALLRIGHT HONEY- BUT BE CAREFUL

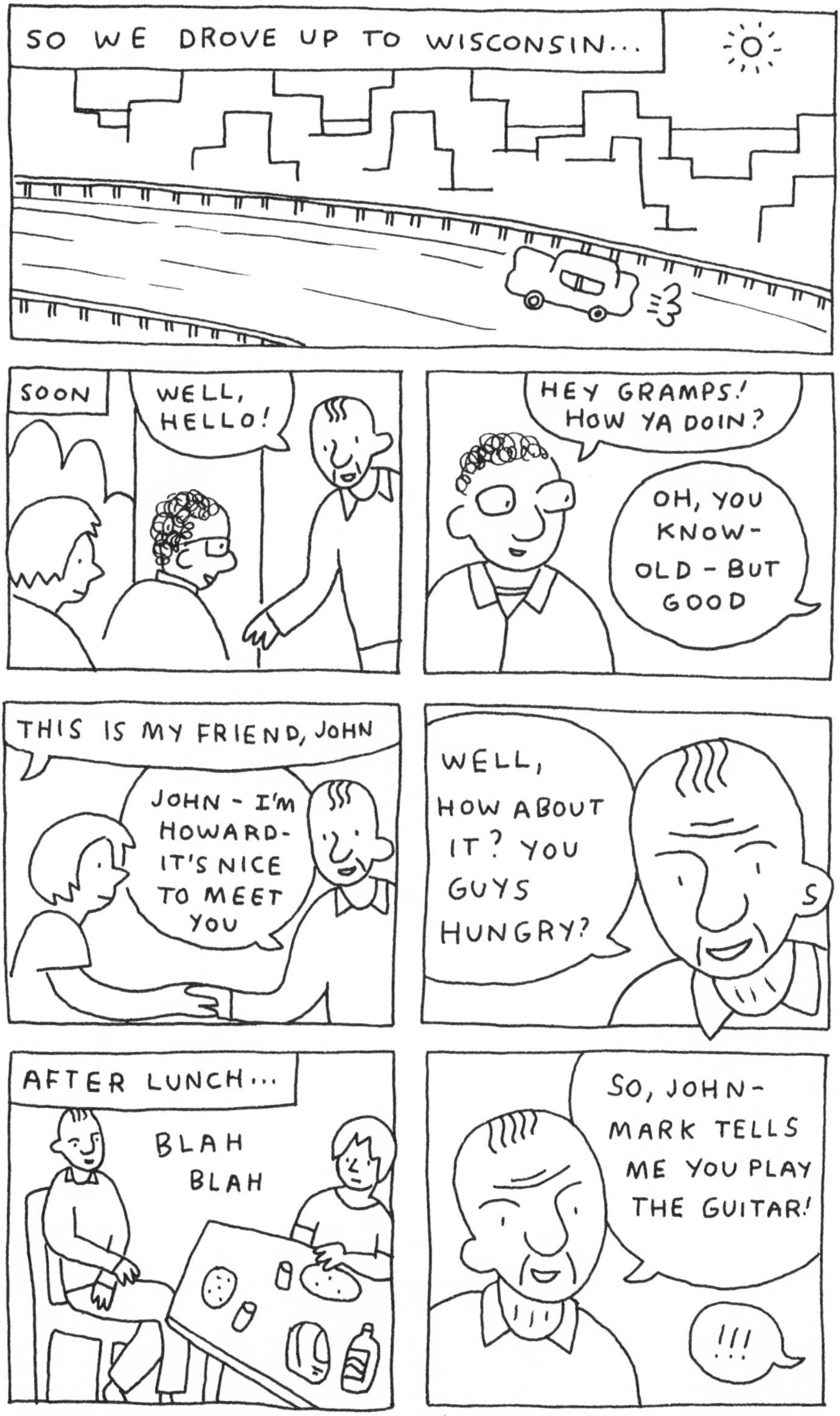
SO WE DROVE UP TO WISCONSIN...
SOON
WELL, HELLO!
HEY GRAMPS! HOW YA DOIN?
OH, YOU KNOW- OLD - BUT GOOD
THIS IS MY FRIEND, JOHN
JOHN - I'M HOWARD- IT'S NICE TO MEET YOU
WELL, HOW ABOUT IT? YOU GUYS HUNGRY?
AFTER LUNCH...
BLAH BLAH
SO, JOHN- MARK TELLS ME YOU PLAY THE GUITAR!
!!!

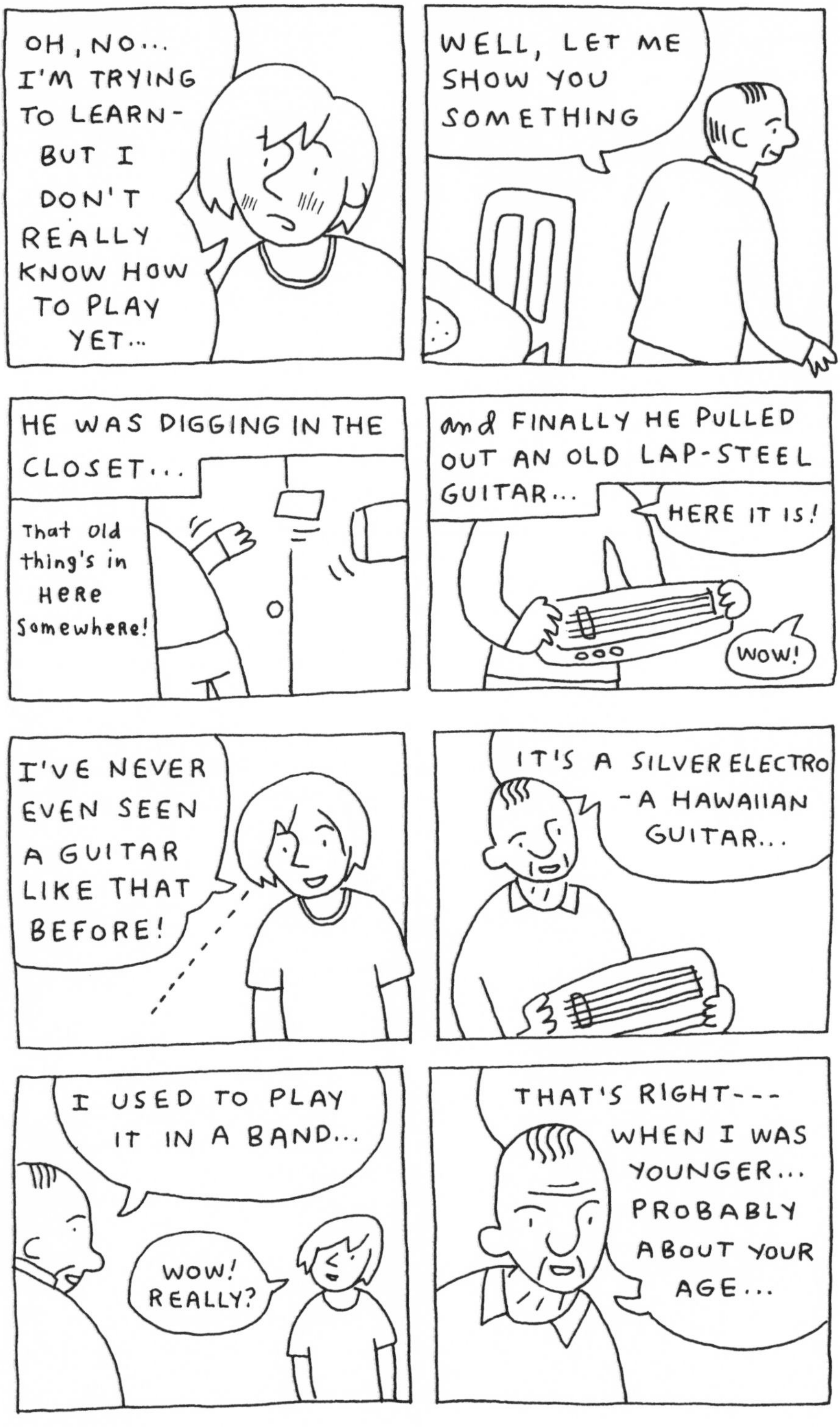
OH, NO... I'M TRYING TO LEARN- BUT I DON'T REALLY KNOW HOW TO PLAY YET...
WELL, LET ME SHOW YOU SOMETHING
HE WAS DIGGING IN THE CLOSET...
That old thing's in Here Somewhere!
and FINALLY HE PULLED OUT AN OLD LAP-STEEL GUITAR...
HERE IT IS!
WOW!
I'VE NEVER EVEN SEEN A GUITAR LIKE THAT BEFORE!
IT'S A SILVER ELECTRO -A HAWAIIAN GUITAR...
I USED TO PLAY IT IN A BAND...
WOW! REALLY?
THAT'S RIGHT--- WHEN I WAS YOUNGER... PROBABLY ABOUT YOUR AGE...

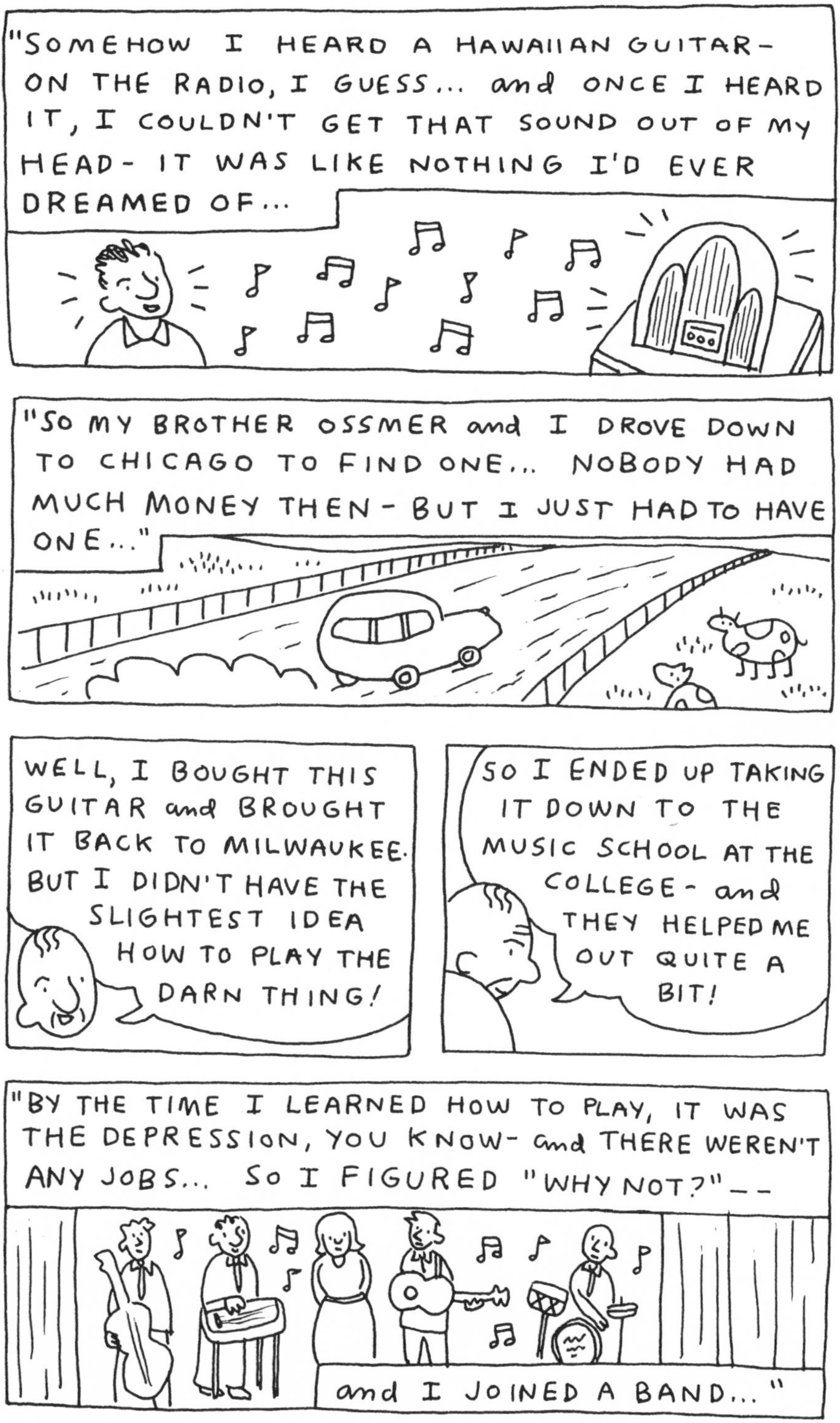
"SOMEHOW I HEARD A HAWAIIAN GUITAR - ON THE RADIO, I GUESS... and ONCE I HEARD IT, I COULDN'T GET THAT SOUND OUT OF MY HEAD - IT WAS LIKE NOTHING I'D EVER DREAMED OF...
"SO MY BROTHER OSSMER and I DROVE DOWN TO CHICAGO TO FIND ONE... NOBODY HAD MUCH MONEY THEN - BUT I JUST HAD TO HAVE ONE..."
WELL, I BOUGHT THIS GUITAR and BROUGHT IT BACK TO MILWAUKEE. BUT I DIDN'T HAVE THE SLIGHTEST IDEA HOW TO PLAY THE DARN THING!
SO I ENDED UP TAKING IT DOWN TO THE MUSIC SCHOOL AT THE COLLEGE - and THEY HELPED ME OUT QUITE A BIT!
"BY THE TIME I LEARNED HOW TO PLAY, IT WAS THE DEPRESSION, YOU KNOW - and THERE WEREN'T ANY JOBS... SO I FIGURED "WHY NOT?" --
and I JOINED A BAND..."

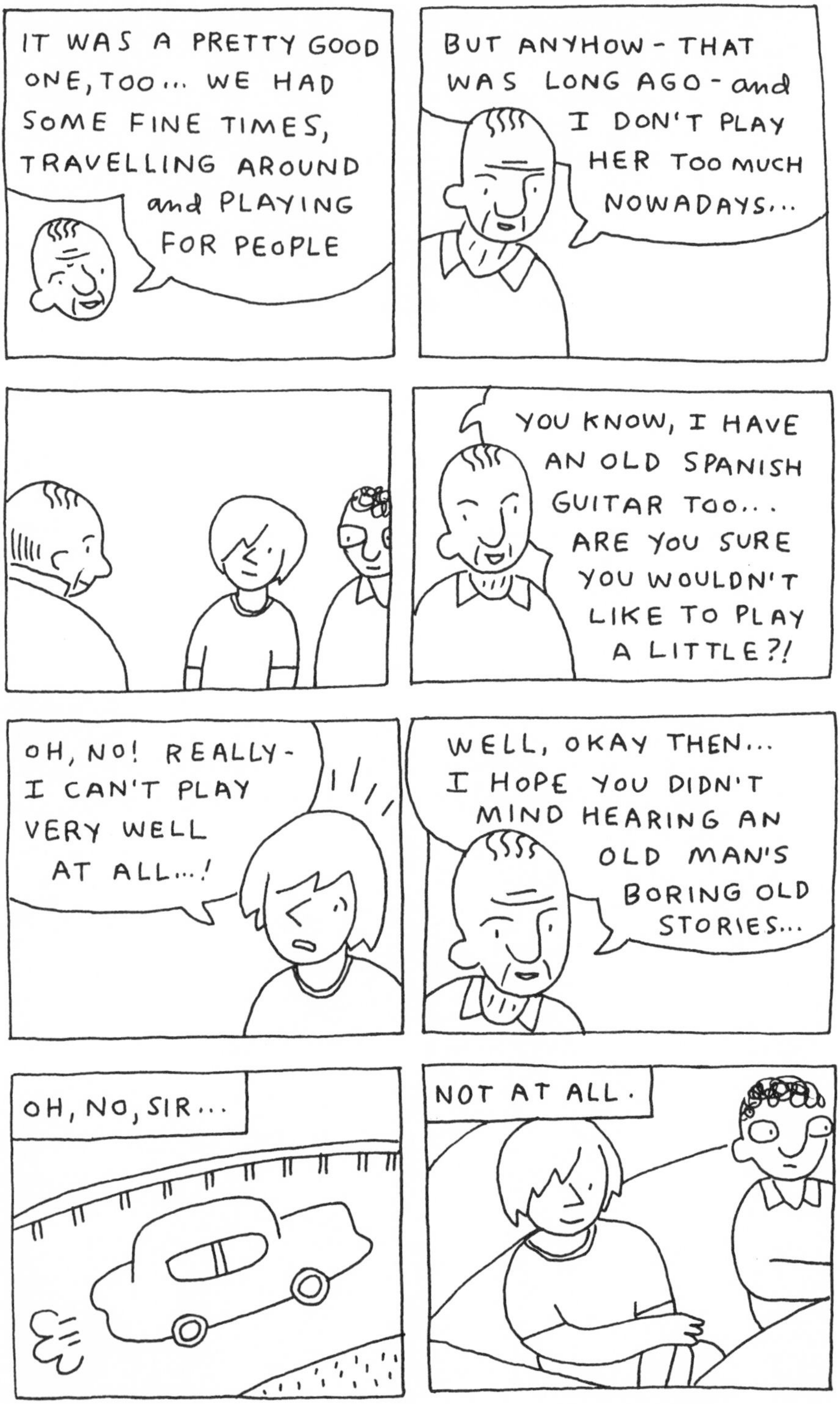
IT WAS A PRETTY GOOD ONE, TOO... WE HAD SOME FINE TIMES, TRAVELLING AROUND and PLAYING FOR PEOPLE
BUT ANYHOW - THAT WAS LONG AGO - and I DON'T PLAY HER TOO MUCH NOWADAYS...
YOU KNOW, I HAVE AN OLD SPANISH GUITAR TOO... ARE YOU SURE YOU WOULDN'T LIKE TO PLAY A LITTLE?!
OH, NO! REALLY - I CAN'T PLAY VERY WELL AT ALL...!
WELL, OKAY THEN... I HOPE YOU DIDN'T MIND HEARING AN OLD MAN'S BORING OLD STORIES...
OH, NO, SIR...
NOT AT ALL.

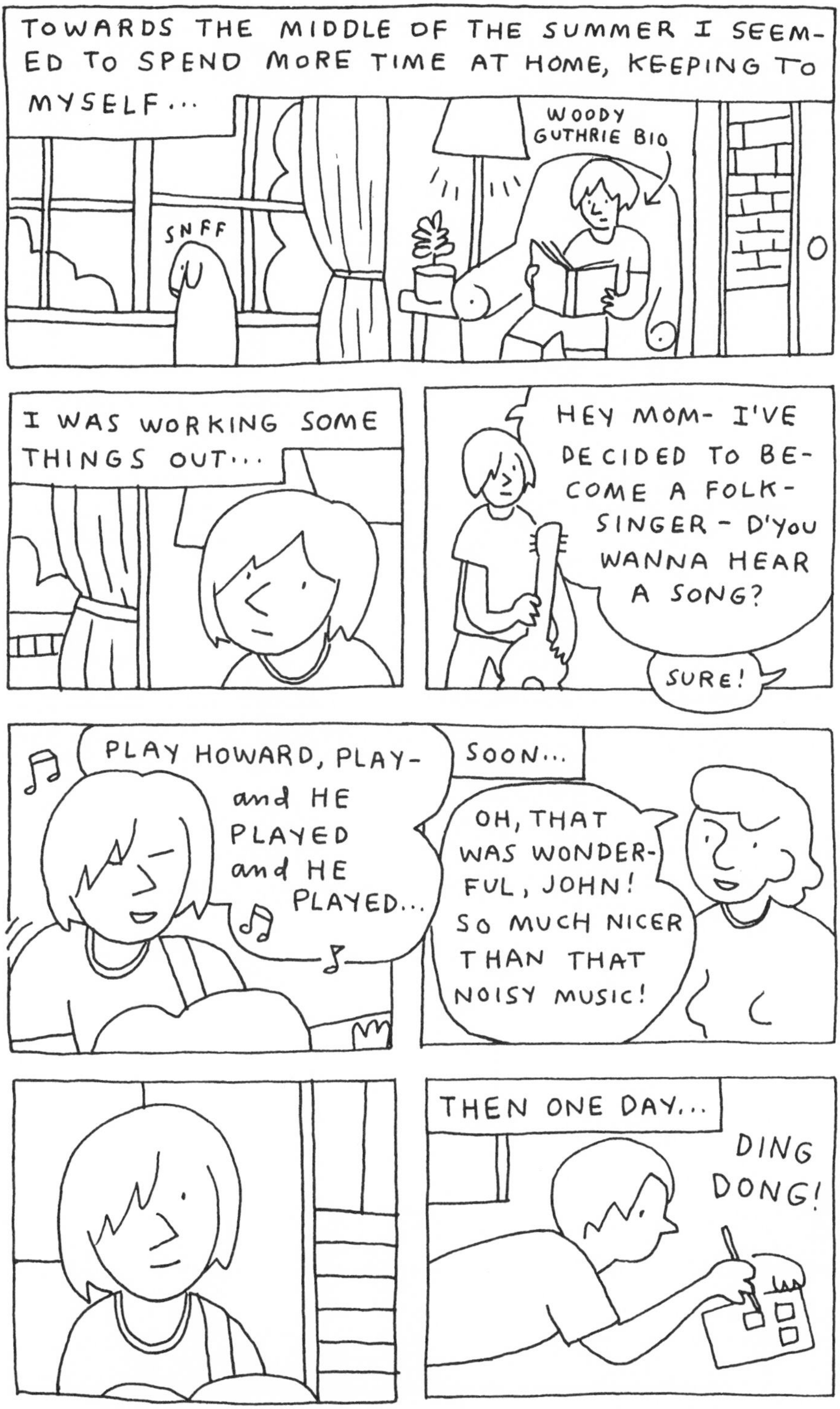
TOWARDS THE MIDDLE OF THE SUMMER I SEEMED TO SPEND MORE TIME AT HOME, KEEPING TO MYSELF...
SNFF
WOODY GUTHRIE BIO
I WAS WORKING SOME THINGS OUT...
HEY MOM- I'VE DECIDED TO BECOME A FOLK-SINGER - D'YOU WANNA HEAR A SONG?
SURE!
PLAY HOWARD, PLAY- and HE PLAYED and HE PLAYED...
SOON...
OH, THAT WAS WONDERFUL, JOHN! SO MUCH NICER THAN THAT NOISY MUSIC!
THEN ONE DAY...
DING DONG!

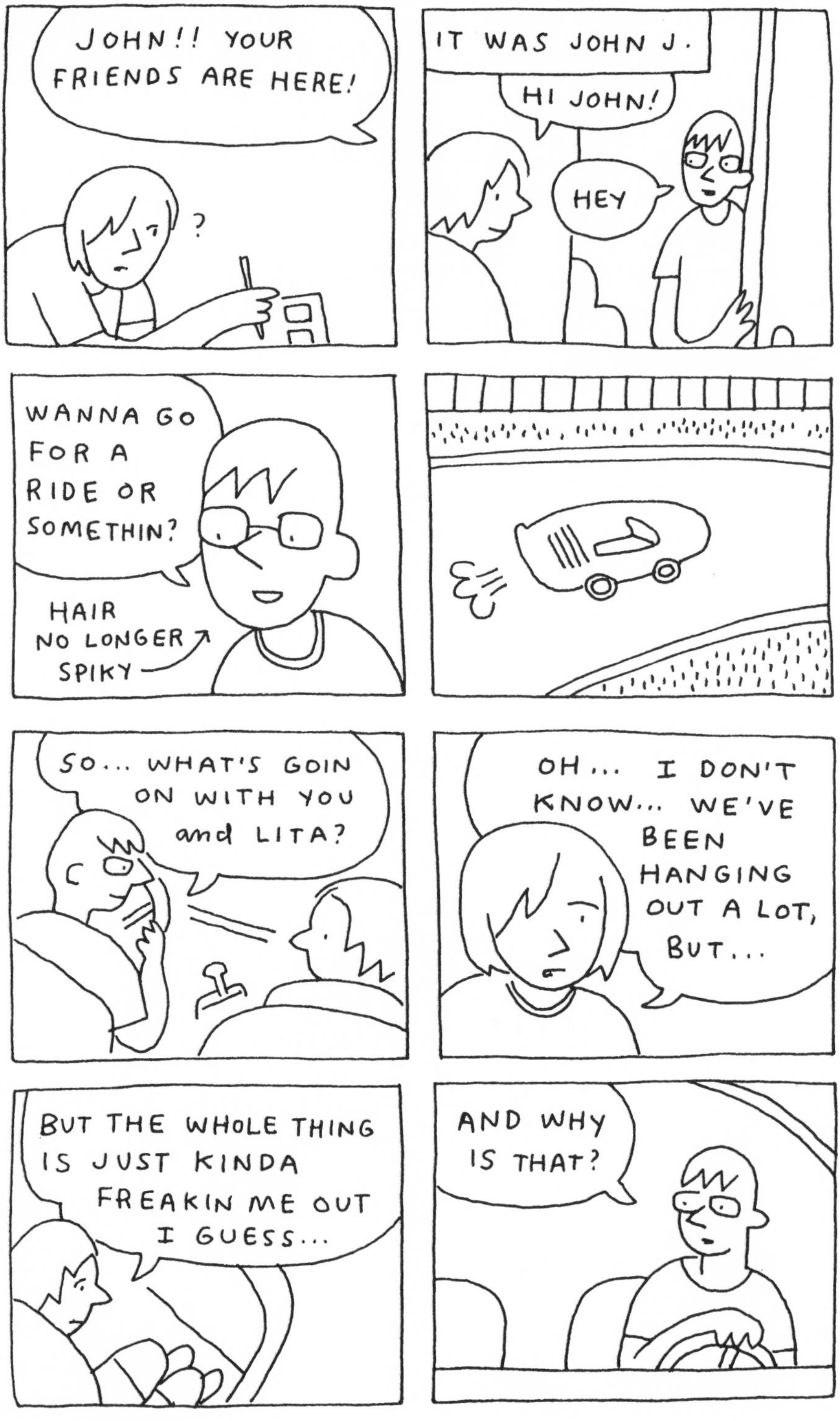
JOHN!! YOUR FRIENDS ARE HERE!
?
IT WAS JOHN J.
HI JOHN!
HEY
WANNA GO FOR A RIDE OR SOMETHIN?
HAIR NO LONGER SPIKY
SO... WHAT'S GOIN ON WITH YOU and LITA?
OH... I DON'T KNOW... WE'VE BEEN HANGING OUT A LOT, BUT...
BUT THE WHOLE THING IS JUST KINDA FREAKIN ME OUT I GUESS...
AND WHY IS THAT?

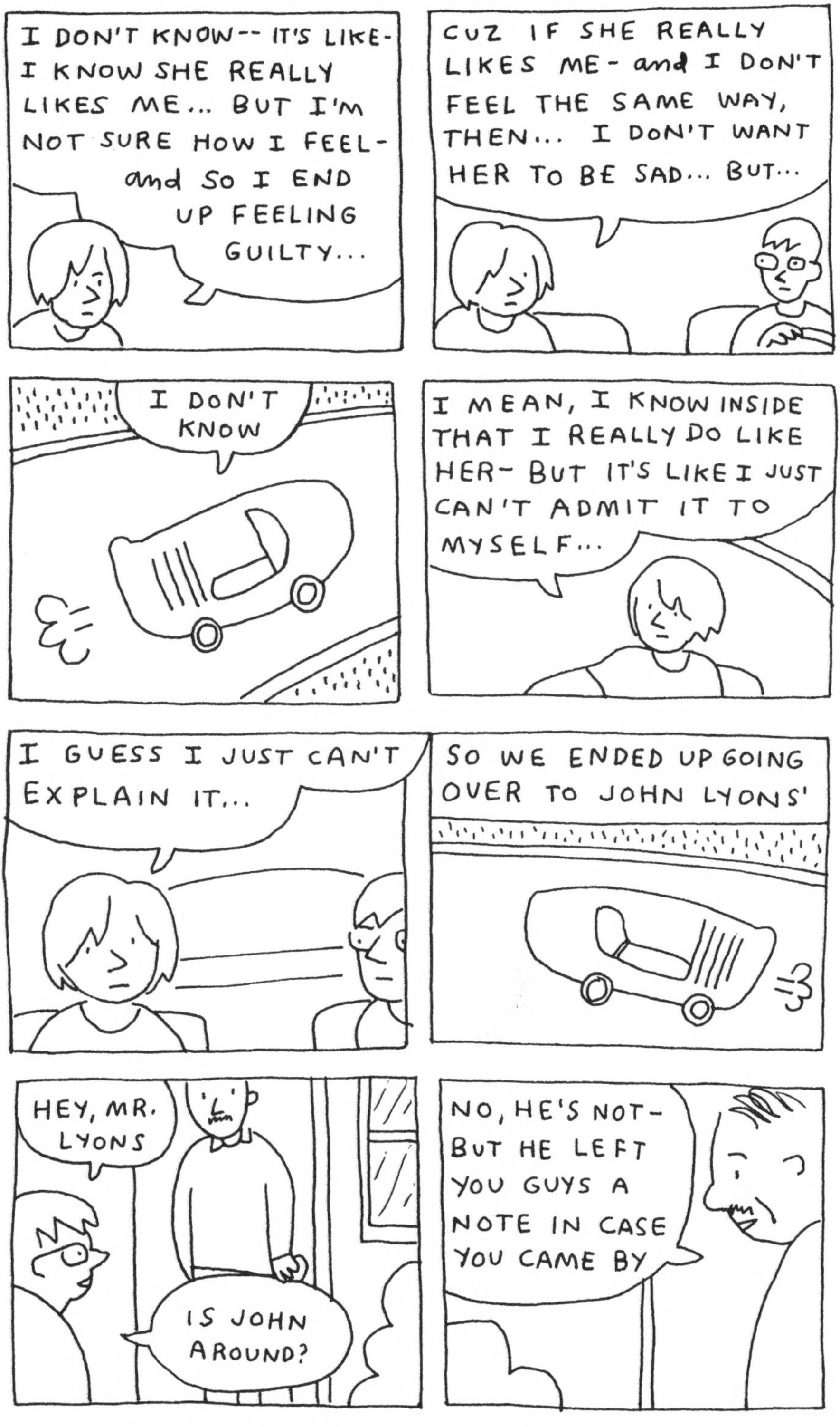

I DON'T KNOW-- IT'S LIKE- I KNOW SHE REALLY LIKES ME... BUT I'M NOT SURE HOW I FEEL- and SO I END UP FEELING GUILTY...
CUZ IF SHE REALLY LIKES ME- and I DON'T FEEL THE SAME WAY, THEN... I DON'T WANT HER TO BE SAD... BUT...
I DON'T KNOW
I MEAN, I KNOW INSIDE THAT I REALLY DO LIKE HER- BUT IT'S LIKE I JUST CAN'T ADMIT IT TO MYSELF...
I GUESS I JUST CAN'T EXPLAIN IT...
SO WE ENDED UP GOING OVER TO JOHN LYONS'
HEY, MR. LYONS
IS JOHN AROUND?
NO, HE'S NOT- BUT HE LEFT YOU GUYS A NOTE IN CASE YOU CAME BY

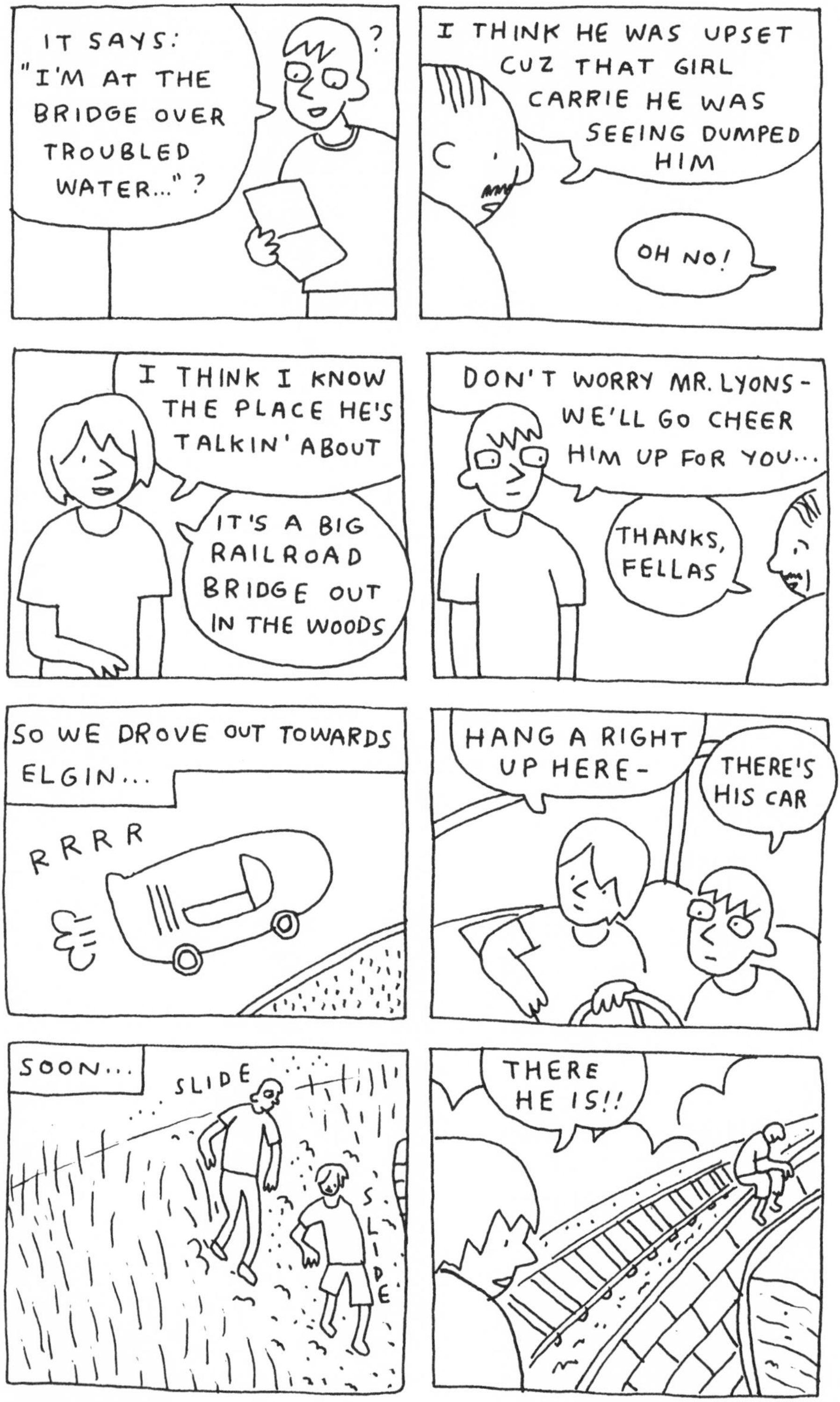
IT SAYS: "I'M AT THE BRIDGE OVER TROUBLED WATER..." ?
?
I THINK HE WAS UPSET CUZ THAT GIRL CARRIE HE WAS SEEING DUMPED HIM
OH NO!
I THINK I KNOW THE PLACE HE'S TALKIN' ABOUT
IT'S A BIG RAILROAD BRIDGE OUT IN THE WOODS
DON'T WORRY MR. LYONS- WE'LL GO CHEER HIM UP FOR YOU...
THANKS, FELLAS
SO WE DROVE OUT TOWARDS ELGIN...
RRRR
HANG A RIGHT UP HERE-
THERE'S HIS CAR
SOON...
SLIDE
SLIDE
THERE HE IS!!

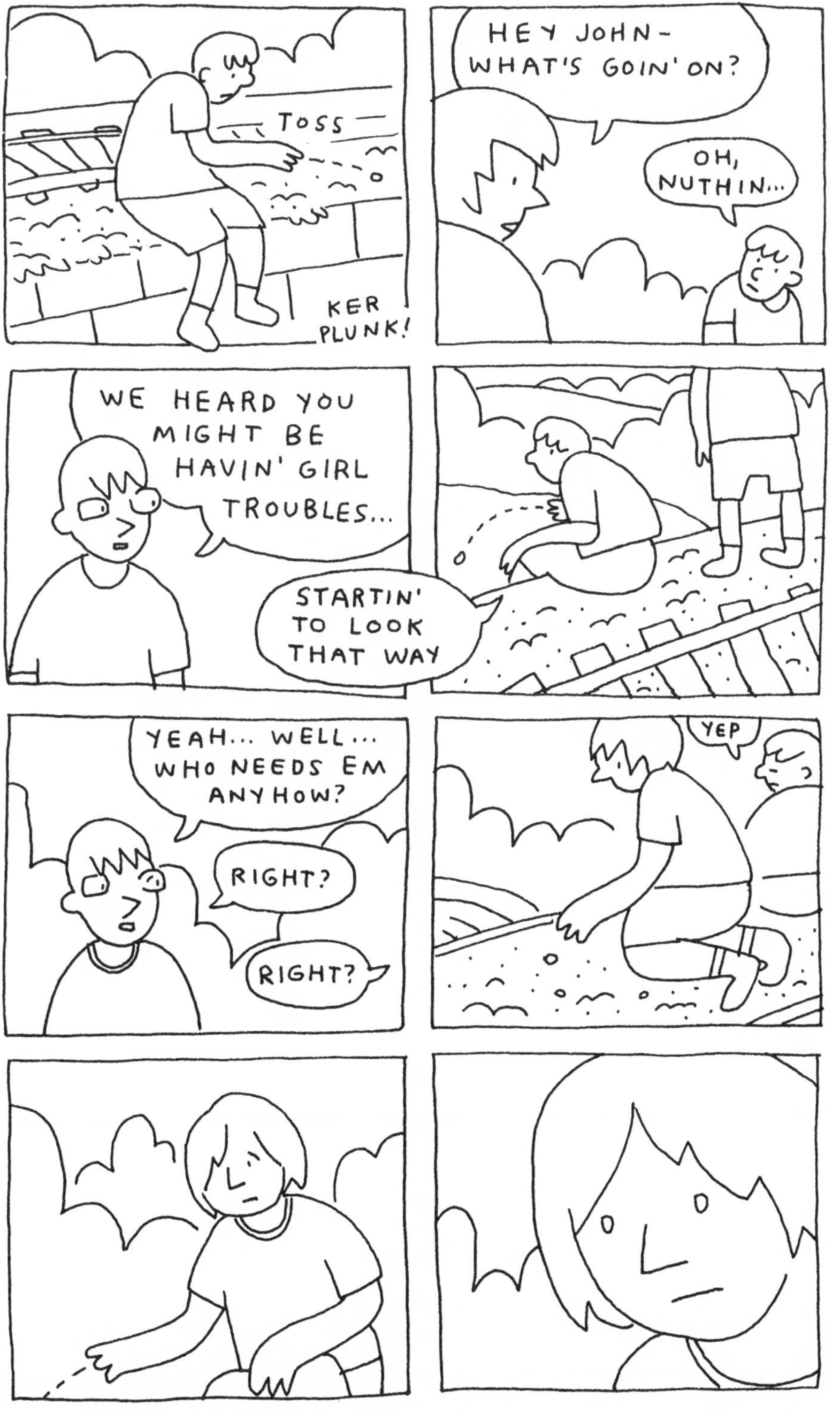
TOSS
KER PLUNK!
HEY JOHN- WHAT'S GOIN' ON?
OH, NUTHIN...
WE HEARD YOU MIGHT BE HAVIN' GIRL TROUBLES...
STARTIN' TO LOOK THAT WAY
YEAH... WELL... WHO NEEDS EM ANYHOW?
RIGHT?
RIGHT?
YEP

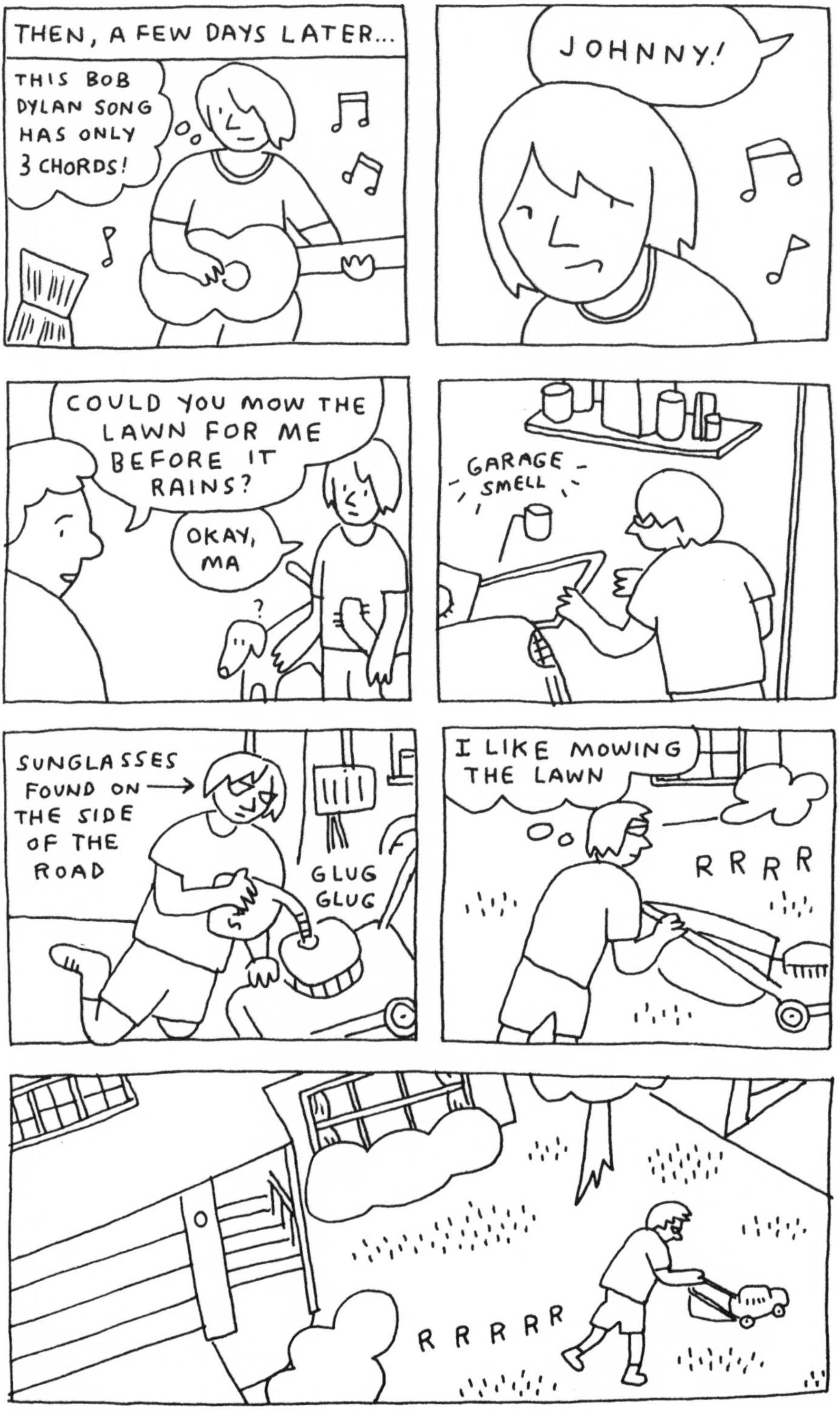
THEN, A FEW DAYS LATER...
THIS BOB DYLAN SONG HAS ONLY 3 CHORDS!
JOHNNY!
COULD YOU MOW THE LAWN FOR ME BEFORE IT RAINS?
OKAY, MA
?
GARAGE SMELL
SUNGLASSES FOUND ON THE SIDE OF THE ROAD
GLUG GLUG
I LIKE MOWING THE LAWN
RRRR
RRRRR

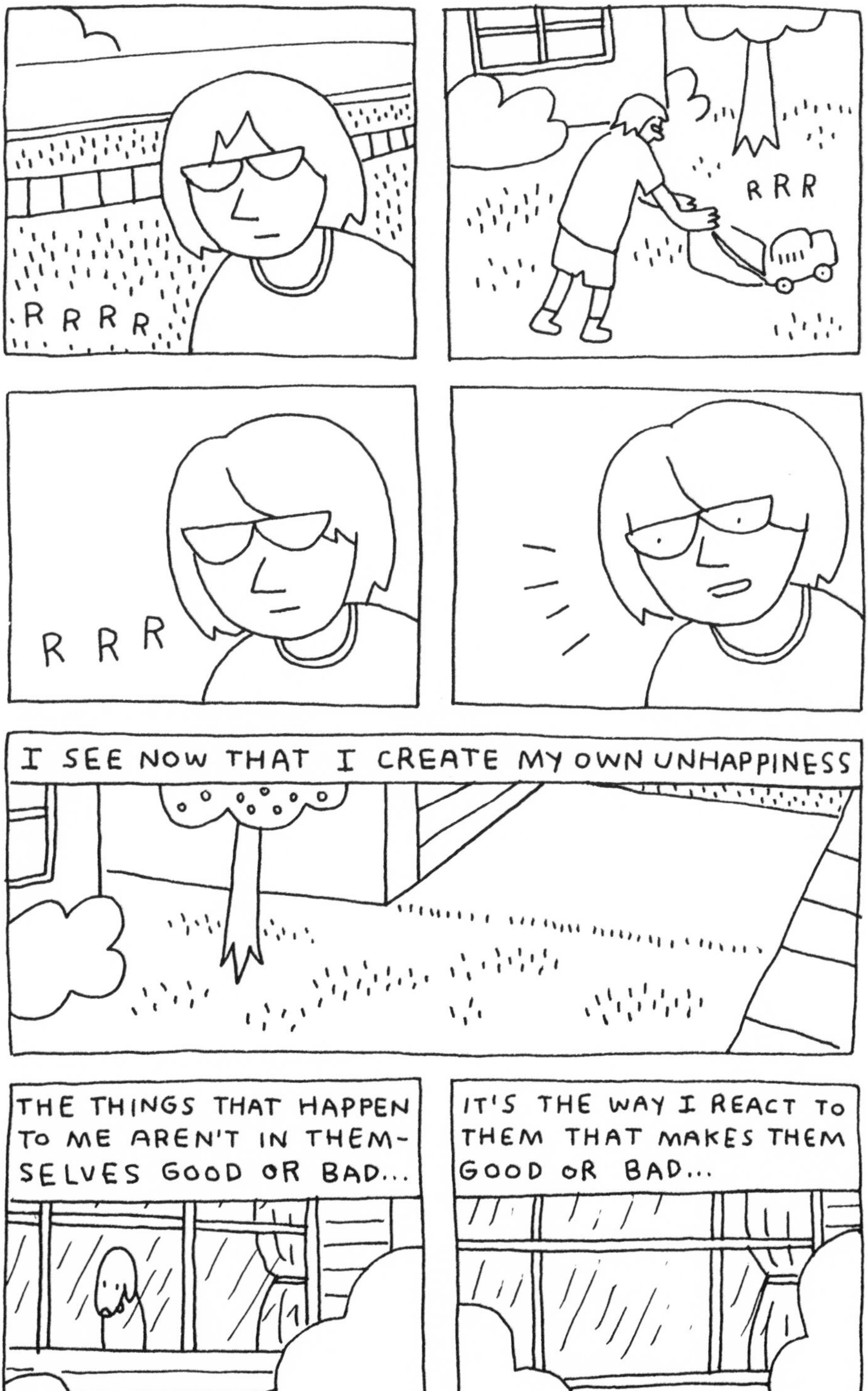
RRRR
RRR
RRR
I SEE NOW THAT I CREATE MY OWN UNHAPPINESS
THE THINGS THAT HAPPEN TO ME AREN'T IN THEMSELVES GOOD OR BAD...
IT'S THE WAY I REACT TO THEM THAT MAKES THEM GOOD OR BAD...

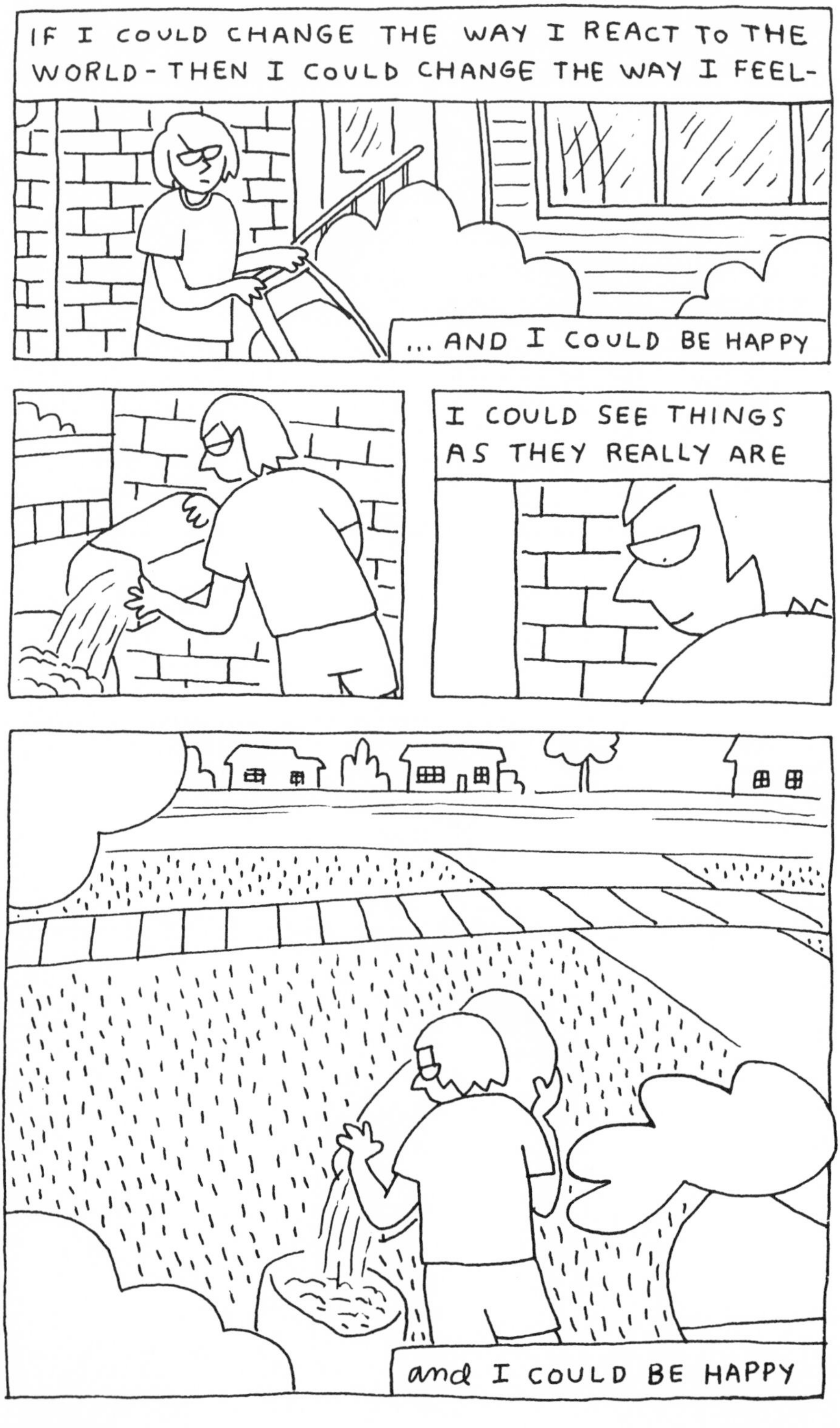
IF I COULD CHANGE THE WAY I REACT TO THE WORLD - THEN I COULD CHANGE THE WAY I FEEL-
... AND I COULD BE HAPPY
I COULD SEE THINGS AS THEY REALLY ARE
and I COULD BE HAPPY

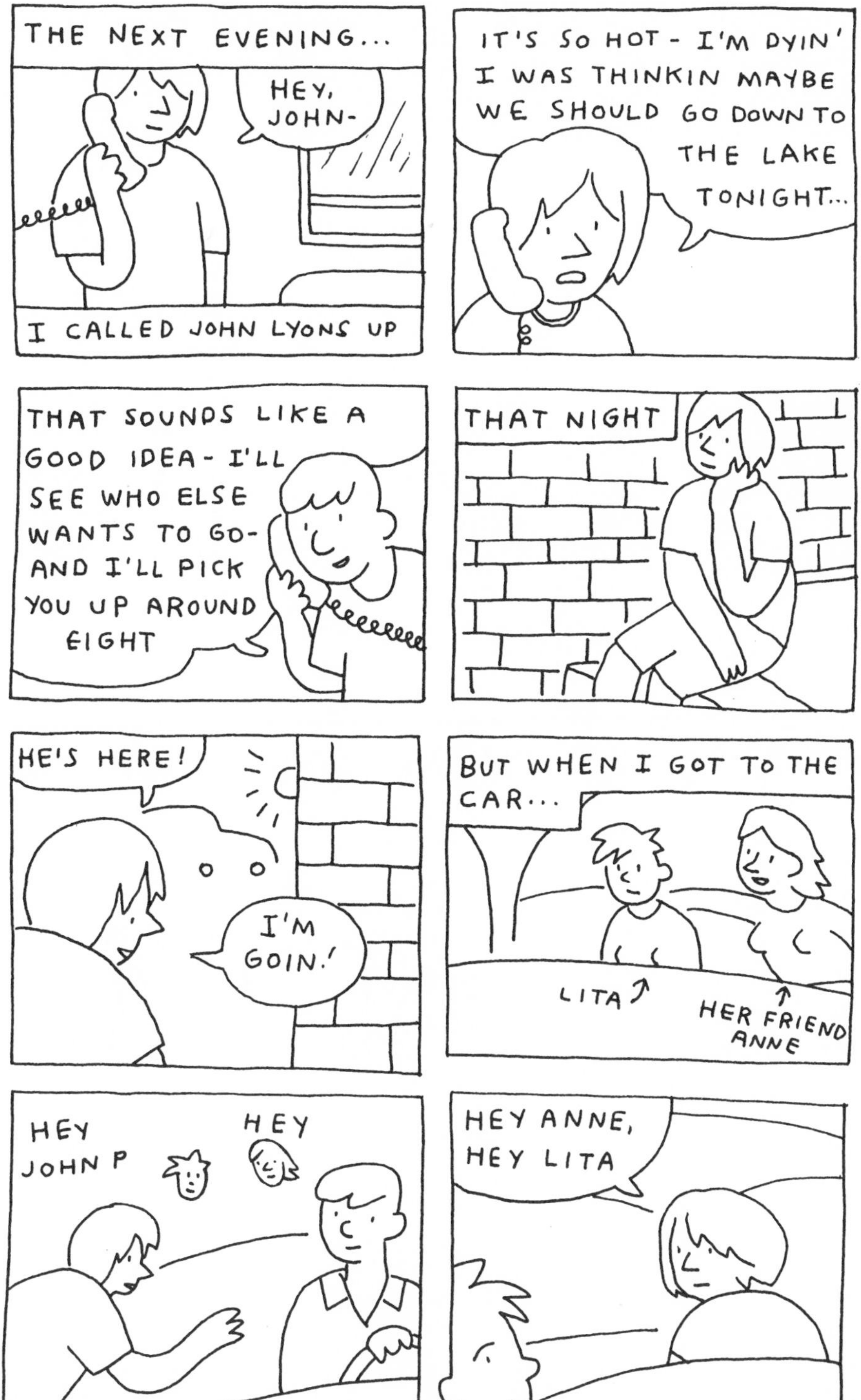
THE NEXT EVENING...
HEY, JOHN-
I CALLED JOHN LYONS UP
IT'S SO HOT - I'M DYIN' I WAS THINKIN MAYBE WE SHOULD GO DOWN TO THE LAKE TONIGHT...
THAT SOUNDS LIKE A GOOD IDEA - I'LL SEE WHO ELSE WANTS TO GO - AND I'LL PICK YOU UP AROUND EIGHT
THAT NIGHT
HE'S HERE!
I'M GOIN!
BUT WHEN I GOT TO THE CAR...
LITA
HER FRIEND ANNE
HEY JOHN P
HEY
HEY ANNE, HEY LITA

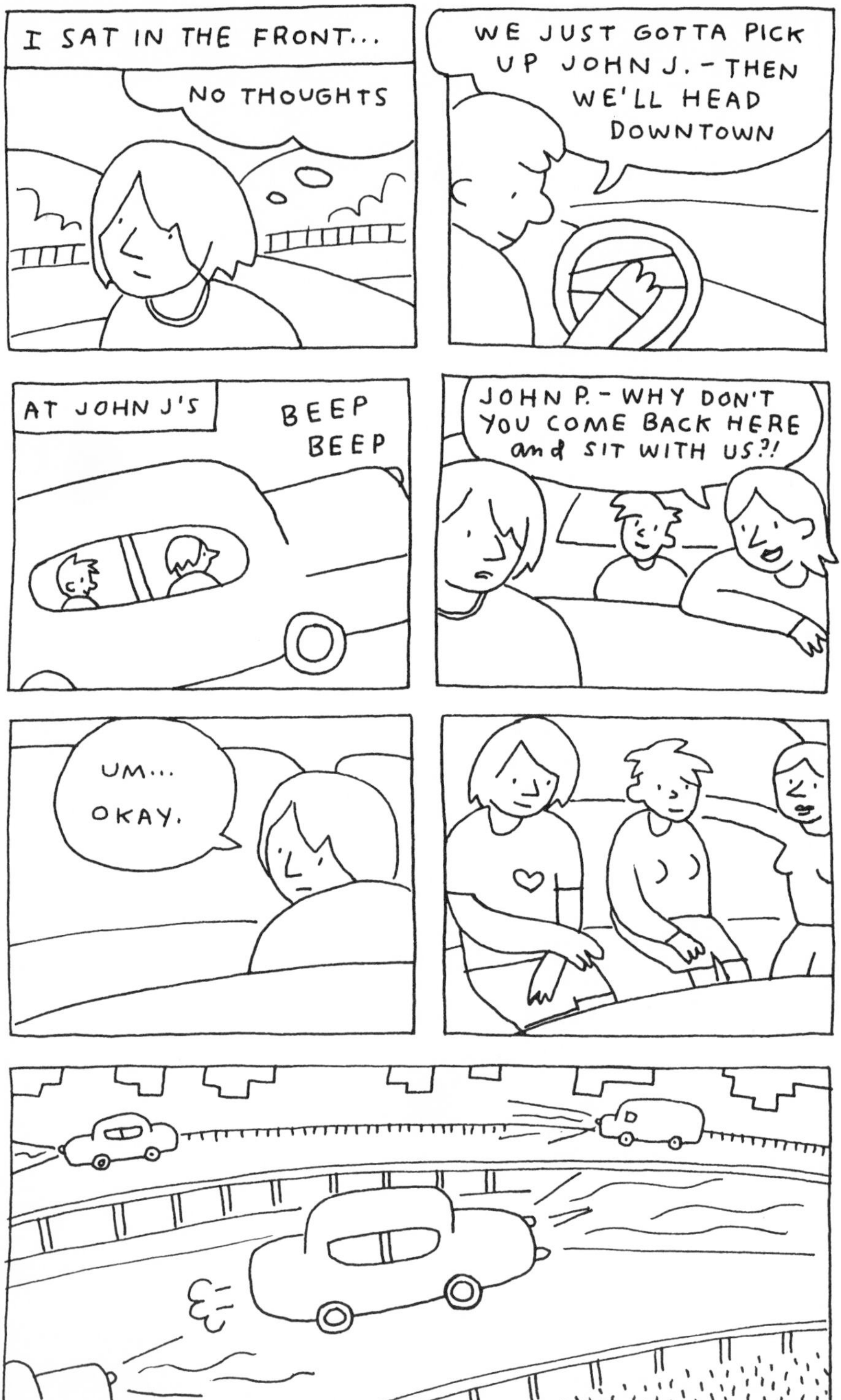
I SAT IN THE FRONT...
NO THOUGHTS
WE JUST GOTTA PICK UP JOHN J. - THEN WE'LL HEAD DOWNTOWN
AT JOHN J'S
BEEP BEEP
JOHN P. - WHY DON'T YOU COME BACK HERE and SIT WITH US?!
UM... OKAY.

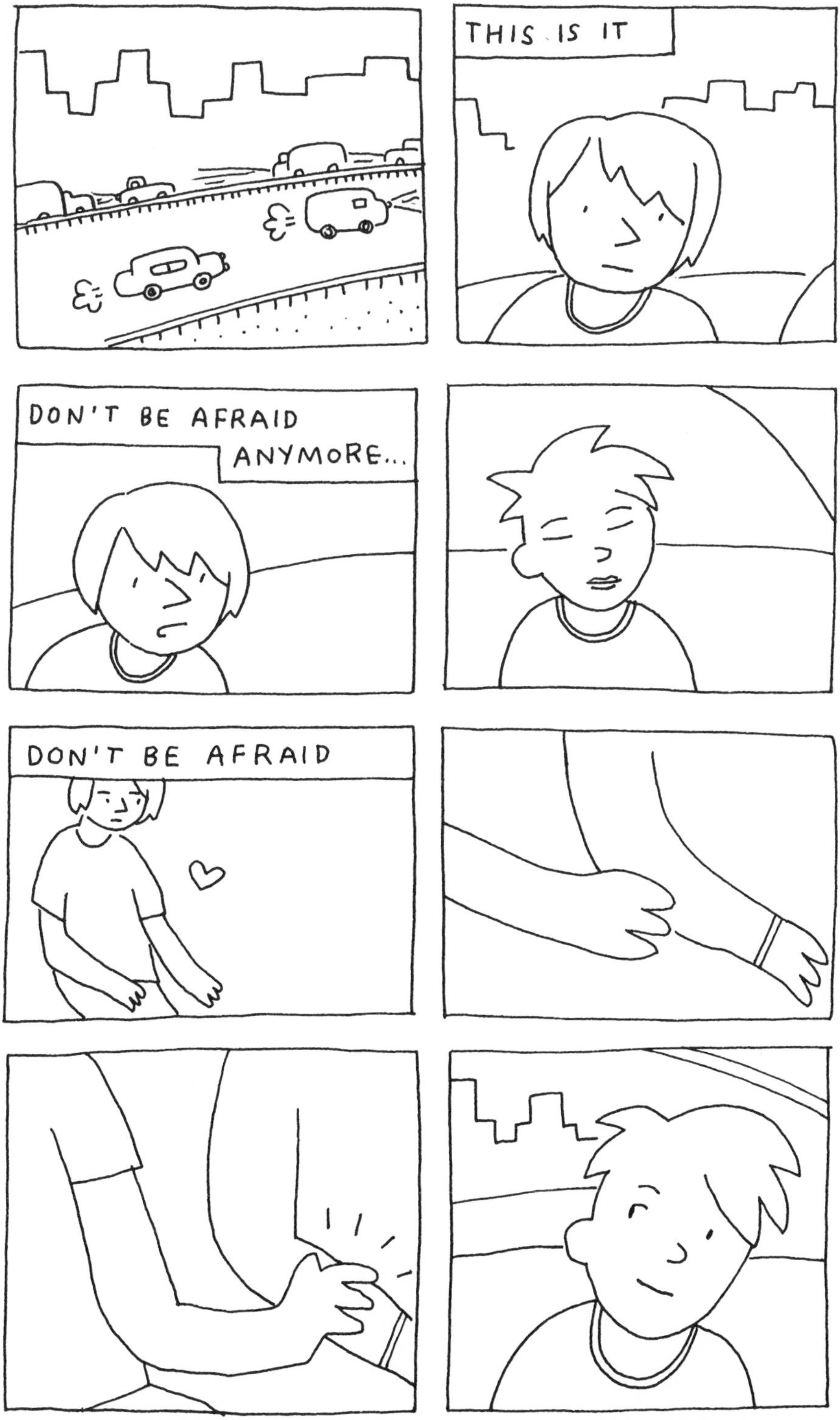
THIS IS IT
DON'T BE AFRAID ANYMORE...
DON'T BE AFRAID

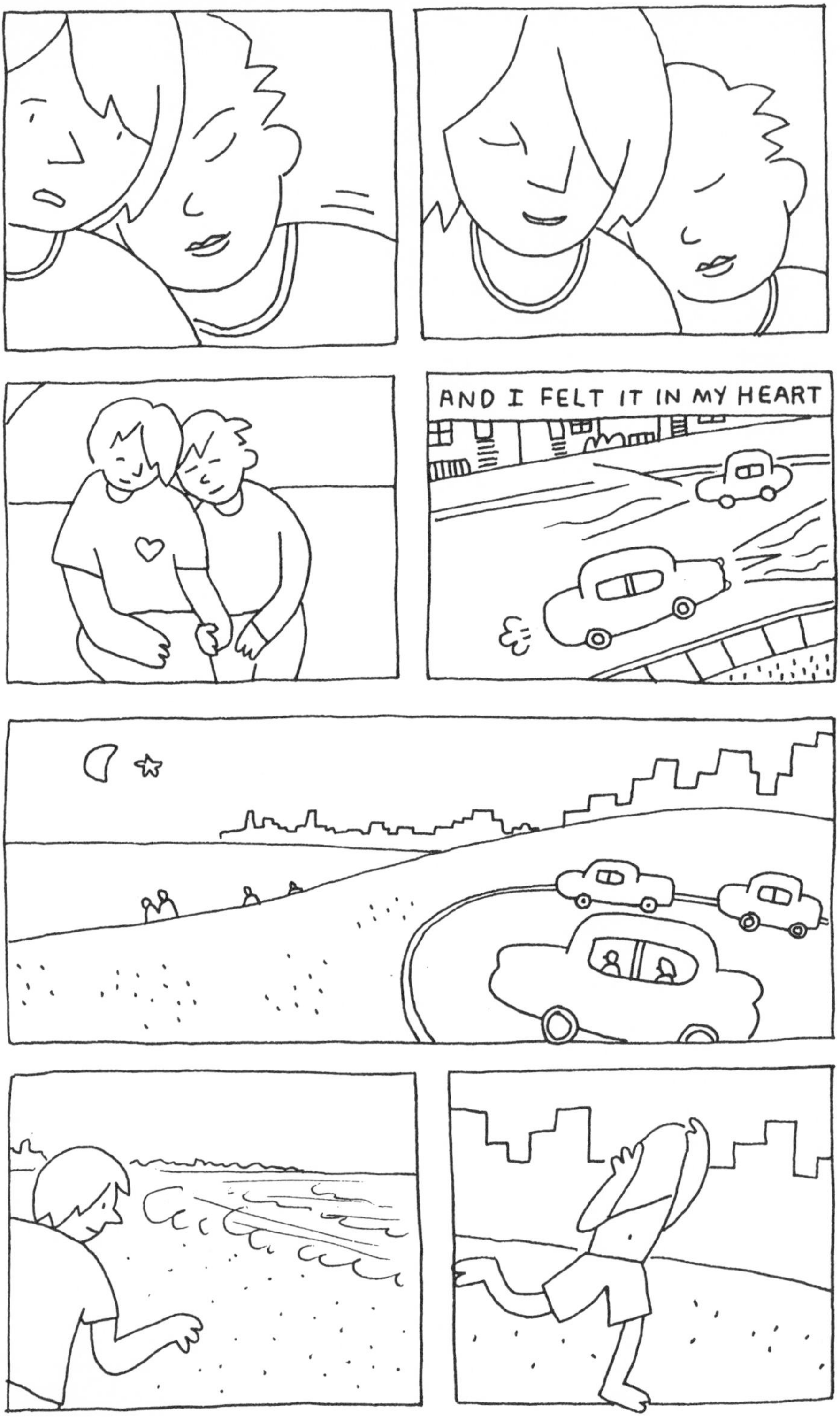
AND I FELT IT IN MY HEART

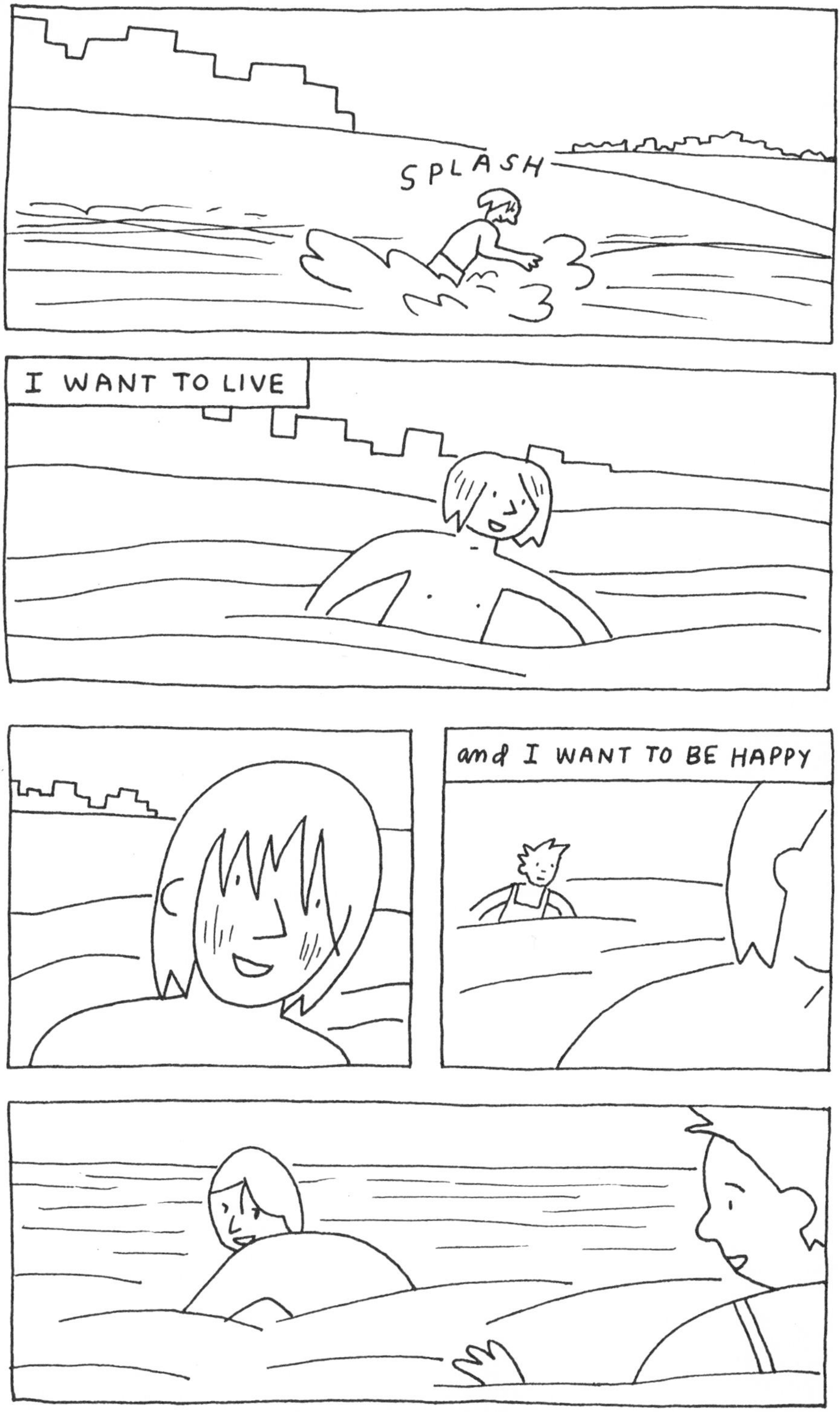
SPLASH
I WANT TO LIVE
and I WANT TO BE HAPPY

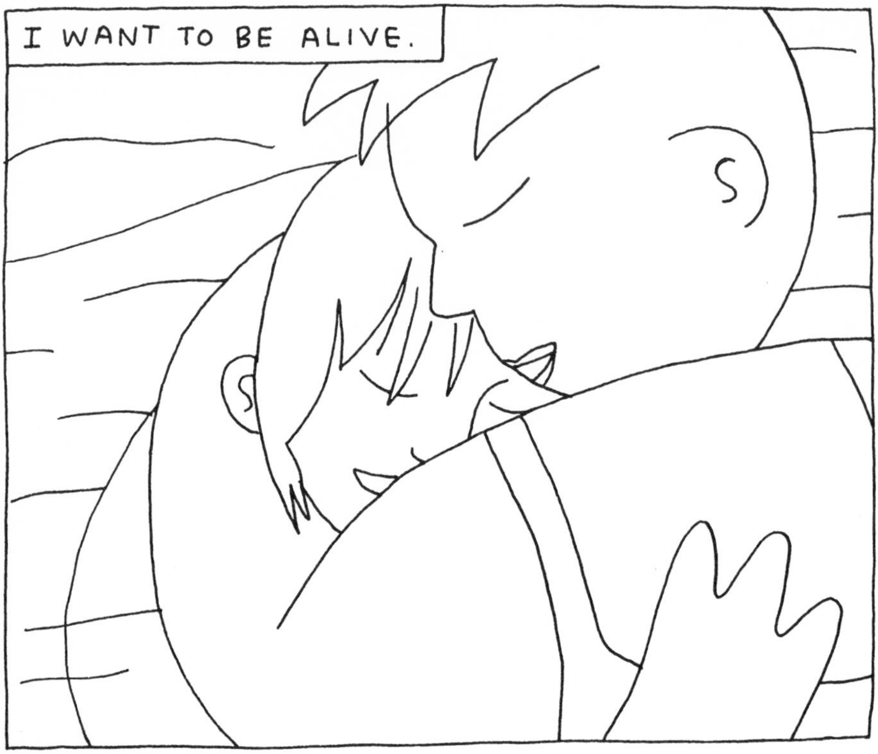
I WANT TO BE ALIVE.

John PoRcellino
1996-1998

Escape to Wisconsin

Escape to Wisconsin

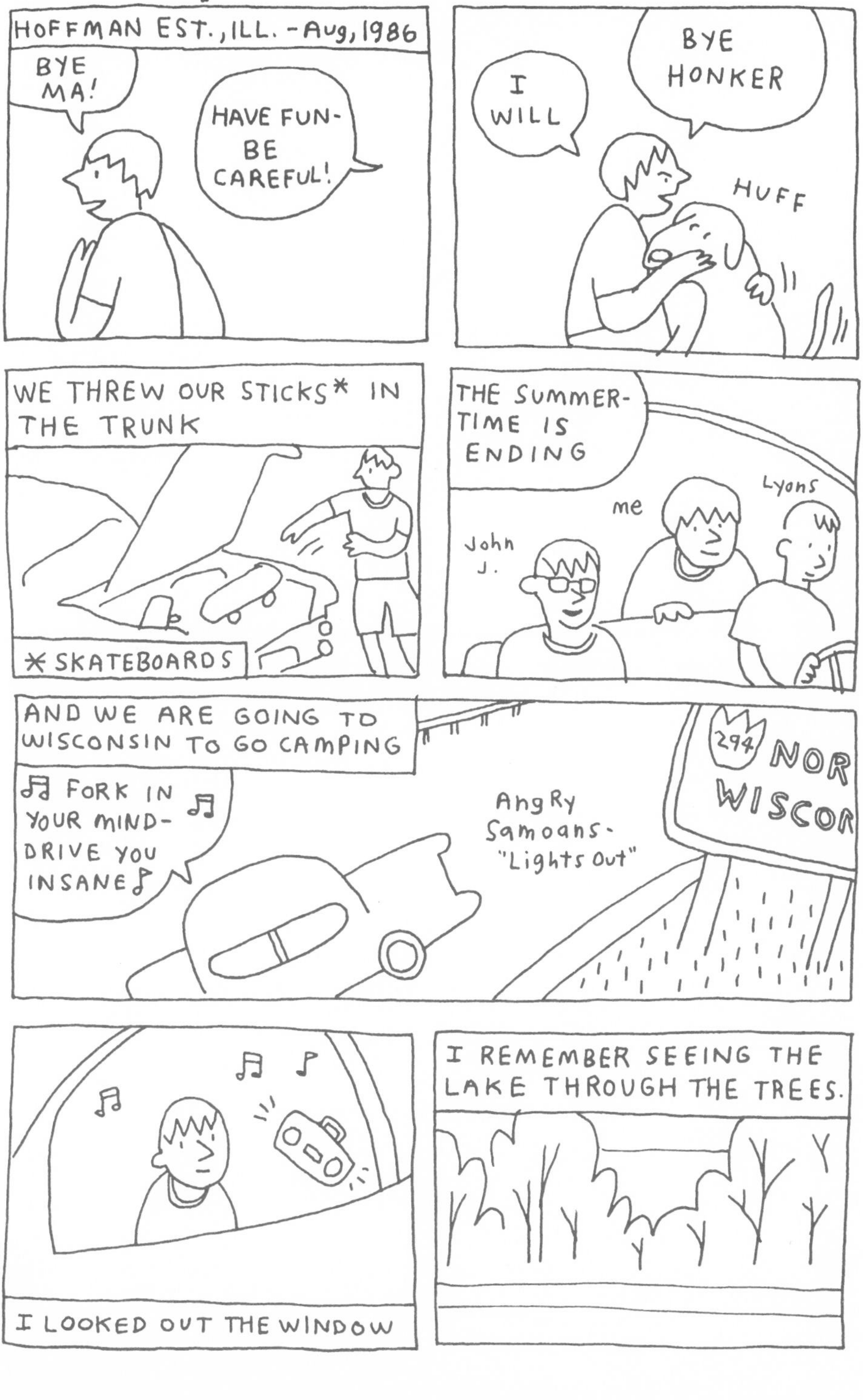

HOFFMAN EST., ILL. - Aug, 1986
BYE MA!
HAVE FUN- BE CAREFUL!
I WILL
BYE HONKER
HUFF
WE THREW OUR STICKS* IN THE TRUNK
* SKATEBOARDS
THE SUMMER-TIME IS ENDING
John J.
me
Lyons
AND WE ARE GOING TO WISCONSIN TO GO CAMPING
FORK IN YOUR MIND- DRIVE YOU INSANE
Angry Samoans- "Lights Out"
294
NOR
WISCON
I LOOKED OUT THE WINDOW
I REMEMBER SEEING THE LAKE THROUGH THE TREES.

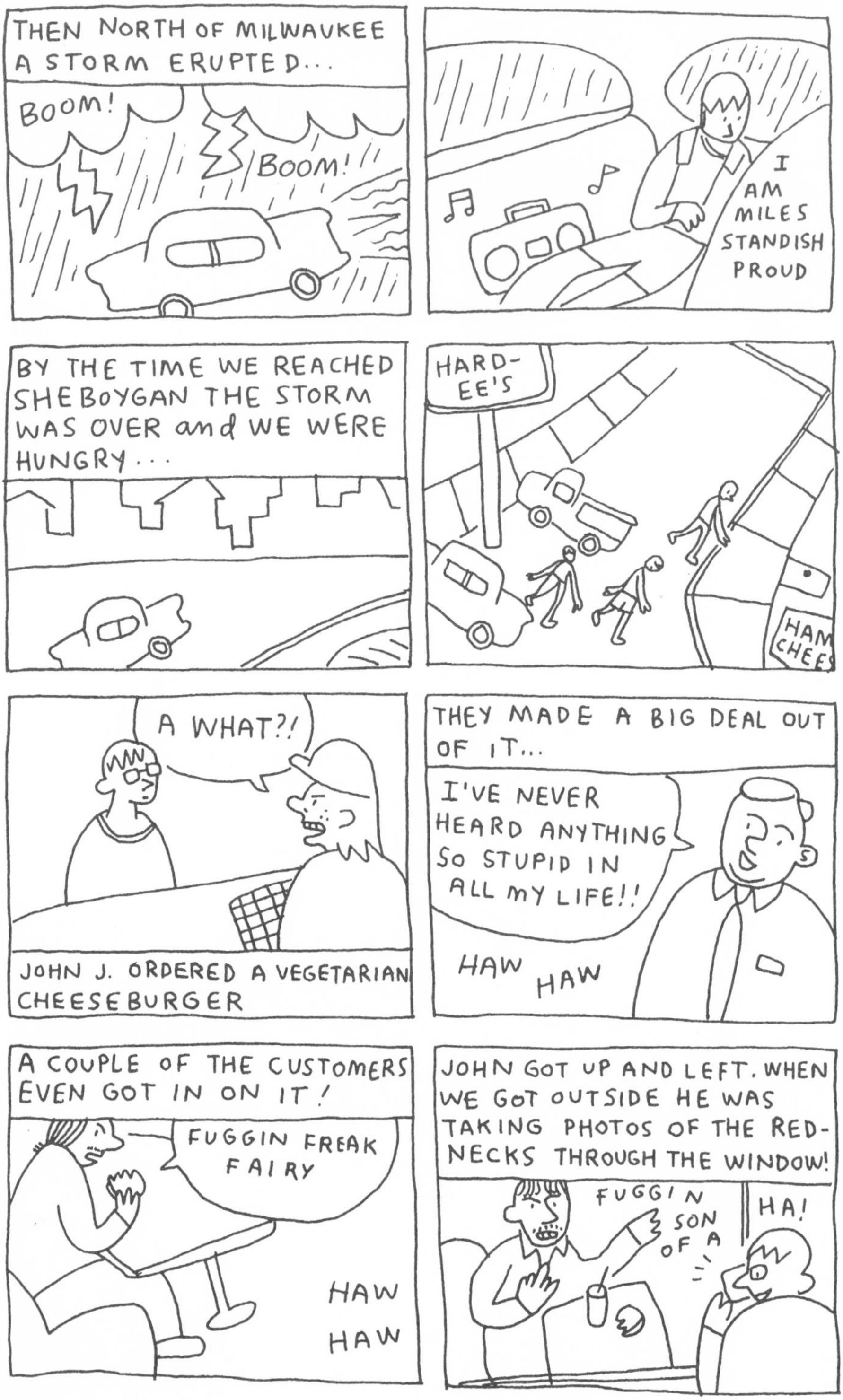
THEN NORTH OF MILWAUKEE A STORM ERUPTED...
BOOM!
BOOM!
I AM MILES STANDISH PROUD
BY THE TIME WE REACHED SHEBOYGAN THE STORM WAS OVER and WE WERE HUNGRY...
HARD-EE'S
A WHAT?!
JOHN J. ORDERED A VEGETARIAN CHEESEBURGER
THEY MADE A BIG DEAL OUT OF IT...
I'VE NEVER HEARD ANYTHING SO STUPID IN ALL MY LIFE!!
HAW HAW
A COUPLE OF THE CUSTOMERS EVEN GOT IN ON IT!
FUGGIN FREAK FAIRY
HAW HAW
JOHN GOT UP AND LEFT. WHEN WE GOT OUTSIDE HE WAS TAKING PHOTOS OF THE RED-NECKS THROUGH THE WINDOW!
FUGGIN SON OF A
HA!

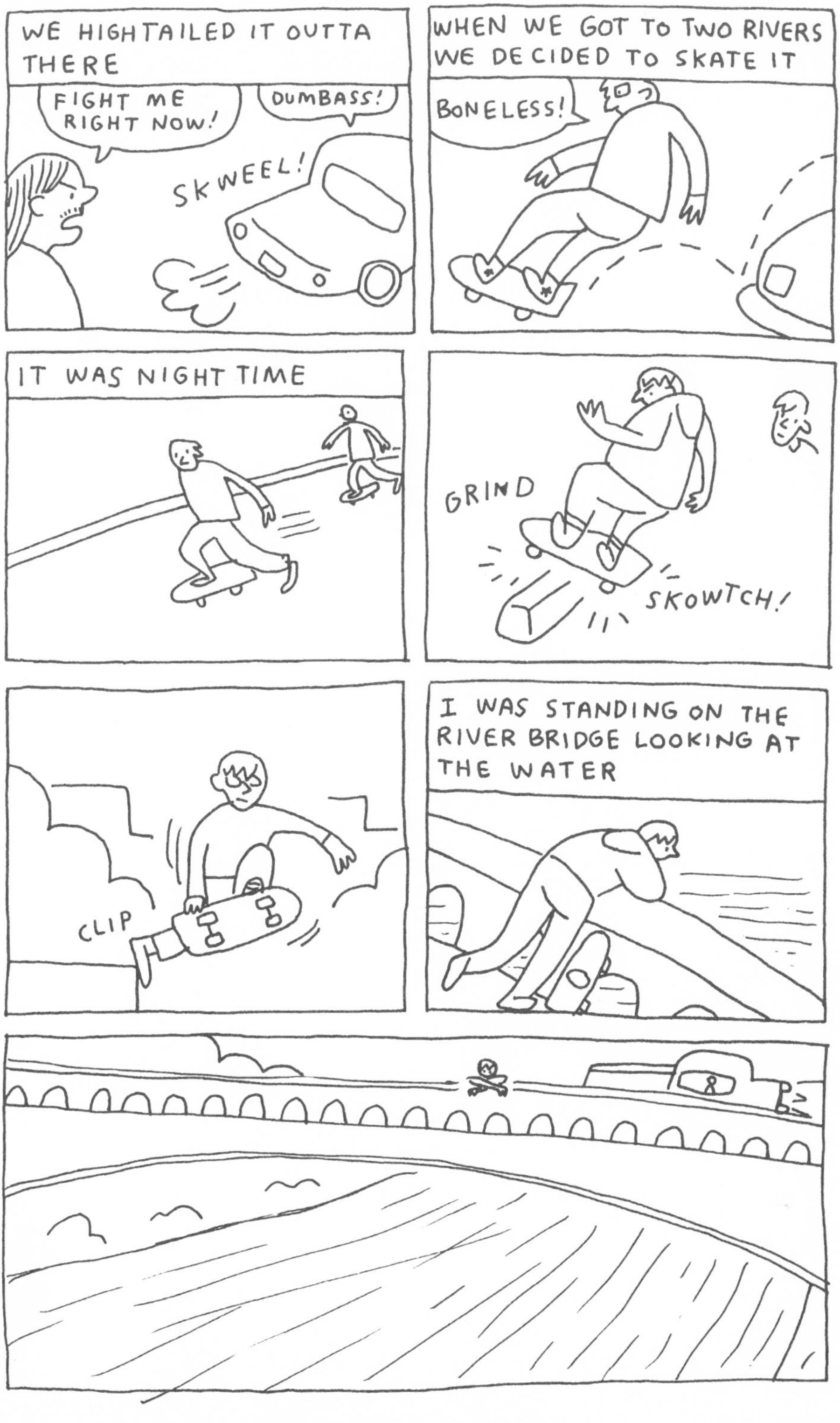
WE HIGHTAILED IT OUTTA THERE
FIGHT ME RIGHT NOW!
DUMBASS!
SKWEEL!
WHEN WE GOT TO TWO RIVERS WE DECIDED TO SKATE IT
BONELESS!
IT WAS NIGHT TIME
GRIND
SKOWTCH!
CLIP
I WAS STANDING ON THE RIVER BRIDGE LOOKING AT THE WATER

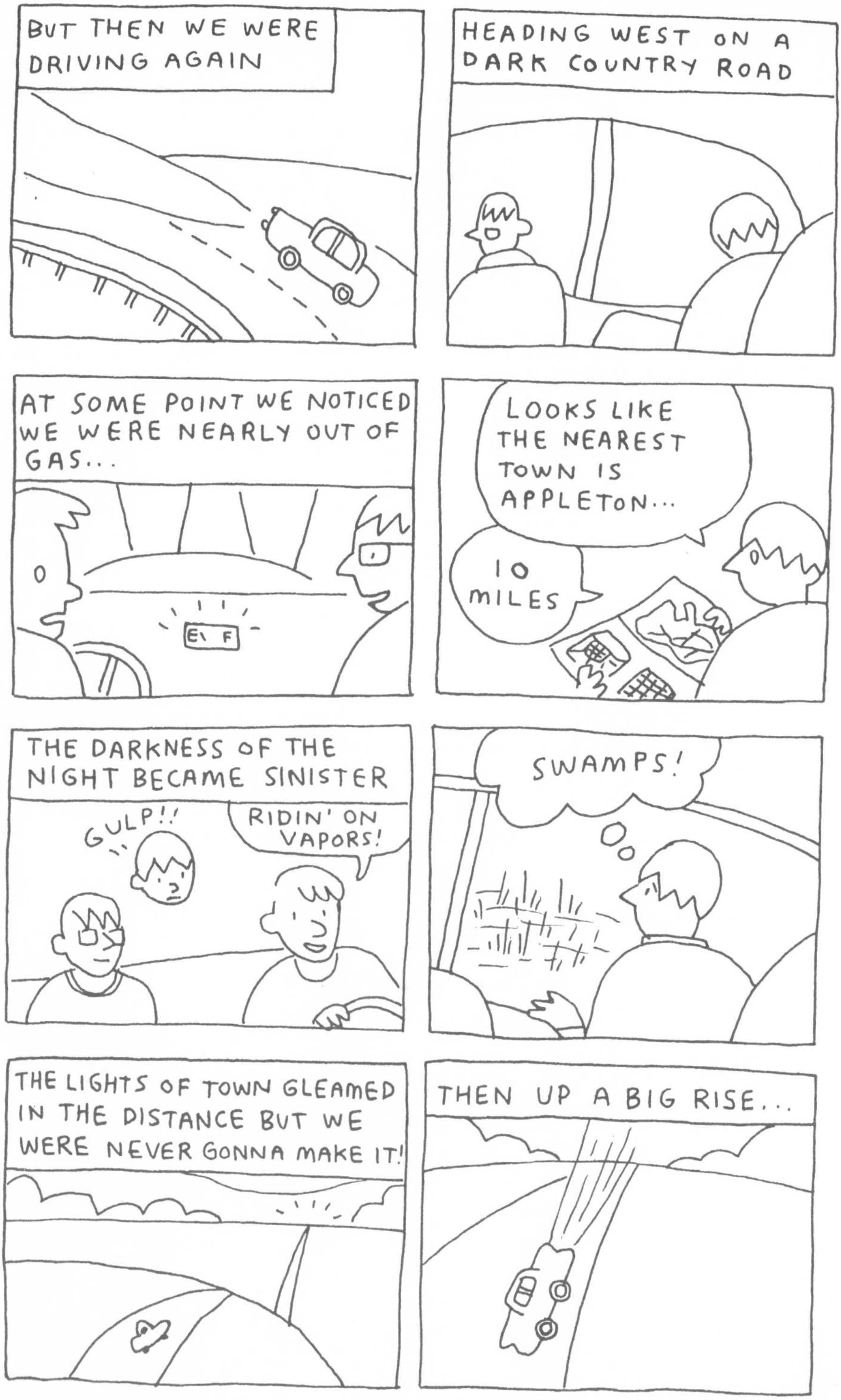
BUT THEN WE WERE DRIVING AGAIN
HEADING WEST ON A DARK COUNTRY ROAD
AT SOME POINT WE NOTICED WE WERE NEARLY OUT OF GAS...
E F
LOOKS LIKE THE NEAREST TOWN IS APPLETON...
10 MILES
THE DARKNESS OF THE NIGHT BECAME SINISTER
GULP!!
RIDIN' ON VAPORS!
SWAMPS!
THE LIGHTS OF TOWN GLEAMED IN THE DISTANCE BUT WE WERE NEVER GONNA MAKE IT!
THEN UP A BIG RISE...

and APPLETON...

WE GASSED UP and DROVE INTO TOWN...

THIS IS VERY WEIRD

APPLETON WAS ONE OF THOSE PLACES WHERE THE ONLY ENTERTAINMENT WAS "CRUISING" IN CIRCLES AROUND THE TOWN SQUARE

Hmm...

WE PARKED THE CAR and STARTED SKATING

-OLLIE!

CLIP

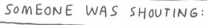

WE WERE SKATING PAST ALL THE PEOPLE IN THEIR CARS...

SOMEONE WAS SHOUTING:

CAREFUL! THEY HATE SKATERS HERE!

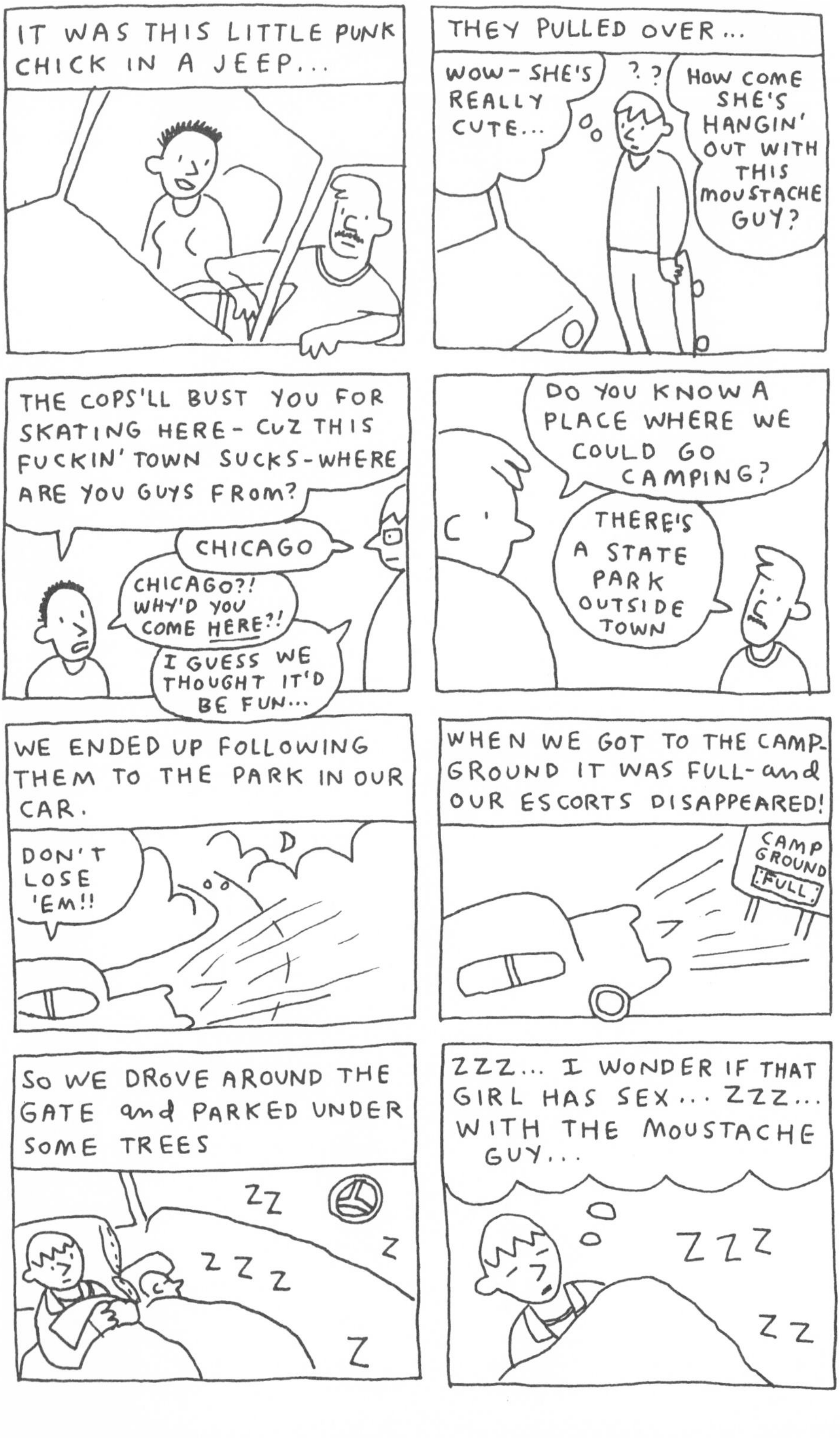
IT WAS THIS LITTLE PUNK CHICK IN A JEEP...
THEY PULLED OVER...
WOW - SHE'S REALLY CUTE...
??
HOW COME SHE'S HANGIN' OUT WITH THIS MOUSTACHE GUY?
THE COPS'LL BUST YOU FOR SKATING HERE - CUZ THIS FUCKIN' TOWN SUCKS - WHERE ARE YOU GUYS FROM?
CHICAGO
CHICAGO?! WHY'D YOU COME HERE?!
I GUESS WE THOUGHT IT'D BE FUN...
DO YOU KNOW A PLACE WHERE WE COULD GO CAMPING?
THERE'S A STATE PARK OUTSIDE TOWN
WE ENDED UP FOLLOWING THEM TO THE PARK IN OUR CAR.
DON'T LOSE 'EM!!
WHEN WE GOT TO THE CAMPGROUND IT WAS FULL - and OUR ESCORTS DISAPPEARED!
CAMP GROUND
FULL
SO WE DROVE AROUND THE GATE and PARKED UNDER SOME TREES
ZZ
Z
ZZZ
Z
ZZZ... I WONDER IF THAT GIRL HAS SEX... ZZZ... WITH THE MOUSTACHE GUY...
ZZZ
ZZ

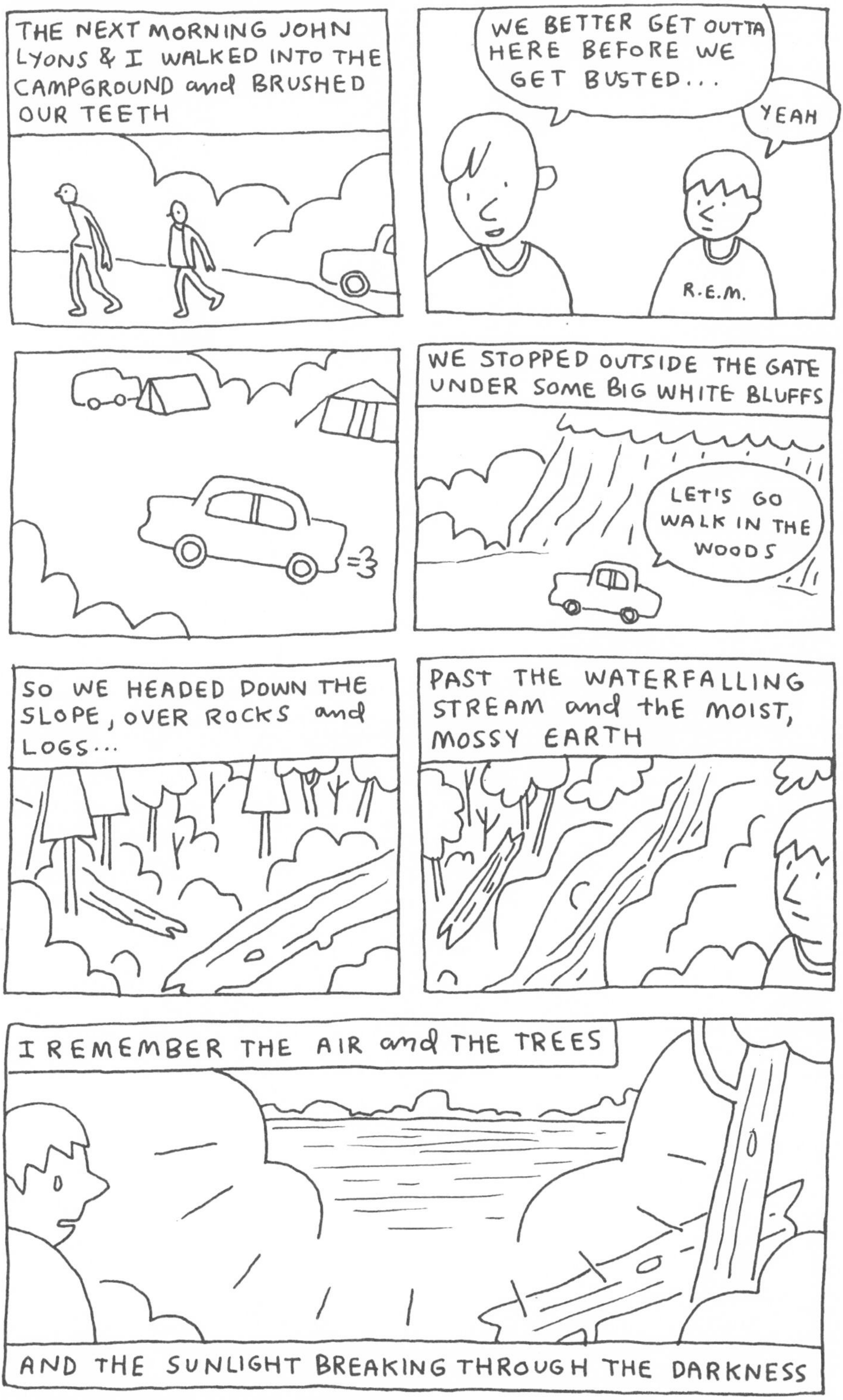
THE NEXT MORNING JOHN LYONS & I WALKED INTO THE CAMPGROUND and BRUSHED OUR TEETH
WE BETTER GET OUTTA HERE BEFORE WE GET BUSTED...
YEAH
R.E.M.
WE STOPPED OUTSIDE THE GATE UNDER SOME BIG WHITE BLUFFS
LET'S GO WALK IN THE WOODS
SO WE HEADED DOWN THE SLOPE, OVER ROCKS and LOGS...
PAST THE WATERFALLING STREAM and the MOIST, MOSSY EARTH
I REMEMBER THE AIR and THE TREES
AND THE SUNLIGHT BREAKING THROUGH THE DARKNESS

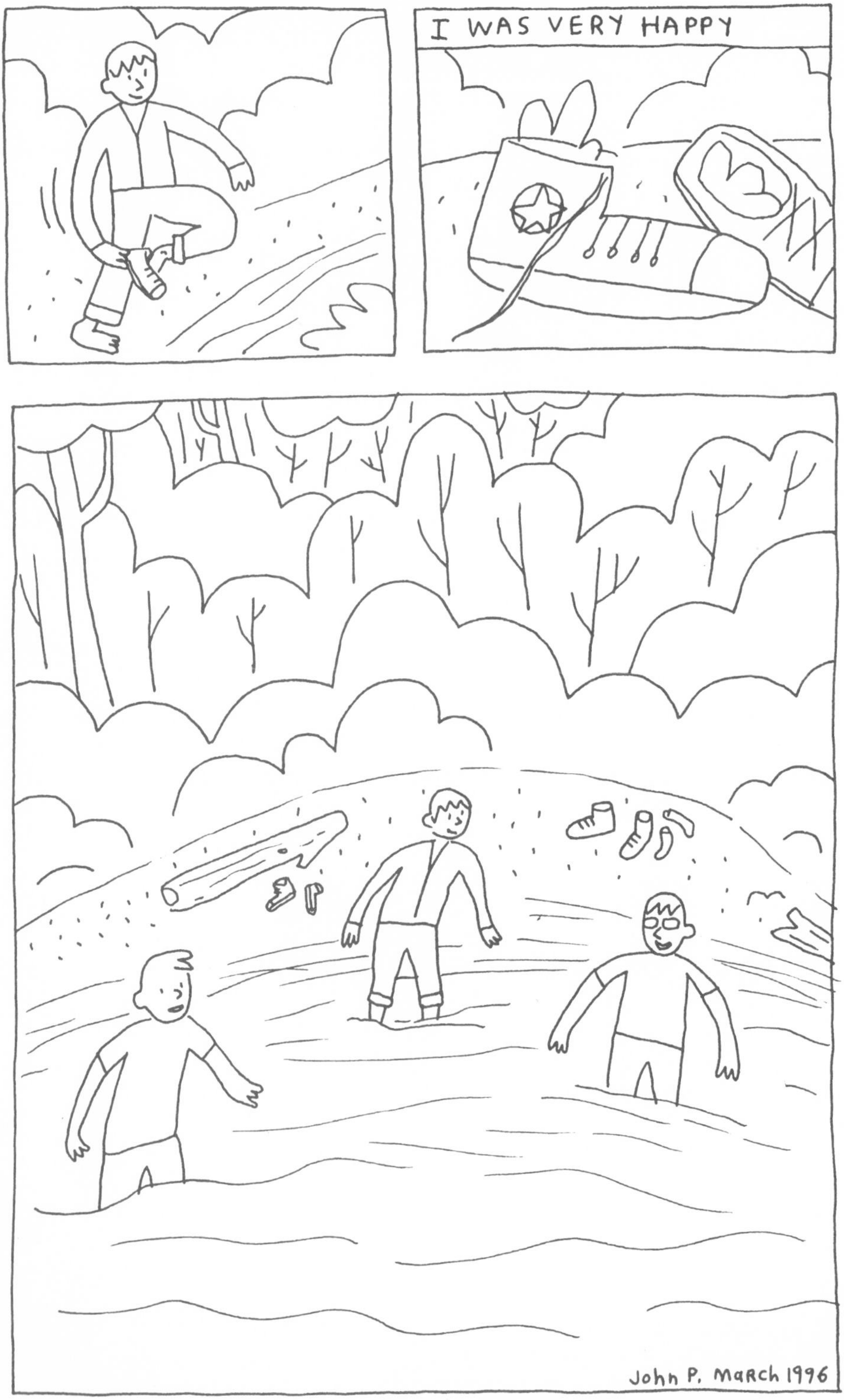
I WAS VERY HAPPY
John P. March 1996

Resume and Relevant Information

NAME   John Anthony Porcellino

NATIONALITY   Mutt (Italian, Polish, Bohemian-American)

PLACE OF BIRTH   Chicago, Illinois

DATE OF BIRTH   September 18, 1968 8:07 PM

EDUCATION   (Schools attended, special courses of study, degrees and years)
Hitch Elementary, Chicago (1973); St. Constance School, Chicago (1974-1979);
Armstrong Elementary, Hoffman Estates, Ill. (1979); Eisenhower Jr High, H.E.
(1980-1982); Hoffman Estates High School (1982-1986); Northern Illinois
University, DeKalb, Ill. (1986-1990) Degree; Bachelor of Fine Arts. American
Health Science University, Aurora, Colo. (2003-2005). School of Hard Knocks
(1990-present).

MARRIED   June 29, 2003 to Miss Camilia Misun Oh of Columbus, Ohio.

GROUPS / ORGANIZATIONS   Member: Hyperacusis Network; Great Plains
Zen Center.

SUMMARY OF PRINCIPLE OCCUPATIONS AND/OR JOBS   Over the
course of my life I have engaged in numerous and varied activities for profit,
including: Ice cream scooper, Grocery bagger, Warehouse worker, Stock Boy,
Gas station attendant, United States Census Enumerator, Assembly line worker,
Clown, Illustrator, Man who holds up Oriental Rugs at auction, Mailroom clerk,
Glass cleaner, Janitor, Warehouse foreman, Mosquito Abatement Technician and
Entrepreneur.

INTERESTS   Applied Arts and Sciences; Metaphysics.

HOBBIES   Reading, Board Games, Hiking.

SPORTS   Go Bears

ARRESTS / CONVICTIONS   Failure to Yield Turning Left, (1988); Illegal Use of a Sound Amplification Device (Band), (1989).

PLEASE GIVE A BRIEF RESUME OF YOUR LIFE   Had beautiful, mysterious boyhood in Jefferson Park, on the Northwest side of Chicago. My father was a lawyer and my mother was a nurse. Happy memories of monster movies, playing and fighting with my sister Joanne. In kindergarten made early friends Robert and Marco. Played baseball everyday in summer, football everyday in winter, at the playlot at Foster and Austin. Went to Catholic Grammar school; church, Jesus. Family picnics at Holidays, playing in my Grandmother's basement. Developed nosebleeds in 5th grade, began reading voraciously and drawing comics. Mad Magazine. Family moved out to Hoffman Estates, Illinois during the summer of 1979.

Fighting with boys in the new neighborhood, discovered girls. Spent days and evenings playing in the fields and woods, climbing trees, falling in creeks. Started listening to Rock Music (Beatles only). Backyard Football; Soccer. Reading, drawing comics.

High school days; played football, soon became enemy of the Jocks. Gradually establishing counter-culture persona; grew hair long; sarcasm; absurdism. Reading and drawing comics. Listened to Classic Rock (Yes, Led Zeppelin), then New Wave. Puberty and first girlfriend; became extremely depressed and angry. I hated my high school, felt complete alienation from my teachers and my schoolmates. Depression deepened, discovered Punk Rock and my life was changed. Played in punk-noise band Bryce Hammer. Began physical self-abuse to alleviate psychological despair; suicidal. Started first real fanzine, Zo-Zo. Writing obsessively, mainly nonsense stories and poetry. Comics. Developing rebel-artist stance; clashes with teachers, administration. Survived and graduated in June of 1986.

Depression worsening; long hopeless nights of despair. Suicidal, lost virginity on August 12, 1986. College; comics and poetry. Started Art and Poetry fanzine Cehsoikoe. Fell in love; got a broken heart that lasted six years. Depression worsens, begin drinking. Series of mystical visions and experiences reestablishes my faith in God and Meaning. I start King-Cat Comics & Stories, May 1989, begin Painting furiously in an attempt to understand my life. Self-esteem rising. Experiments with hallucinogenic drugs; world view radically altered by my experiences. I begin to ascend out of the darkness of the previous seven years.

After college graduation I begin working in a warehouse in DeKalb, focusing my energies at night and weekends on King-Cat. Lived hermetic existence in apartment on 11th Street, felt first inner peace since puberty. In June of 1992 I quit my job and move across country to Denver, Colorado.

Dedicating myself to my comics and independent living, I begin seeking a way to survive in an increasingly unforgiving society. Living in such a beautiful place restores my love of nature and the outdoors. Cross country road trips. Another series of mystical events propels my spiritual life forward. Unexplained illnesses drive me deeper inside, spurring another chain of circumstances that simultaneously confuse and enlighten me. Comics.

Reunite with old sweetheart Kera Schaley; we marry in September 1996. Road trips through the desert. Severe illness over the summer of 1997 culminates in hospitalizations and life saving surgery. Recovery. Return to Illinois to be near family and roots. Continued struggles with physical and emotional difficulties result in psychological collapse, summer 1998. Spiritual life focuses and deepens. Doctors, Nurses, health improves. Move to Elgin; marriage fails, March 1999. Psychotherapy, King-Cat, journaling. Divorce finalized September, '99.

Next several years spent in isolation, working on comics; spiritual study. Solitary explorations of the woods and fields of my youth. Mental condition worsening: anxiety, depression and obsessive-compulsive disorder. Time passes, comics.

In Spring of 2001 begin long-distance correspondence with Misun Oh; we fall in love. She joins me in Elgin and we make plans to return to Denver. Final days in Illinois spent with family and friends; arrive in Colorado, December '02. Research into causes of mental illness, experimentation with various nutritional therapies; condition begins to improve. Married June, 2003 at the Botanical Gardens in Denver. In December we pack up once more and move to San Francisco.

In California, I push myself intently into comics. Mental state wavering; health struggles, exhaustion. King-Cat celebrates its 15th anniversary, May 2004. Flowers. Walking in the park, on City Streets. Now.

CURRENT PHOTO

2/11/05

CURRENT PHOTO

MAISIE KUKOC